fat-free

healthy ways with a favourite cuisine

ITALIAN

fat-free

healthy ways with a favourite cuisine

ITALIAN

contributing editor:
ANNE SHEASBY

Over 160 no-fat or low-fat recipes
for tempting, tasty and healthy eating

Consulting Editor: Anne Sheasby

TED SMART

This edition published in 2003 by The Book People Ltd
Hall Wood Avenue
Haydock
ASt Helens WA11 9UL

Produced by Anness Publishing Limited
Hermes House, 88–89 Blackfriars Road,
London SE1 8HA

A CIP catalogue record for this book is available from the British Library.

Publisher: Joanna Lorenz
Project Editor: Felicity Forster
Consultant Editor: Anne Sheasby
Nutritional Analysis: Jill Scott
Recipes: Catherine Atkinson, Carla Capalbo, Kit Chan, Jacqueline Clarke,Maxine Clarke, Frances Cleary, Carol Clements, Roz Denny, Matthew Drennan, Joanna Farrow, Christine France, Sarah Gates, Shirley Gill, Carole Handslip, Christine Ingram, Patricia Lousada, Norma MacMillan, Sue Maggs, Elizabeth Martin, Sarah Maxwell, Janice Murfitt, Annie Nichols, Angela Nilsen, Maggie Pannell, Louise Pickford, Jennie Shapter, Anne Sheasby, Hilaire Walden, Laura Washburn, Steven Wheeler, Kate Whiteman, Judy Williams, Elizabeth Wolf-Cohen, Jeni Wright

Photographers: Karl Adamson, Edward Allwright, David Armstrong, Steve Baxter, Nicki Dowey, James Duncan, Michelle Garret, Amanda Heywood, Tim Hill, David Jordan, Dave King, Don Last, Patrick McLeavey, Michael Michaels, Thomas Odulate, Peter Reilly, William Lingwood
Jacket Photographer: William Lingwood
Jacket Stylist: Helen Trent
Jacket Home Economist: Lucy McKelvie
Designers: Nigel Partridge, Ian Sandom
Indexer: Helen Snaith
Editorial Reader: Marion Wilson

Printed and bound in Hong Kong

10 9 8 7 6 5 4 3 2 1

CONTENTS

INTRODUCTION

Italians are passionate about their food and always enjoy spending time preparing, cooking and eating food with family and friends. Food is one of their greatest pleasures and Italians are fortunate to be able to enjoy many regional variations in the food and dishes they eat. Italian food is thought by many of us to be laden with calories and fat, but in fact the same appealing scope and variety of flavours from Italy can be enjoyed as part of a healthy, low-fat cuisine.

Many traditional Italian foods such as the abundance of fresh Mediterranean sun-ripened vegetables, fresh herbs and many different types of pasta are naturally low in fat, making them ideal to enjoy as part of a low-fat eating plan. Quality and freshness of foods are both of great importance to the Italians and much of the fresh produce eaten in Italy is grown or produced locally. When it comes to cooking foods such as vegetables, they are often cooked in simple ways to bring out their delicious and natural flavours.

Olive oil is the primary fat used for cooking in Italy and it is also commonly used for dressing foods such as salads. Olive oil is a "healthier" type of fat which is high in monounsaturated fat and low in saturated fat and so long as it is used in moderation, it can also be enjoyed as part of a low-fat diet.

Some other typical Italian ingredients, such as pancetta, salami, Parmesan and mozzarella, are high in fat but are easily substituted with lower-fat foods such as lean bacon and reduced-fat mozzarella, or, in many recipes, the quantity of the high-fat food can often simply be reduced to lower the fat content of the dish.

BELOW: Italian food is packed with flavour and colour, and can be amazingly low in fat too.

ABOVE: Pasta, rice, olive oil, nuts, cheese, meat, olives, garlic, and fresh fruit and vegetables can all be enjoyed as part of a low-fat Italian diet.

In Italy, pasta and rice dishes form a large part of the cuisine and both are ideal for a low-fat diet as they are naturally high in carbohydrates and low in fat, so long as the sauce served with the pasta or the other ingredients used for a rice dish such as a risotto are also low in fat!

Most of us eat fats in some form or another every day and we all need a small amount of fat in our diet to maintain a healthy, balanced eating plan. However, most of us eat far too much fat and we should all be looking to reduce our overall fat intake, especially saturated fats.

Weight for weight, dietary fats supply far more energy than all the other nutrients in our diet and if you eat a diet that is high in fat but don't exercise sufficiently to use up that energy, you will gain weight.

By cutting down on the amount of fat you eat and making easy changes to your diet, such as choosing the right types of fat, using low-fat and fat-free products whenever possible and making simple changes to the way you prepare and cook food, you will soon be reducing your overall fat intake and enjoying a much healthier lifestyle – and you'll hardly notice the difference!

As you will see from this cookbook, it is certainly practicable to eat and enjoy Italian food as part of a low-fat eating plan. We include lots of useful and informative advice, including an introduction to basic healthy eating guidelines; helpful hints and tips on low-fat and fat-free ingredients and low-fat or fat-free cooking techniques; practical tips on how to reduce fat and saturated fat in your diet; an interesting insight into the traditional Italian kitchen and the types of ingredients and foods most commonly used in everyday Italian cooking, as well as an appealing selection of over 160 delicious and easy-to-follow low-fat Italian recipes for all the family to enjoy.

Each recipe includes a nutritional breakdown, providing at-a-glance calorie and fat contents per serving. All the recipes in this cookbook are very low in fat – each containing five grams of fat or less per serving, some containing less than one gram of fat per serving.

You will be surprised and delighted at this tempting collection of recipes which ranges from soups, starters and salads to main-course pasta dishes, breads and desserts. All the recipes contain less fat than similar traditional Italian recipes and yet they are packed full of Italian flavour and appeal. This practical cookbook will give you a valuable insight into low-fat and Italian cookery and will enable you to enjoy Italian food that is healthy, delicious and nutritious as well as being low in fat.

BELOW: Fresh fruits are an ideal choice for fat-free cooking because they are naturally low in fat. They can be used in both sweet and savoury Italian dishes.

HEALTHY EATING GUIDELINES

A healthy diet is one that provides us with all the nutrients we need. By eating the right types, balance and proportions of foods, we are more likely to feel healthy, have plenty of energy and a higher resistance to disease that will help prevent us from developing illnesses such as heart disease, cancers, bowel disorders and obesity.

By choosing a variety of foods every day, you will ensure that you are supplying your body with all the essential nutrients, including vitamins and minerals, it needs. To get the balance right, it is important to know just how much of each type of food you should be eating.

There are five main food groups, and it is recommended that we should eat plenty of fruit and vegetables (at least five portions a day, not including potatoes) and foods such as cereals, pasta, rice and potatoes; moderate amounts of meat, fish, poultry and dairy products, and only small amounts of foods containing fat or sugar. By choosing a good balance of foods from these groups every day, and by choosing lower-fat or lower-sugar alternatives, we will be supplying our bodies with all the nutrients they need for optimum health.

The Five Main Food Groups

- Fruit and vegetables
- Rice, potatoes, bread, pasta and other cereals
- Meat, poultry, fish and alternative proteins, such as peas, beans and lentils
- Milk and other dairy foods
- Foods that contain fat and foods that contain sugar

Above: By choosing a variety of foods from the five main food groups, you will ensure that you are supplying your body with all the nutrients it needs.

The Role and Importance of Fat in Our Diet

Fats shouldn't be cut out of our diets completely. We need a small amount of fat for general health and well-being – fat is a valuable source of energy, and also helps to make foods more palatable to eat. However, if you lower the fats, especially saturated fats, in your diet, it may help you to lose weight as well as reducing your risk of developing some diseases, such as heart disease.

Aim to limit your daily intake of fats to no more than 30–35 per cent of the total number of calories. Since each gram of fat provides nine calories, your total daily intake should be no more than around 70g fat. Your total intake of saturated fats should be no more than approximately ten per cent of the total number of calories.

Types of Fat

All fats in our foods are made up of building blocks of fatty acids and glycerol and their properties vary according to each combination.

There are two main types of fat, which are referred to as saturated and unsaturated. The unsaturated group of fats is divided into two further types – polyunsaturated and monounsaturated fats.

There is usually a combination of these types of fat (saturated, polyunsaturated and monounsaturated) in foods that contain fat, but the amount of each type varies from one kind of food to another.

Saturated Fats

These fats are usually hard at room temperature. They are not essential in the diet, and should be limited, as they are linked to increasing the level of cholesterol in the blood, which in turn can increase the likelihood that heart disease will develop.

The main sources of saturated fats are animal products, such as fatty meats, and spreading fats, such as butter and lard, that are solid at room temperature. However, there are also saturated fats of vegetable origin, notably coconut and palm oils, and some margarines and oils, which, when processed, change the nature of the fat from unsaturated fatty acids to saturated ones. These fats are labelled "hydrogenated vegetable oil" and should be limited. Saturated fats are also found in many processed foods, such as crisps and savoury snacks, as well as biscuits and cakes.

Below: A selection of foods containing the three main types of fat: saturated, polyunsaturated and monounsaturated fats. Small quantities of poly- and monounsaturated fats can help to reduce the level of cholesterol in the blood.

Polyunsaturated Fats

There are two types of polyunsaturated fats: those of vegetable or plant origin (omega 6), such as sunflower oil, soft margarine and seeds, and those from oily fish (omega 3), such as salmon, herring, mackerel and sardines. Both fats are usually liquid at room temperature. Small quantities of polyunsaturated fats are essential for good health and are thought to help reduce the blood cholesterol level.

Monounsaturated Fats

Monounsaturated fats are also thought to have the beneficial effect of reducing the blood cholesterol level and this could explain why in some Mediterranean countries there is such a low incidence of heart disease. Monounsaturated fats are found in foods such as olive oil, rapeseed oil, some nuts such as almonds and hazelnuts, oily fish and avocado pears.

Cutting Down on Fats and Saturated Fats in the Diet

About one-quarter of the fat we eat comes from meat and meat products, one-fifth from dairy products and margarine and the rest from cakes, biscuits, pastries and other foods.

It is relatively easy to cut down on obvious sources of fat in the diet, such as butter, oils, margarine, cream, whole milk and full-fat cheese, but we also need to know about – and check our consumption of – "hidden" fats. Hidden fats can be found in foods such as cakes, crisps, biscuits and nuts.

By being aware of which foods are high in fats and particularly saturated fats, and by making simple changes to your diet, you can reduce the total fat content of your diet quite considerably.

Whenever possible, choose reduced-fat or low-fat alternatives to foods such as milk, cheese and salad dressings, and fill up on very low-fat foods, such as fruit and vegetables, and foods that are high in carbohydrates, such as pasta, rice, bread and potatoes.

Cutting down on fat doesn't mean sacrificing taste. It's easy to follow a healthy-eating plan without having to forgo all your favourite foods.

EASY WAYS TO CUT DOWN ON FAT AND SATURATED FAT IN THE DAILY DIET

There are lots of simple no-fuss ways of reducing the fat in your diet. Just follow the simple "eat less – try instead" suggestions below to discover how easy it is.

- EAT LESS – Butter, margarine, other spreading fats and cooking oils.
- TRY INSTEAD – Low-fat spread or very low-fat spread. If you must use butter or hard margarine, make sure they are softened at room temperature and spread them very thinly, or try fat-free spreads such as low-fat soft cheese for sandwiches and toast.
- EAT LESS – Fatty meats and high-fat products, such as meat pâtés, burgers, pies and sausages.
- TRY INSTEAD – Low-fat meats, such as chicken, turkey and venison. Use only the leanest cuts of meats such as lamb, beef and pork. Always cut and discard any visible fat and skin from meat before cooking. Choose reduced-fat sausages and meat products and eat fish more often. Try using low-fat protein products such as peas, beans, lentils, Quorn or tofu in place of meat in recipes.
- EAT LESS – Full-fat dairy products such as whole milk, cream, butter, hard margarine, crème fraîche, whole milk yogurts and hard cheese.

BELOW: Chicken and fish are low in fat; always use only the leanest cuts of meats.

ABOVE: Look for reduced-fat hard cheeses, low-fat yogurts and skimmed milk.

- TRY INSTEAD – Semi-skimmed or skimmed milk and milk products, low-fat yogurts, low-fat fromage frais and low-fat soft cheeses, reduced-fat hard cheeses such as Cheddar, and reduced-fat creams and crème fraîche.
- EAT LESS – Hard cooking fats, such as lard or hard margarine.
- TRY INSTEAD – Polyunsaturated or monounsaturated oils, such as olive, sunflower or corn oil for cooking (but don't use too much).
- EAT LESS – Rich salad dressings, such as full-fat mayonnaise, salad cream or French dressing.
- TRY INSTEAD – Reduced-fat or fat-free mayonnaise or dressings. Make salad dressings at home with low-fat yogurt or fromage frais.
- EAT LESS – Fried foods.
- TRY INSTEAD – Fat-free cooking methods such as grilling, microwaving, steaming or baking whenever possible. Try cooking in a non-stick wok with only a very small amount of oil. Always roast or grill meat or poultry on a rack.
- EAT LESS – Deep-fried chips and sautéed potatoes.
- TRY INSTEAD – Low-fat starchy foods such as pasta, couscous and rice. Choose baked or boiled potatoes, or cook oven chips occasionally.
- EAT LESS – Added fat in cooking.
- TRY INSTEAD – To cook with little or no fat. Use heavy-based or good quality non-stick pans so that the food doesn't stick. Try using a small amount of spray oil in cooking to control exactly how much fat you are using. Use fat-free or low-fat ingredients for cooking, such as fruit juice, low-fat or fat-free stock, wine or even beer.
- EAT LESS – High-fat snacks, such as crisps, tortilla chips, fried snacks and pastries, chocolate cakes, muffins, doughnuts, sweet pastries and biscuits.
- TRY INSTEAD – Low-fat and fat-free fresh or dried fruits, breadsticks or vegetable sticks. Make your own home-baked low-fat cakes and bakes. Buy low-fat and reduced-fat versions of biscuits.

BELOW: Rice is very low in fat and there are many varieties to choose from.

FAT-FREE COOKING METHODS

It's extremely easy to cook without fat – whenever possible, grill, bake, microwave and steam foods without the addition of fat, or try stir-frying without fat – try using a little low-fat or fat-free stock, wine or fruit juice instead.

• By choosing heavy-based or good quality cookware, you'll find that the amount of fat needed for cooking foods can be kept to an absolute minimum. When making casseroles or meat sauces such as Bolognese, dry fry the meat to brown it and then drain off all the excess fat before adding the other ingredients. If you do need a little fat for cooking, choose an oil that is high in unsaturates such as corn, sunflower, olive or rapeseed oil and always use as little as possible.

• When baking low-fat cakes and bakes, use good quality bakeware which doesn't need greasing before use, or use non-stick baking parchment and only lightly grease before lining.

• Look out for non-stick coated fabric sheet. This re-usable non-stick material is amazingly versatile. It can be cut to size and used to line cake tins, baking sheets or frying pans. Heat-resistant up to 290°C/550°F and microwave-safe, it will last for up to five years.

BELOW: Always cut and discard any visible fat and skin from meat before cooking.

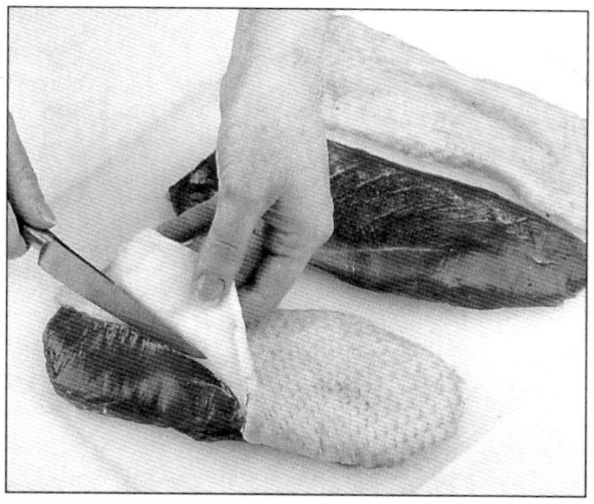

ABOVE: Marinating helps to tenderize meat as well as adding flavour and colour.

• When baking foods such as chicken or fish, rather than adding a knob of butter to the food, try baking it in a loosely sealed parcel of foil or greaseproof paper and adding some wine or fruit juice and herbs or spices before sealing the parcel.

• When grilling foods, the addition of fat is often unnecessary. If the food shows signs of drying, lightly brush with a small amount of unsaturated oil, such as sunflower or corn oil.

• Microwaved foods rarely need the addition of fat, so add herbs or spices for extra flavour and colour.

• Steaming or boiling are easy, fat-free ways of cooking many foods, especially vegetables, fish and chicken.

• Try poaching foods, such as chicken, fish and fruit, in low-fat or fat-free stock or syrup – it is another easy, fat-free cooking method.

• Try braising vegetables in the oven in low-fat or fat-free stock, wine or simply water with the addition of some herbs.

• Sauté vegetables in low-fat or fat-free stock, wine or fruit juice instead of oil.

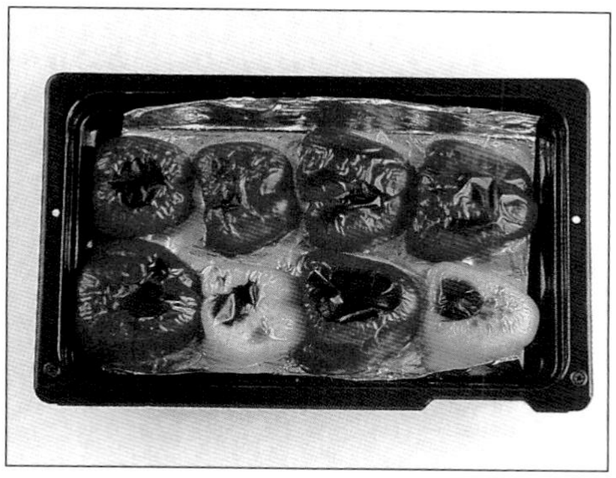

ABOVE: Vegetables can be grilled without adding any fat at all.

• Cook vegetables in a covered saucepan over a low heat with a little water so they cook in their own juices.

• Marinate food such as meat or poultry in mixtures of alcohol, herbs or spices, and vinegar or fruit juice. This will help to tenderize the meat and add flavour and colour. In addition, the leftover marinade can be used to baste the food occasionally while it is cooking.

• When serving vegetables such as boiled potatoes, carrots or peas, resist the temptation to add a knob of butter or margarine. Instead, sprinkle with chopped fresh herbs or ground spices.

LOW-FAT SPREADS IN COOKING

There is a huge variety of low-fat, reduced-fat and half-fat spreads available in our supermarkets, along with some spreads that are very low in fat. Generally speaking, the very low-fat spreads with a fat content of around 20 per cent or less have a high water content and so are unsuitable for cooking and only suitable for spreading.

INGREDIENTS

VEGETABLES

Vegetables play an important role in Italian cooking and, as many vegetables are also naturally low in fat, they are ideal for use in low-fat Italian cooking.

AUBERGINES

Aubergines are a popular vegetable in Italian cooking. Many different types can be found in Italian markets, the deep purple, elongated variety being the most common. Choose firm aubergines with tight, glossy skins, that feel heavy for their size.

RIGHT: Deep purple aubergines

BELOW: Clockwise from top left: beans, courgettes, potatoes, tomatoes, asparagus, carrots, peppers, broccoli and mangetouts.

COURGETTES

LEFT: Courgettes

Courgettes are widely used in Italy, both as a vegetable and for their deep yellow flowers. They are available all year round but are at their best in spring and summer. The smaller and skinnier the courgettes are, the better they taste. Choose courgettes that are firm with glossy green skins and avoid those which are soft or have blemished skins. Courgettes are low in calories and fat and provide some vitamin C. They are used in many low-fat Italian dishes, and are, for example, served raw in salads, cooked with other Mediterranean vegetables such as peppers and tomatoes, or simply stuffed and oven-baked.

FENNEL

Fennel has become a very popular vegetable and is used widely in low-fat Italian cooking. Bulb or Florence fennel resembles a fat white celery root and has a delicate but distinctive flavour of aniseed and a crisp, refreshing texture. Fennel is available all year round. If possible, buy it with its topknot of feathery fronds, which you can chop and use as a herb or as a garnish. Choose fennel bulbs that feel firm with crisp white outer layers that are not wizened or yellowish. It should have a delicate, fresh scent of aniseed and the texture of green celery. Whole fennel bulbs will keep in the fridge for up to one week. Once cut, use them immediately or the cut surfaces will discolour and soften. Fennel is naturally low in calories and fat and is enjoyed in low-fat dishes throughout Italy. It is served raw in salads, lightly dressed with a vinaigrette, or sautéed, baked or braised in similar ways to celery. It is particularly good served with white fish.

RIGHT: Fennel

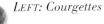

LEFT: Porcini mushrooms

MUSHROOMS

During the spring and autumn months, throughout the Italian countryside keen fungi collectors are spotted searching for the flavourful edible wild mushrooms that are a popular delicacy of Italy. Cultivated mushrooms, such as button mushrooms, are rarely eaten in Italy, and Italians prefer to use dried or preserved wild fungi with their robust earthy taste. The most popular and highly prized mushroom used in Italian cooking is the porcini or cep which is also readily available dried. Other popular wild mushrooms used in Italy include field mushrooms and chanterelles.

Cultivated mushrooms and ceps can be eaten raw (in salads or lightly dressed), but other edible wild mushrooms should be cooked before eating. In Italy, mushrooms may simply be lightly grilled or baked or added to many dishes, such as sauces, stocks, soups and risottos.

ONIONS

Onions are an essential part of low-fat Italian cooking. Many varieties are grown, including white, mild yellow, baby and red onions. Choose firm onions that show no signs of sprouting green leaves. Onions should have thin, almost papery skins that are unblemished. Onions are naturally low in calories and fat and they are used in numerous low-fat Italian dishes. They can be served raw in salads, stuffed and baked or, in the case of baby onions, cooked in a sweet and sour sauce of sugar and wine vinegar and served cold or hot.

LEFT: Red onion

PEPPERS

Generically known as capsicums, peppers come in a variety of colours including green (these are unripe red peppers), red, yellow, orange, white and purplish-black, all of which have the same sweetish flavour and crunchy texture and can be eaten raw or cooked.

ABOVE: Mixed peppers

Each region of Italy has its own low-fat specialities using peppers. These include raw or lightly cooked peppers added to salads, roasted and lightly dressed peppers, and stuffed and oven-baked peppers.

TOMATOES

It is impossible to imagine low-fat Italian cooking without tomatoes. Tomatoes are cultivated all over Italy and are incorporated into the cooking of every region. In Italy, many types of tomatoes are grown, from plum to cherry tomatoes, and they are at their best in summer. Choose bright, firm, ripe tomatoes, with tight, unwrinkled, unblemished skins and a good aroma. Ripe tomatoes will keep well for several days in the fridge, but always bring tomatoes to room temperature before serving to enjoy them at their best.

Tomatoes are naturally low in calories and fat and provide a good source of vitamin C. Tomatoes can be enjoyed raw or cooked and they are often served with fresh basil leaves with which they have a great affinity. Tomatoes add flavour and colour to almost any savoury low-fat dish and can be enjoyed simply chopped and added to salads or made into a topping for bruschetta. They can be grilled, lightly fried, baked, stuffed or stewed and made into sauces and soups. Canned or bottled peeled plum tomatoes, passata and tomato purée or paste are also widely used in low-fat Italian cooking to add flavour, colour and texture to many dishes.

RIGHT: Vine-ripened tomatoes

Fruit and Nuts

Above: Citrus fruits are an Italian favourite and can be used for both sweet and savoury recipes, melons make an excellent accompaniment to Parma ham as an antipasto, and cherries - usually preserved in syrup - are used in desserts.

The Italians prefer to enjoy fruits and nuts when they are in season and much of the fresh produce available in Italy is grown or produced locally. Most types of fruit are naturally low in fat and so play a significant part in low-fat Italian cooking to create some delicious dishes.

Figs

Figs are grown all over Italy and there are two main types, green and purple. Both have thin, tender skins and very sweet, succulent red flesh. Choose fruits that are soft and yielding but not squashy. Fresh figs are low in calories and fat and provide some vitamin C. Fresh figs are delicious served on their own as a typical low-fat Italian dessert, but they can also be enjoyed raw or poached in both sweet and savoury low-fat dishes.

Left: Purple figs

Lemons

Lemons are grown all over Italy and their aromatic flavour enhances many low-fat Italian dishes. Depending on the variety, lemons may have a thick indented skin, or be perfectly smooth. Their appearance does not affect the flavour, but they should feel heavy for their size. Buy unwaxed lemons if you intend to use the zest in recipes. Lemons will keep in the fridge for up to two weeks. They are low in calories and fat and provide a good source of vitamin C. Lemons are very versatile and the juice and/or zest is added to many low-fat Italian dishes. Lemon is used in cold drinks, to add flavour to dressings and sauces, freshly squeezed over cooked fish or lean meat to add flavour, or as an aromatic flavouring for low-fat cakes and bakes.

Left: Lemons

Melons

Many different varieties of sweet aromatic melons are grown in Italy, the most common types being cantaloupe melons and watermelons. The best way to tell whether a melon is ripe is to smell it; it should have a mild, sweet scent. If it smells highly perfumed and musky it will be over-ripe. The fruit should feel heavy for its size and the skin should not be bruised or damaged. Gently press the rind with your thumbs at the stalk end; it should give a little. Melons are low in calories and fat and provide some vitamin C. Typically, Italians enjoy melon as a low-fat starter, simply served on its own or with wafer-thin slices of Parma ham, or as a tasty dessert served on its own or in a fresh fruit salad, sorbet or granita.

Below: Watermelon

ABOVE: The Italian climate is perfect for growing oranges; they add a bright splash of colour to salads and desserts.

ORANGES

Many varieties of oranges are grown in Sicily and southern Italy, the best-known Sicilian oranges being the small blood oranges with their bright ruby-red flesh. Other types include sweet navel and bitter oranges. Choose unwaxed oranges if you intend to use the zest in recipes. Oranges are naturally low in calories and fat and provide a good source of vitamin C. Oranges are served in both sweet and savoury low-fat dishes across Italy, including in salads, desserts, sorbets or granitas.

PEACHES AND NECTARINES

Peaches and nectarines with their sweet juicy flesh are summer fruits grown in Italy. Both fruits are available in either yellow or white fleshed varieties, all of which are succulent, juicy and full of flavour. They are naturally low in calories and fat and provide some vitamin C. Peaches and nectarines are interchangeable in recipes and are delicious served as a dessert fruit but can also be macerated in fortified wine or spirits or poached in white wine or syrup to create a typical low-fat Italian dessert. They are also delicious served with raspberries or made into fruit drinks, low-fat ice creams and sorbets.

ABOVE: Peaches

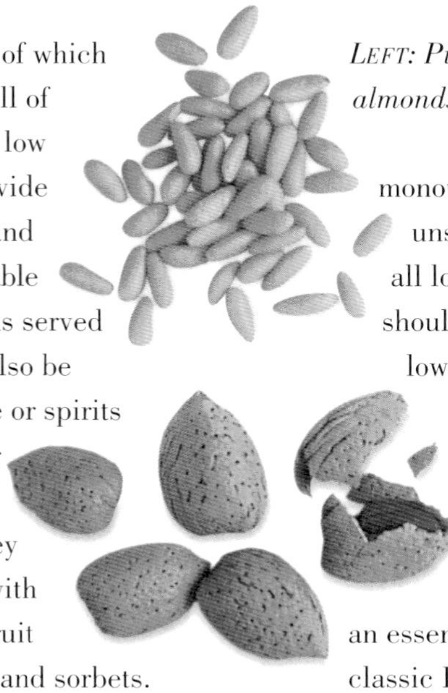

LEFT: Pine nuts (top) and almonds (below)

ALMONDS AND OTHER NUTS

Two varieties of almonds are grown in Italy – sweet and bitter almonds. Sweet almonds are the most common and are eaten on their own or used in cooking and baking. Bitter almonds are not edible in their raw state and are used to flavour liqueurs such as amaretto. In Italy, sweet almonds are enjoyed raw as a dessert or dried and blanched, slivered or ground for use in cakes, bakes and confectionery. Dried sweet almonds are the most common type used in many countries. Almonds are high in monounsaturated fat and low in saturated fat.

Other nuts, such as hazelnuts, walnuts and pistachios, are also grown and harvested in Italy and are used in many sweet and savoury dishes, including desserts, confections, cakes and bakes. Hazelnuts are usually dried before use, whereas walnuts can be enjoyed fresh or dried and pistachios are eaten raw or roasted. As with many nuts, they are all high in fat, although the type of fats they contain are the "healthier" types - either monounsaturated or poly-unsaturated fats. They are all low in saturated fat but should be used sparingly in low-fat cooking.

PINE NUTS

Pine nuts or pine kernels are very popular in Italy and are an essential ingredient in the classic Italian pesto sauce. They can be eaten either raw or toasted and are used in both sweet and savoury dishes. Pine nuts are high in polyunsaturated fat and low in saturated fat and they should be used in moderation.

BELOW: Almonds are an extremely versatile ingredient, used raw or to flavour cakes and liqueurs. Red and white Italian grapes are particularly refreshing on a hot day; they have a wonderful Muscat flavour.

Pasta

Pasta is the one ingredient that probably sums up the essence of Italian cooking, and it is an essential part of many Italian meals. It is a wonderfully simple, nutritious and low-fat food which is available in a whole wealth of shapes and sizes. There are two basic types of pasta, dried and fresh.

Fresh Pasta

Home-made fresh pasta is usually made by hand using superfine plain white flour enriched with eggs. It is often wrapped around a low-fat stuffing of lean meat, fish, vegetables or low-fat cheese to make filled pasta such as ravioli or tortellini, or layered with lean meat or vegetable sauces to make a tasty low-fat lasagne. Commercially-made fresh pasta is made with durum wheat, water and eggs. The flavour and texture of all fresh pasta is very delicate, so it is best suited to slightly more creamy, low-fat sauces.

LEFT: Angel's hair pasta

Dried Pasta

Dried pasta is produced from a dough made from hard durum wheat. It is then shaped into numerous different forms, from long, thin spaghetti to elaborate spirals and frilly bow shapes. Dried pasta can be made from basic pasta dough, which consists of durum wheat and water, or it can be made from a dough enriched with eggs or coloured and flavoured with ingredients such as spinach, herbs, tomatoes or squid ink. Dried pasta has a nutty flavour and should always retain a firm texture when cooked. It is generally used in preference to fresh pasta for thinner-textured, more robust, low-fat sauces.

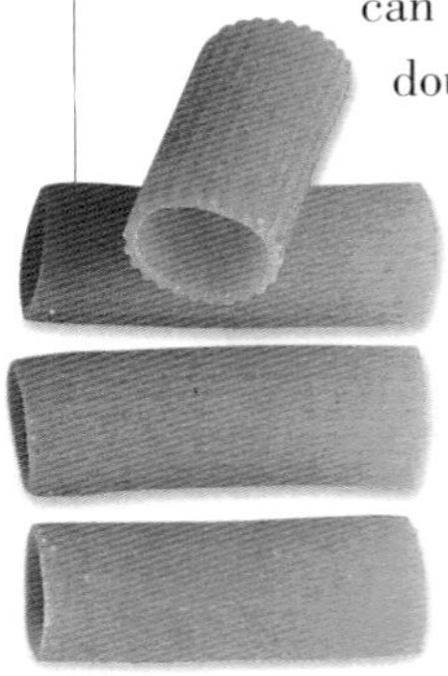

LEFT: Dried rigatoni

ABOVE: Fresh pasta comes in a wide variety of interesting shapes, sizes and colours.

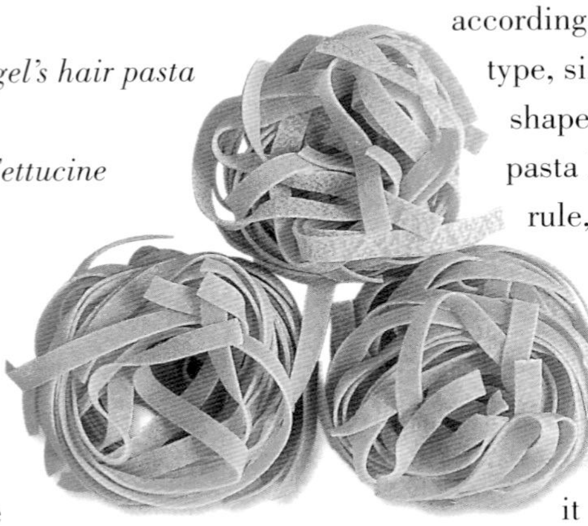

RIGHT: Fettucine

Buying and Storing Pasta

Choose dried pasta that is made from Italian durum wheat and store it in a cool, dry place. Once opened, dried pasta will keep for weeks in an airtight container. Home-made fresh pasta will only keep for a couple of days, but it also freezes very well. Commercially made fresh pasta (fresh pasta that is available in a chilled compartment in the supermarket) is pasteurized and vacuum-packed, so it will keep in the fridge for about two weeks, or it can be frozen for up to six months. When buying coloured and flavoured pasta, make sure that it has been made with natural ingredients.

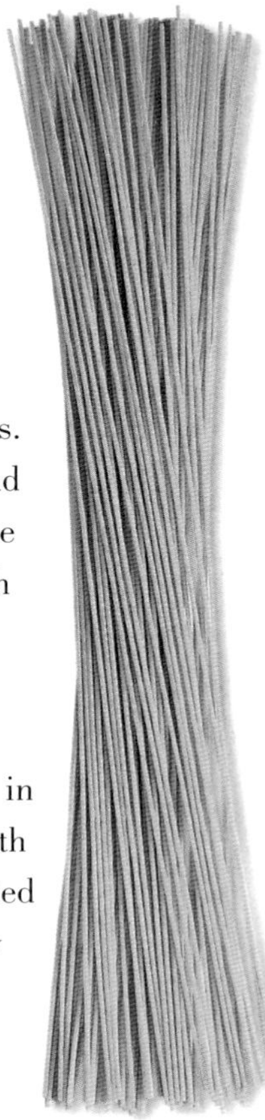

RIGHT: Dried spaghetti

Cooking Pasta

All pasta must be cooked in a large saucepan filled with plenty of fast-boiling, salted water. Cooking times vary according to the type, size and shape of the pasta but, as a general rule, filled pasta takes about 12 minutes, dried pasta needs 8–10 minutes and fresh pasta only 2–3 minutes. All pasta should be cooked until it is *al dente*, or still firm to the bite. Always test pasta for readiness just before you think it should be done as it can easily overcook. To stop it cooking, take the pan off the heat and run a little cold water into it, then drain the pasta and serve.

Pasta Varieties

Pasta shapes can be divided roughly into four categories: long strands or ribbons, flat, short and filled. When choosing the appropriate pasta for a sauce, there are no hard-and-fast rules; almost any pasta is suitable for a low-fat sauce.

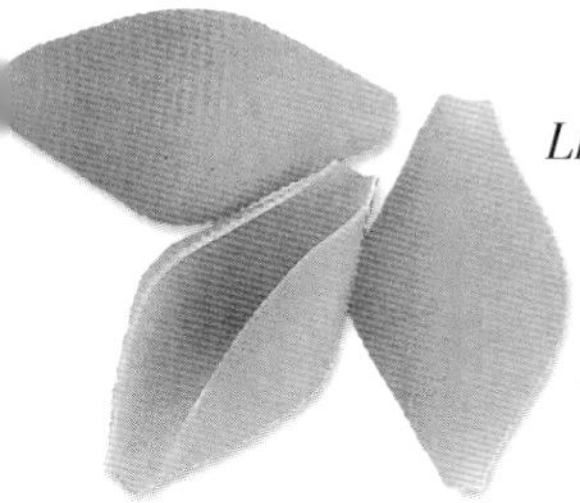

LEFT: Conchiglie

BELOW: Tomato and spinach orecchiette

Short Pasta

Short pasta covers a wide variety of shapes, the more common types being macaroni, rigati, rigatoni and tubetti. Pasta shapes vary and the list is almost endless, with some wonderfully descriptive names. There are cappellacci (little hats), orecchiette (little ears) or maltagliati (badly cut) and penne (quills), conchiglie (little shells), farfalle (bows) and lumache (snails).

Long or Ribbon Pasta

The best-known long variety is spaghetti, which also comes in a thinner version, spaghettini, and the flatter linguine, which means "little tongues". Bucatini are thicker and hollow – perfect for trapping low-fat sauces in the cavity. Ribbon pasta is wider than the strands and fettucine, tagliatelle and trenette all fall into this category. Dried tagliatelle is usually sold folded into nests, which unravel during cooking. Pappardelle are the widest ribbon pasta; they are often served with a low-fat rabbit sauce. The thinnest pasta strands are vermicelli (little worms) and ultra-fine capelli d'angelo (angel's hair).

Flat Pasta

In Italy, fresh flat pasta is often called maccheroni, not to be confused with the short tubes of macaroni with which we are familiar. Lasagne and cannelloni are larger flat rectangles of pasta, used for layering or rolling round a low-fat filling; dried cannelloni are already formed into wide tubes. Layered pasta dishes like this are cooked in the oven.

RIGHT: Lasagne

BELOW: Multi-coloured tagliatelle

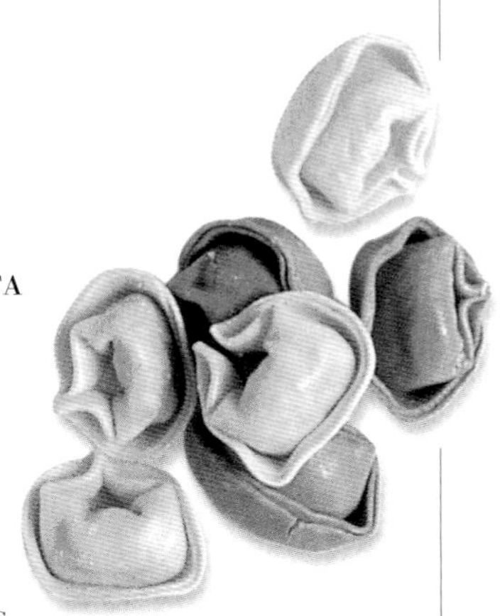

RIGHT: Tortelli

Filled Pasta

Dried and fresh filled pastas are available in many varieties and there are dozens of names for filled pasta, but the only difference lies in the shape and size. Ravioli are square, tortelli and agnolotti are usually round, while tortellini and anellini are ring-shaped. Fillings for fresh and dried pasta include lean meat, pumpkin, artichokes, ricotta and spinach, seafood, chicken and mushrooms.

Gnocchi

Gnocchi fall into a different category from other pasta, being similar to small dumplings. They can be made from semolina (milled durum wheat), flour, potatoes or ricotta and spinach and may be shaped like elongated shells, ovals, cylinders or flat discs, or roughly shredded into strozzapreti (priest stranglers). Gnocchi are extremely light and almost melt in the mouth and can be served like any pasta, as a low-fat first course, in clear soup or as an accompaniment to the main course.

RIGHT: Gnocchi

Bread, Rice, Grains and Pulses

Above: Ciabatta

Rice, grains and pulses form the basis of many delicious and nutritious low-fat Italian dishes and fresh bread is always served in Italy as a tasty, low-fat accompaniment to every meal.

In Italy, no meal is ever served without bread. There are numerous different types of Italian breads with many regional variations. Several varieties, such as ciabatta and focaccia are readily available from bakers or supermarkets.

Rice and grains are staple foods in Italy and are almost as important as pasta in Italian cooking. Italy relied heavily on these low-fat, protein-rich foods when luxuries such as meat were in short supply, and a whole host of wholesome and delicious low-fat recipes were developed using these modest ingredients.

Many beans and pulses, both fresh and dried, are naturally low in fat and are used widely in low-fat Italian cooking, providing the basis for a variety of delicious dishes.

Ciabatta

These flattish, slipper-shaped loaves with squared or rounded ends are made with olive oil and are often flavoured with fresh or dried herbs, olives or sun-dried tomatoes. They have an airy texture inside and a pale, crisp crust. Ciabatta is delicious served warm and is excellent for low-fat sandwiches.

Focaccia

Focaccia is a dimpled flat bread similar to pizza dough which is traditionally lightly oiled and baked in a wood oven. A whole traditional focaccia from an Italian bakery weighs several kilos and is sold by weight, cut into manageable pieces. A variety of low-fat ingredients can be worked into the dough or served as a topping - onions, rosemary or oregano, lean ham or olives.

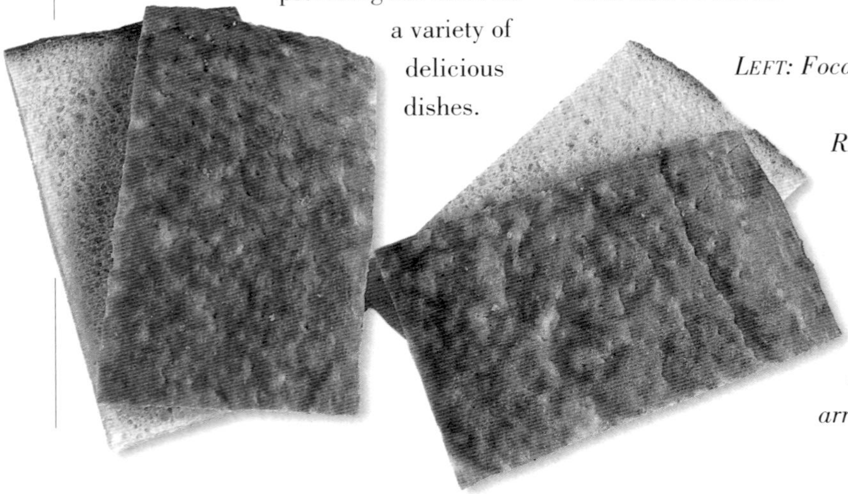

Left: Focaccia

Rice

Italy produces a great variety of rice including the short-grain carnaroli and arborio rice, which make the best risottos. Italian rice is classified by size, ranging from the shortest, roundest ordinario (used for puddings), to semifino (for soups and salads), then fino and finally the longer grains of the finest risotto rice, superfino.

Rice is used in many low-fat Italian dishes. Baked rice dishes are also popular or plain boiled rice may simply be served on its own.

The most famous of all Italian rice dishes, however, is risotto. A good risotto can be made only with superfine rice and provides a delicious low-fat Italian meal. All risottos are basically prepared in the same way, although they can be flavoured with an almost endless variety of exciting ingredients.

Buy only superfine risotto rice for use in Italian risottos. Shorter grain rice is best reserved for making soups and puddings. Store uncooked rice in an airtight container in a cool, dry place. The rice will keep for several months.

Right: Risotto rices like these arborio varieties are famous in Italy, and can be flavoured with an almost endless array of ingredients.

ABOVE: Fine polenta

POLENTA

For centuries, polenta has been a staple low-fat food of northern Italy. Polenta is a grainy yellow flour which is a type of cornmeal made from ground maize. It is then cooked into a kind of porridge and used in a variety of ways. There are two main types of polenta – coarse and fine.

Polenta is very versatile and can be used to create many delicious low-fat dishes. It is most often served in Italy as a first course but it can also be used as a vegetable dish or main course. Plain boiled polenta can be served on its own to make a satisfying dish. It goes well with lean meats and game or it can be cooled and cut into squares before being grilled or baked and served with a low-fat sauce or topping.

Quick-cooking polenta, which can be prepared in only five minutes, and ready-prepared blocks of cooked polenta are also available, but traditional polenta only takes about 20 minutes to cook, so it is best to buy this for its superior texture and flavour. Once opened, polenta will keep in an airtight container for at least one month.

LEFT: Dried cannellini beans

ABOVE: Canned borlotti beans

LEFT: Canned black-eyed beans

HARICOT BEANS

Haricot beans are eaten all over Italy, the most popular varieties being borlotti beans, cannellini beans (a type of kidney bean) and black-eyed beans. All these are eaten in hearty low-fat stews, with pasta, in low-fat soups or salads or simply cooked and served as a side dish.

Both fresh and dried beans are available in Italy and canned varieties make an acceptable substitute. Once opened, store dried beans in an airtight container in a cool, dry place for up to one year.

BROAD BEANS

Broad beans are at their best when eaten fresh from the pod in late spring or early summer when they are small and very tender, or cooked and skinned later in the season. They are popular in Italy and are excellent served with lean ham, in other low-fat dishes such as risotto or simply served as a vegetable accompaniment. Dried broad beans, which need pre-cooking, are also used in Italian dishes such as low-fat soups and stews.

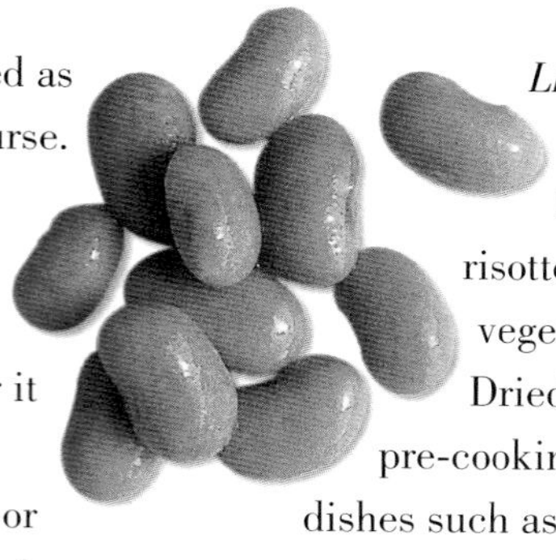

LEFT: Canned broad beans

CHICK-PEAS

Chick-peas, which are round, golden pulses shaped rather like hazelnuts, and which have a distinctive, nutty flavour, are also popular in low-fat Italian cooking. Chick-peas are cooked and used in the same way as haricot beans and they can also be served cold and lightly dressed to make a tasty salad.

LENTILS

Lentils grow in pods although they are always sold podded and dried. Italian lentils are the small brown variety which do not break up during cooking and are often mixed with pasta or rice to create delicious and satisfying low-fat dishes. They are also delicious served cold, lightly dressed or in nutritious soups. Whole brown, green or puy lentils can also be used.

ABOVE: Dried chick-peas

RIGHT: Dried brown lentils

Meat, Poultry and Fish

Although meat and poultry did not feature largely in Italian cooking until more recent years, a variety of lean cuts and a range of fish are used in many appetizing low-fat Italian dishes.

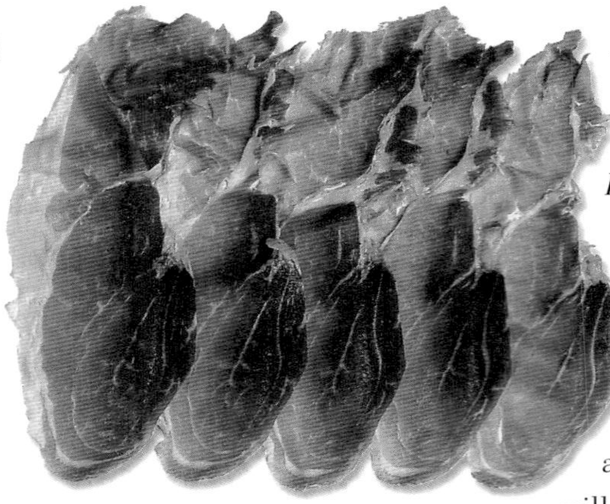

Left: Prosciutto di Parma

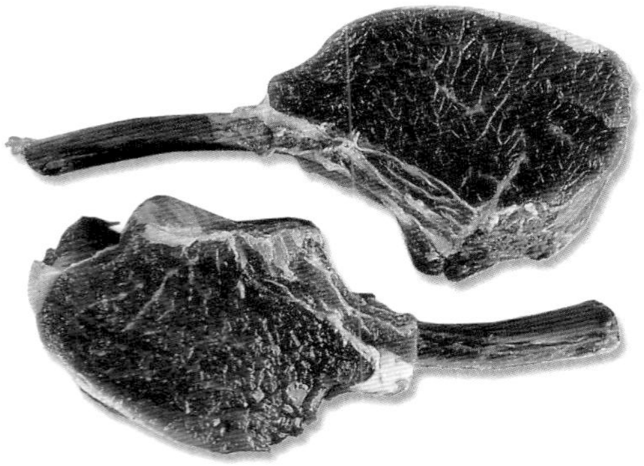

Right: Lamb cutlets

Cured Meats

Italy is famous for its prosciutto crudo – salted and dried ham that requires no cooking. The most famous of these hams is prosciutto di Parma, or Parma ham, which has a medium fat content, but is served in wafer-thin slices, so can be incorporated into low-fat Italian dishes.

Pancetta, bresaola, mortadella and salami are also popular Italian cured meats. Meats such as pancetta, mortadella and salami are high in fat and should be used sparingly in low-fat Italian recipes. Bresaola has a similar fat content to prosciutto or Parma ham.

Below: Bresaola

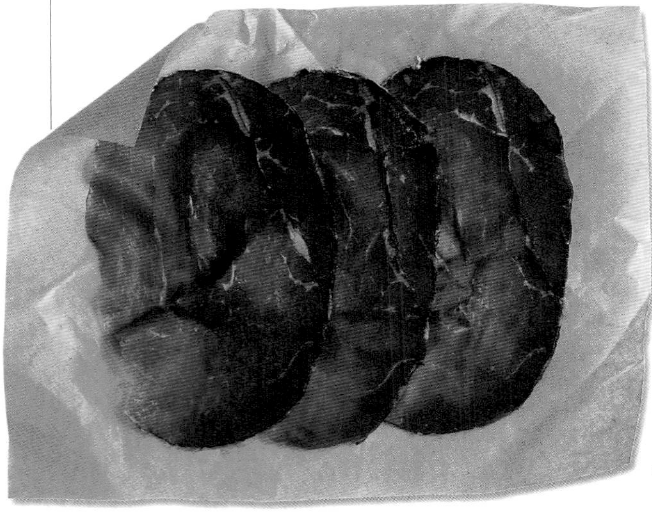

Beef

Lean, thick T-bone steaks are a popular choice in Italy and are often simply grilled over wood fires. Beef olives are also popular and leftover cooked lean beef can be sliced and made into a tasty salad. Less tender cuts of beef are usually braised, stewed or minced and used for a whole variety of tasty low-fat Italian dishes. Choose lean cuts of beef which are naturally low in fat or choose extra-lean minced beef.

Above: Minced beef

Chicken and Turkey

Poultry is a popular food in Italy and is used to create a huge variety of simple and delicious, low-fat Italian dishes. Factory farming does exist in Italy but many flavoursome free-range birds are also available. Chicken and turkey are usually filleted for quick cooking, and removing and discarding the skin before cooking ensures the meat is very lean.

Lamb

Lambs in Italy are bred mainly in the southern region and they are slaughtered at different ages, resulting in distinctive flavours. Young spring lambs are often spit-roasted whole or used for roasting or grilling. Older lamb has a stronger flavour and is suitable for roasting or stewing. Choose lean cuts of lamb for low-fat cooking to keep the fat content down.

Pork

A lot of Italian pork is transformed into hams, sausages and salamis, but fresh pork is also enjoyed all over Italy. Lean

Below: Chicken

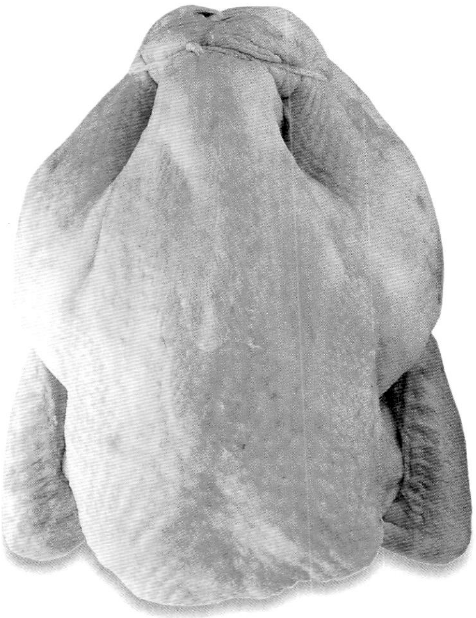

Above: Rabbit

pork chops or cutlets can be grilled or braised with herbs or artichokes for a tasty, low-fat meal. Loin of pork can be braised in milk or roasted with rosemary or sage. Choose lean cuts of pork and remove and discard any visible fat before cooking to keep the fat content low.

Rabbit

Rabbit often replaces chicken or veal in low-fat Italian cooking. The meat is very pale and is naturally lean and low in fat. Wild rabbit has a stronger flavour; farmed rabbit is very tender and has a much more delicate flavour. Farmed rabbit can replace chicken or turkey in almost any low-fat recipe. Wild rabbit can be stewed or braised either in white wine or Marsala, or with aubergines, lean bacon and tomatoes. It can also be roasted simply with root vegetables or fresh herbs.

Fish

Italy's extensive coastal waters are host to a large variety of fish and shellfish of every description, many of which are unknown outside Italy. Italians like their seafood very fresh and tend to cook it simply. Large fish are usually grilled, barbecued or baked, smaller whole fish may be stuffed and grilled or baked, and small fry are often lightly pan-fried.

Popular fish in Italy include white fish such as monkfish, cod and sole and oily fish such as salmon, swordfish, tuna, trout or sardines. Some fish are dried, salted or preserved in oil, the most popular being tuna which is packed in olive oil. Salted dried cod is also a favourite which is often made into soups and stews.

White fish is very low in fat and is ideal for use in low-fat Italian cooking. Remove and discard the skin to keep the fat content low. Oily fish such as tuna and swordfish are also naturally low in fat and although oily fish such as salmon is higher in fat, it is higher in the "healthier" types of fat – poly-unsaturated and monounsaturated fats – and low in saturated fat.

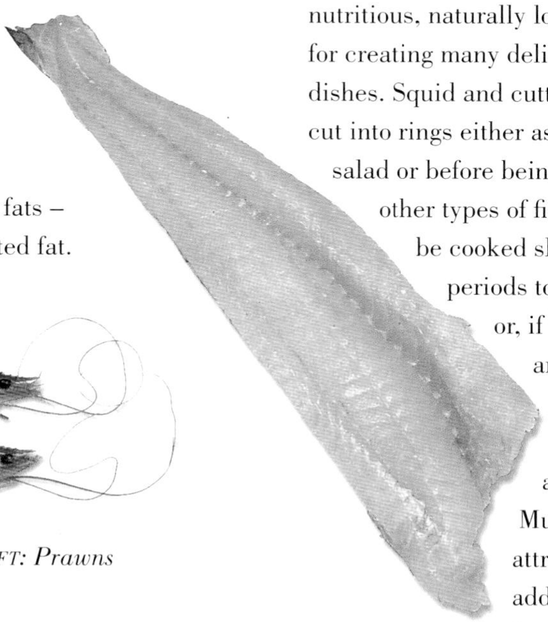

Right: Cod fillet

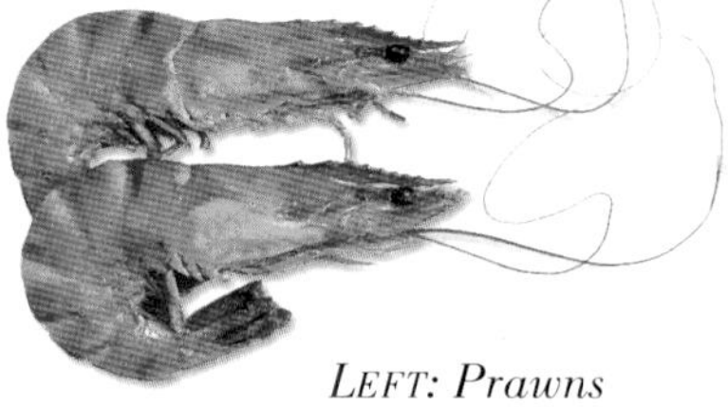

Left: Prawns

Shellfish

The Italians enjoy a huge variety of shellfish and crustaceans from their coastal waters and almost all seafood is considered edible, from mussels, clams and scallops to octopus, squid, razor-shells and sea snails. Shrimps and prawns come in all sizes and colours, from vibrant red to pale grey, while crustaceans range from bright orange crawfish to blue-black lobsters.

Above: Fish and shellfish like sardines and mussels are often simply grilled or fried, or used as the basis of a soup or stew.

Most shellfish and crustaceans are nutritious, naturally low in fat and ideal for creating many delicious low-fat Italian dishes. Squid and cuttlefish are served cut into rings either as part of a seafood salad or before being lightly fried with other types of fish. Octopus tend to be cooked slowly for long periods to tenderize them or, if very small ones are available, these can be cooked in the same way as squid.

Mussels make an attractive and tasty addition to many low-fat pasta and fish dishes, salads and pizza toppings. They are especially good served with a low-fat garlicky tomato sauce. Shrimps and prawns can be boiled and served with lemon juice and olive oil or in salads. They can also be grilled or barbecued and served with tomato sauce or rice.

Dairy Products

Dairy products such as butter and cheeses play a part in low-fat Italian cooking but due to their generally high fat content they should only be used in small amounts.

Left: Butter

Right: Mozzarella

Butter

Although olive oil is the primary fat used for cooking in Italy, butter is used more commonly in northern Italian cookery. The quantity of butter used in recipes in this book has been kept to a minimum as butter is very high in fat, particularly saturated fat. Choose a polyunsaturated or mono-unsaturated margarine in place of butter if you prefer. Although the fat content of these margarines is similar to butter, the fats are "healthier" types. Very low-fat spreads are not suitable for cooking; only use these for spreading.

Cheeses

Italy has a great variety of cheese, ranging from fresh, mild cheese such as mozzarella to mature hard cheeses such as Parmesan. All types of milk are used, including cow's, ewe's, goat's and buffalo's and some cheeses are made from a mixture of milks. Other popular types of Italian cheese include Pecorino, Provolone, Bel Paese, Fontina, ricotta, Gorgonzola and mascarpone.

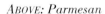

Many of the Italian cheeses are suitable for cooking and are used in a wide variety of dishes. However, many are also high in fat, especially saturated fat, but if used in moderation can be incorporated into low-fat Italian cuisine. Strong-flavoured cheeses, such as Parmesan, can be used in smaller quantities and other cheeses, such as mozzarella, are available in reduced-fat versions.

Above: Parmesan

Parmesan

Parmesan is the best-known and most important of the Italian hard cheeses. There are two basic types – Parmigiano Reggiano and Grana Padano – but the former is infinitely superior. A little finely grated Parmesan adds delicious flavour to many dishes from pasta and polenta to risotto and minestrone.

Left: Pecorino studded with peppercorns

Right: Ricotta

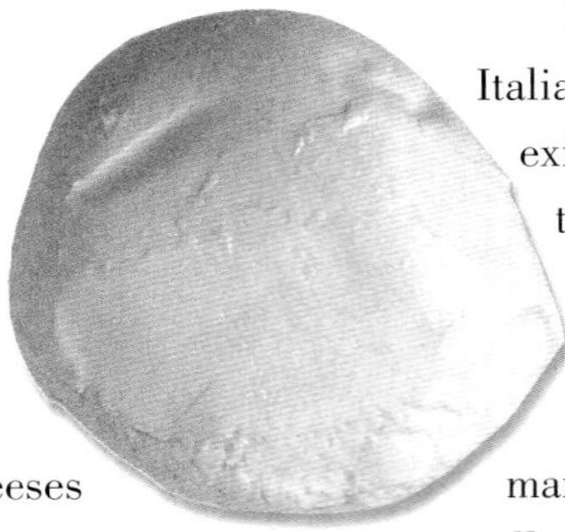

Mozzarella

Italian cooking could hardly exist without mozzarella, the pure white egg-shaped fresh cheese, whose melting quality makes it perfect for so many dishes. The best mozzarella is made in the area around Naples, using water buffalo's milk. Reduced-fat mozzarella is also readily available and is ideal for use in low-fat Italian cooking. It is delicious in sandwiches or served with fresh red tomatoes and green basil (*insalata tricolore*, or three-colour salad). When cooked, mozzarella becomes uniquely stringy and is ideal for topping pizzas.

Ricotta

Ricotta is a fresh, soft cheese made from cow's, ewe's or goat's milk. It is used widely in Italy for both sweet and savoury recipes. Ricotta has a medium fat content so should be used in moderation in low-fat Italian cooking. It has an excellent texture and a mild flavour, so it makes a perfect vehicle for seasonings such as black pepper, nutmeg or chopped fresh herbs. It is also puréed with cooked spinach to make a classic filling for ravioli, cannelloni or lasagne. It is often used in desserts and it can be sweetened and then served with fresh fruit.

Olive Oil and Flavourings

Olive oil and flavourings play an important role in Italian cooking. They are ideal for combining with staples such as rice and pasta to create speedy and nutritious low-fat meals.

Olive Oil

Olive oil is perhaps the single most important ingredient in an Italian kitchen. The best olive oil is extra virgin, which must have an acidity level of less than one per cent. It is ideal for using "raw" in salad dressings, uncooked sauces and for drizzling lightly over vegetables. Virgin olive oil has a higher acidity level and less refined flavour and is used as a condiment or for general cooking. Unclassified or pure olive oil is refined, then blended with virgin oil to add flavour and is ideal for cooking and baking.

Olive oil is high in monounsaturated fat and low in saturated fat and should be used in moderation when preparing low-fat Italian recipes.

Left: Extra virgin olive oil

Below: Balsamic vinegar

Above: A selection of Italian flavourings is essential for the authentic Italian store cupboard. Here we see a variety of oils, sun-dried tomatoes and tomato paste, passata, anchovies, capers and balsamic vinegar.

Right: A mixture of black and green olives

Balsamic Vinegar

Balsamic vinegar is the king of vinegars and is made in the area around Modena in Italy. It is the boiled and concentrated juice of local trebbiano grapes, which is aged over a very long period to give it a slightly syrupy texture and a rich, deep mahogany colour. Balsamic vinegar is used as a dressing or to finish a delicate sauce for white fish, poultry or calf's liver.

Olives

Black and green olives are used in low-fat Italian cooking, and both types are available whole or pitted, sold loose, in jars or vacuum-packed. Olives are added to many low-fat Italian dishes, such as salads and sauces. Olives are quite high in monounsaturated fat and low in saturated fat, but should be used in moderation.

Pesto

Green pesto is traditionally made with fresh basil, pine nuts, Parmesan and olive oil, but a red version based on sweet red peppers is also available. It can be home-made or bought ready-made in jars or fresh in tubs. Pesto can be added to hot pasta or gnocchi, risottos, tomato sauces or tomato-based soups. However, pesto is high in fat and should be used sparingly.

Sun-dried Tomatoes

Wrinkled red sun-dried tomatoes are available dry in packets or preserved in oil in jars. Dry-packed tomatoes are lower in fat than the oil-packed ones and are used in many low-fat Italian dishes to add flavour and colour. They can be eaten on their own as a snack, or soaked in hot water until soft, then added to numerous dishes including low-fat sauces, soups, egg and vegetable dishes.

Right: Sun-dried tomatoes

Herbs and Spices

Herbs and spices are vital to low-fat Italian cooking. Their aromatic flavour adds depth and interest to numerous dishes. Many wild herbs grow in the Italian countryside and are often incorporated into low-fat Italian recipes. Buy growing herbs in their pots if you can as this ensures the herbs are as fresh as possible. Better still, grow herbs in your own kitchen garden, in tubs or on windowsills and enjoy the convenience of a continuous supply.

ABOVE: Always use fresh herbs whenever you can. Their aromatic flavour adds depth and interest to all Italian cooking.

Basil

Basil, with its intense aroma and fresh, pungently sweet flavour, is associated with low-fat Italian cooking more than any other herb. There are many varieties of fresh basil but sweet basil is the most common. It is an essential ingredient of pesto, but it is also used in low-fat soups, salads, white fish and seafood dishes and almost any dish based on tomatoes, with which it has a great affinity. It is best added at the end of cooking.

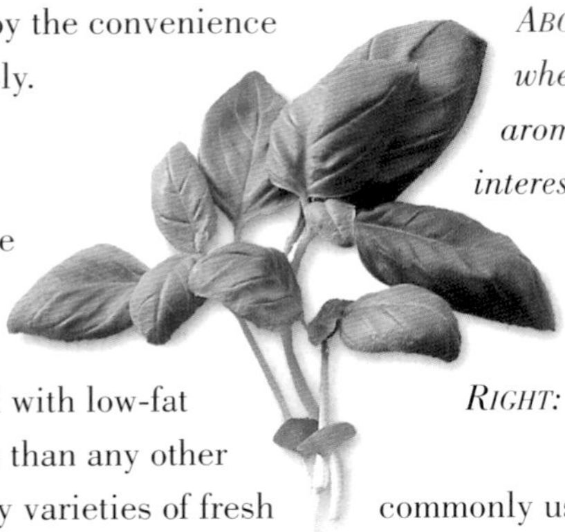

LEFT: Basil

Marjoram and Oregano

These two highly aromatic herbs are closely related (oregano is the wild variety), but marjoram has a much milder flavour. Marjoram is more commonly used in northern Italy, to flavour meat, poultry, vegetables and low-fat soups, while oregano is widely used in the south to flavour low-fat tomato dishes, vegetables and pizza. Choose plants which have fresh-looking leaves of good colour and even size.

ABOVE: Marjoram

Parsley

Italian parsley is the flat leaf variety which has a more robust flavour than curly parsley. It is used in low-fat savoury dishes such as soups, sauces, stocks, stews and risottos. Chopped parsley or whole leaves may also be used as a garnish. If flat leaf parsley is not available, curly parsley makes a good substitute. Choose parsley which has a good, fresh green colour.

RIGHT: Parsley

Rosemary

Spiky evergreen rosemary bushes, with their attractive blue flowers, grow wild all over Italy. The herb has a delicious, highly aromatic flavour which can easily overpower a dish, so should be used sparingly. Rosemary combines well with roast or grilled lean lamb, veal and chicken. It is also used to enhance low-fat dishes such as those based on baked fish and tomato. Some rosemary branches added to the charcoal on a barbecue impart a lovely flavour to whatever is being cooked.

RIGHT: Rosemary

Sage

Wild sage grows in profusion in the Italian countryside. There are several varieties, all of which have a slightly bitter, aromatic flavour, which contrasts well with lean meat such as pork, veal and chicken. Sage should be used sparingly and combines well with almost all low-fat meat and vegetable dishes, including minestrone, calf's liver and white haricot beans. Choose leaves which look fresh and bright in colour. Fresh sage should be stored in a plastic bag in the fridge for up to one week.

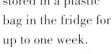

RIGHT: Sage

BELOW: Black peppercorns

BLACK PEPPERCORNS

Black peppercorns are the green berries of a vine which are dried on mats in the sun until they are all wrinkled and black. They are used for seasoning numerous low-fat Italian dishes and are best used freshly ground in a mill or crushed to enjoy their delicious flavour and aroma. Store peppercorns in an airtight container in a cool, dry place.

CHILLIES

Chopped fresh chillies or hot flakes of dried chillies are added to many low-fat Italian dishes. Fresh chillies vary in taste, from mild to fiery hot and they are unusual in that their "hotness" is usually in inverse proportion to their size, so larger, round fleshly varieties are generally milder than the smaller, thin-skinned pointed ones. For a milder spicy flavour, remove and discard the seeds and veins from fresh chillies before use. A small pinch of dried chilli flakes spices up low-fat stews and sauces, particularly those made with tomatoes. For a really hot low-fat pizza, crumble a few dried chilli flakes over the top. Dried chillies are extremely fiery and should be used sparingly.

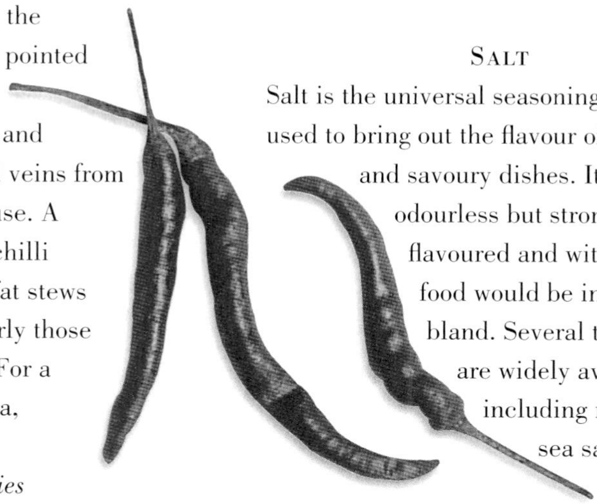

RIGHT: Fresh red chillies

Take care when preparing fresh chillies and always wear rubber or plastic gloves, or wash your hands and utensils thoroughly after use as chillies contain volatile oils which can irritate and burn if they touch sensitive areas, especially the eyes.

SAFFRON

Saffron is the world's most expensive spice and consists of the hand-picked dried stigmas of the saffron crocus. Saffron has a highly aromatic flavour and will impart a rich golden colour to many dishes. In Italy, saffron is mainly used to flavour and colour risottos and it is excellent in low-fat sauces for fish and poultry. It can also be used to flavour biscuits and cakes. Saffron threads are sold in small boxes or jars containing only a few grams, and powdered saffron is also available in jars.

ABOVE: Saffron threads

SALT

Salt is the universal seasoning ingredient used to bring out the flavour of both sweet and savoury dishes. It is odourless but strongly flavoured and without it our food would be insipid and bland. Several types of salt are widely available, including rock salt, sea salt and refined table salt. Due to its strong flavour, salt should be used sparingly in cooking and for seasoning food. Always store salt in an airtight container in a cool, dry place.

LEFT: Fine and coarse sea salt

BELOW: Italian chillies are generally milder than their South American counterparts, but should still be used with caution – it can often be quite difficult to gauge their heat.

THE FAT AND CALORIE CONTENTS OF FOOD

The following figures show the weight of fat (g) and the energy content per 100g/3½oz of each food.

VEGETABLES	FAT (G)	ENERGY
Aubergines, raw	0.4	15Kcals/64kJ
Aubergines, fried in corn oil	31.9	302Kcals/1262kJ
Artichokes, globe, raw	0.2	18Kcals/77kJ
Broccoli, raw	0.9	33Kcals/138kJ
Carrots, raw	0.3	35Kcals/146kJ
Cauliflowers, raw	0.9	34Kcals/142kJ
Chard, Swiss, raw	0.2	19Kcals/81kJ
Chicory, raw	0.6	11Kcals/45kJ
Courgettes, raw	0.4	18Kcals/74kJ
Cucumbers, raw	0.1	10Kcals/40kJ
Fennel, Florence, raw	0.2	12Kcals/50kJ
Mushrooms, raw	0.4	13Kcals/55kJ
Olives, in brine	11.0	103Kcals/422kJ
Onions, raw	0.2	36Kcals/150kJ
Peas, raw	1.5	83Kcals/344kJ
Peppers, red, raw	0.4	32Kcals/134kJ
Potatoes, raw	0.2	75Kcals/318kJ
Radicchio, raw	0.2	14Kcals/58kJ
Spinach, raw	0.8	25Kcals/103kJ
Squashes, butternut	0.1	36Kcals/155kJ
Tomatoes, raw	0.3	17Kcals/73kJ

FRUIT AND NUTS	FAT (G)	ENERGY
Apples, eating, raw	0.1	47Kcals/199kJ
Apricots, raw	0.1	31Kcals/134kJ
Avocados	19.5	190Kcals/748kJ
Bananas	0.3	95Kcals/403kJ
Dried mixed fruit	0.4	268Kcals/1144kJ
Figs, raw	0.3	43Kcals/185kJ
Figs, ready-to-eat (dried)	1.5	209Kcals/889kJ
Grapefruits, raw	0.1	30Kcals/126kJ
Grapes	0.1	60Kcals/257kJ
Melons	0.1	24Kcals/102kJ
Nectarines	0.1	40Kcals/171kJ
Oranges	0.1	37Kcals/158kJ
Peaches	0.1	33Kcals/142kJ
Pears	0.1	40Kcals/169kJ
Almonds	55.8	612Kcals/2534kJ
Brazil nuts	68.2	682Kcals/2813kJ
Cashew nuts, plain	48.2	573Kcals/2374kJ
Chestnuts	2.7	170Kcals/719kJ
Hazelnuts	63.5	650Kcals/2685kJ
Pine nuts	68.6	688Kcals/2840kJ
Pistachio nuts	55.4	601Kcals/2485kJ
Walnuts	68.5	688Kcals/2837kJ

CEREALS AND BAKING	FAT (G)	ENERGY
Brown rice, uncooked	2.8	357Kcals/1518kJ
White rice, uncooked	3.6	383Kcals/1630kJ
Pasta, white, uncooked	1.8	342Kcals/1456kJ
Pasta, wholemeal, uncooked	2.5	324Kcals/1379kJ
Brown bread	2.0	218Kcals/927kJ
White bread	1.9	235Kcals/1002kJ
Wholemeal bread	2.5	215Kcals/914kJ
Sugar, white	0	394Kcals/1680kJ
Chocolate, milk	30.7	520Kcals/2177kJ
Chocolate, plain	28.0	510Kcals/2137kJ
Honey	0	288Kcals/1229kJ
Fruit jam	0	261Kcals/1114kJ

BEANS AND PULSES	FAT (G)	ENERGY
Black-eyed beans, cooked	0.7	116Kcals/494kJ
Broad beans, raw	1.0	59Kcals/247kJ
Butter beans, canned	0.5	77Kcals/327kJ
Chick-peas, canned	2.9	115Kcals/487kJ
Green and brown lentils, cooked	0.7	105Kcals/446kJ
Red kidney beans, canned	0.6	100Kcals/424kJ

MEAT AND MEAT PRODUCTS	FAT (G)	ENERGY	DAIRY, FATS AND OILS	FAT (G)	ENERGY
Bacon rashers, streaky, raw	23.6	276Kcals/1142kJ	Cream, double	48.0	449Kcals/1849kJ
Bacon rashers, lean back, raw	6.7	136Kcals/568kJ	Cream, single	19.1	198Kcals/817kJ
Beef mince, raw	16.2	225Kcals/934kJ	Crème fraîche	40.0	379Kcals/156kJ
Beef mince, extra lean, raw	9.6	174Kcals/728kJ	Reduced-fat crème fraîche	15.0	165Kcals/683kJ
Beef, average, lean, raw	5.1	136Kcals/571kJ	Reduced-fat double cream	24.0	243Kcals/1002kJ
Lamb, average, lean, raw	8.3	156Kcals/651kJ	Milk, skimmed	0.1	33Kcals/140kJ
Pork, average, lean, raw	4.0	123Kcals/519kJ	Milk, whole	3.9	66Kcals/275kJ
Chicken breast, no skin, raw	1.1	106Kcals/449kJ	Cheddar cheese	34.4	412Kcals/1708kJ
Chicken, roasted, meat and skin	12.5	218Kcals/910kJ	Cheddar-type, reduced-fat	15.0	261Kcals/1091kJ
Duck, meat only, raw	6.5	137Kcals/575kJ	Cream cheese	47.4	439Kcals/1807kJ
Duck, roasted, meat, fat, skin	38.1	423Kcals/1750kJ	Fromage frais, plain	7.1	113Kcals/469kJ
Turkey, meat only, raw	1.6	105Kcals/443kJ	Fromage frais, very low-fat	0.2	58Kcals/247kJ
Liver, lamb, raw	6.2	137Kcals/575kJ	Mozzarella cheese	21.0	289Kcals/1204kJ
Salami	39.2	438Kcals/1814kJ	Ricotta cheese	11.0	144Kcals/599kJ
Parma ham	12.7	223Kcals/932kJ	Skimmed milk soft cheese	Trace	74Kcals/313kJ
Liver, calf, raw	3.4	104Kcals/437kJ	Feta cheese	20.2	250Kcals/1037kJ
			Parmesan cheese	32.7	452Kcals/1880kJ
FISH AND SHELLFISH	**FAT (G)**	**ENERGY**	Low-fat yogurt, natural	0.8	56Kcals/236kJ
Anchovies, canned in oil	19.9	280Kcals/1165kJ	Greek yogurt	9.1	115Kcals/477kJ
Clams, canned in brine	0.6	77Kcals/325kJ	Reduced-fat Greek yogurt	5.0	80Kcals/335kJ
Cod fillets, raw	0.7	80Kcals/337kJ	Butter	81.7	737Kcals/3031kJ
Crab, canned	0.5	77Kcals/326kJ	Margarine	81.6	739Kcals/3039kJ
Haddock, raw	0.6	81Kcals/345kJ	Low-fat spread	40.5	39Kcals/1605kJ
Monkfish, raw	0.4	66Kcals/282kJ	Very low-fat spread	25.0	273Kcals/1128kJ
Mussels, raw	1.8	74Kcals/312kJ	Corn oil	99.9	899Kcals/3696kJ
Plaice, raw	1.4	79Kcals/336kJ	Olive oil	99.9	899Kcals/3696kJ
Prawns, boiled	0.9	99Kcals/418kJ	Safflower oil	99.9	899Kcals/3696kJ
Red mullet, raw	3.8	109Kcals/459kJ	Eggs, whole, raw	10.8	147Kcals/612kJ
Sardines, raw	9.2	165Kcals/691kJ	Egg yolk, raw	30.5	339Kcals/1402kJ
Sea bass, raw	2.5	100Kcals/421kJ	Egg white, raw	Trace	36Kcals/153kJ
Squid, raw	1.7	81Kcals/344kJ	Dressing, fat-free	1.2	67Kcals/282kJ
Tuna, canned in brine	0.6	99Kcals/422kJ	Dressing, French	49.4	462Kcals/1902kJ
Tuna, canned in oil	9.0	189Kcals/794kJ	Mayonnaise	75.6	691Kcals/2843kJ
Tuna, raw	4.6	136Kcals/573kJ	Mayonnaise, reduced-calorie	28.1	288Kcals/1188kJ

Information from *The Composition of Foods* (5th Edition 1991) is Crown copyright and is reproduced with
the permission of the Royal Society of Chemistry and the Controller of Her Majesty's Stationery Office.

EQUIPMENT

Many of the utensils in the Italian kitchen are everyday items found in most kitchens, but some specialized ones are particularly useful.

For pasta you need to have a large saucepan for cooking the pasta and a colander for draining, while for making sauces you need only a sharp knife and a cutting board for chopping ingredients and a saucepan for cooking. You will also need a large bowl plus spoons and forks for tossing and serving.

You can make pasta by hand, but a pasta machine will make it much lighter work. Pasta machines come in electric or hand-cranked varieties.

BELOW: If you make pasta frequently, a pasta machine is an excellent buy because it is inexpensive, easy and fun to use, and makes excellent pasta in a very short time.

A special spoon with "teeth" or a perforated ladle are ideal for lifting spaghetti out of the saucepan. If you are making pizza, a cutting wheel will cut it into clean slices.

To keep fat to an absolute minimum, choose heavy-based, good quality cookware which doesn't need greasing before use, or use non-stick baking parchment and only lightly grease the tin before lining it. Also look out for non-stick coated fabric sheet, which is reusable.

Biscuit Cutter

Usually used for cutting biscuit dough into fancy shapes but is equally good for cutting fresh pasta shapes.

Colander

Indispensable for draining hot pasta and cooked vegetables.

Earthenware Pot

Excellent for slow-cooking stews, soups or sauces. It can be used either in the oven or on top of the stove on a gentle heat with a metal heat diffuser under it to prevent cracking. Many shapes and sizes are available. To season a terracotta pot before using it for the first time, immerse it in cold water overnight. Remove from the water and rub the unglazed bottom with a garlic clove. Fill with water and bring slowly to the boil. Discard the water. Repeat, changing the water, until the "earth" taste disappears.

Fluted Pastry Cutter

Good for cutting out fresh pasta shapes or for cutting freshly rolled pastry.

Hand Food Mill

Excellent for soups, sauces and tomato "passata": the pulp passes through the holes of the mill, leaving the seeds and skin behind.

Ice Cream Scoop

Suited to scooping firm and well-frozen ice creams, sorbets and yogurt ices.

Italian Ice Cream Scoop

Good for soft ices or sorbets that are not too solid.

Meat Hammer

Good for pounding escalopes. As well as pounding meat, it can be used to crush nuts and whole spices.

Mortar and Pestle

Useful for hand-grinding spices, rock salt, whole peppercorns, fresh or dried herbs and breadcrumbs.

ABOVE: 1 Earthenware pot, 2 olive stoner, 3 whisk, 4 fluted pastry cutter, 5 biscuit cutters, 6 pasta rolling pin, 7 mortar and pestle, 8 hand food mill, 9 colander, 10 Parmesan cheese knife, 11 pizza cutting wheel, 12 palette knife, 13 spaghetti spoon, 14 meat hammer, 15 pasta machine, 16 wide vegetable peeler, 17 Italian ice cream scoop, 18 ice cream scoop.

OLIVE STONER

Can be used for stoning black or green olives or fresh cherries.

PALETTE KNIFE

Very useful for spreading and smoothing.

PARMESAN CHEESE KNIFE

Break Parmesan off the large cheese wheels using this wedge-shaped tool.

PASTA MACHINE

Many models are available, including sophisticated electric and industrial models. Most have an adjustable roller width and both thin and wide noodle cutters.

PASTA ROLLING PIN

Ideal for rolling out home-made pasta dough. A length of dowelling 5 cm/2 in in diameter can also be used. Smooth the surface with fine sandpaper before using for the first time.

PIZZA CUTTING WHEEL

Useful for cutting slices of pizza, although a sharp knife may also be used.

SPAGHETTI SPOON

The wooden "teeth" catch the spaghetti strands and make cooked spaghetti easier to serve.

WHISK

Excellent for smoothing sauces and beating egg whites.

WIDE VEGETABLE PEELER

Very effective and easy to use for peeling all sizes of vegetable. Can also be used for peeling fruit.

TECHNIQUES

Chicken Stock

This classic, flavourful low-fat stock forms the base for many Italian soups and sauces.

Ingredients

1kg/2¼ lb chicken wings or thighs
1 onion
2 whole cloves
1 bay leaf
1 sprig of fresh thyme
3–4 sprigs of fresh parsley
10 black peppercorns

Makes 1.5 litres/2½ pints/6¼ cups

1 Cut the chicken into pieces and put into a saucepan. Peel the onion and stud it with cloves. Tie the bay leaf, thyme, parsley and peppercorns in a piece of muslin and add to the saucepan with the onion.

2 Pour in 1.75 litres/3 pints/7½ cups cold water. Slowly bring to simmering point, skimming off and discarding any scum which rises to the surface with a slotted spoon. Continue to simmer very gently, uncovered, for 1½ hours.

3 Strain the stock through a sieve into a large bowl and leave until it is cold. Discard the contents of the sieve. Remove and discard any chicken fat from the surface of the stock with a spoon. Keep the stock chilled and covered in the fridge until required, or freeze in usable amounts for up to six months.

Vegetable Stock

Ingredients

2 carrots
2 celery sticks
2 onions
2 tomatoes
10 mushroom stalks
2 bay leaves
1 sprig of fresh thyme
3–4 sprigs of fresh parsley
10 black peppercorns

Makes 1.5 litres/2½ pints/6¼ cups

Cook's Tip

To make fish stock, follow the recipe for chicken stock, substituting fish bones or trimmings for the chicken, and let it simmer for 20–30 minutes.

1 Roughly chop the carrots, celery, onions, tomatoes and mushroom stalks. Place them in a large heavy-based saucepan. Tie the bay leaves, thyme, parsley and peppercorns in a piece of muslin and add to the saucepan.

2 Pour in 1.75 litres/3 pints/7½ cups cold water. Slowly bring to simmering point. Continue to simmer very gently, uncovered, for 1½ hours.

3 Strain the stock through a sieve into a large bowl and leave until it is cold. Discard the contents of the sieve. Keep the stock chilled and covered in the fridge until required, or freeze in usable amounts for up to one month.

Peeling and Seeding Tomatoes

The best tomatoes for cooking are plum tomatoes, which hold their shape well and should have a fine flavour. Try to buy "vine-ripened" varieties as they will be properly ripened. The following method is an efficient way of preparing tomatoes and can be done in advance of making a recipe.

1 Use a sharp knife to cut a small cross on the bottom of the tomato. Turn the tomato over and carefully cut out the core. Immerse the tomato in boiling water for 30 seconds, then transfer to a bowl of cold water using a slotted spoon.

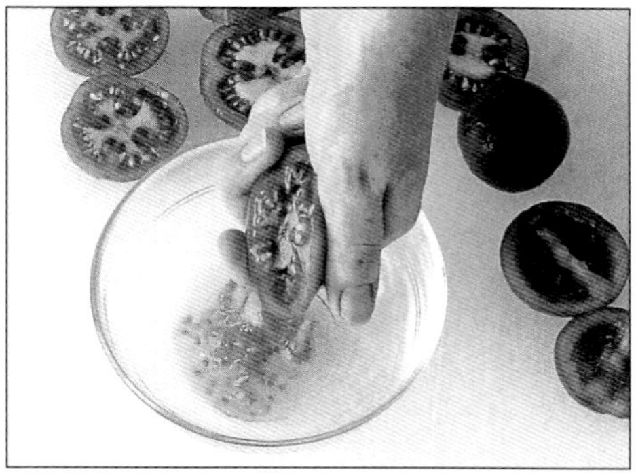

2 Lift out the tomato and peel (the skin should be easy to remove). Cut the peeled tomato in half crossways and squeeze out the seeds.

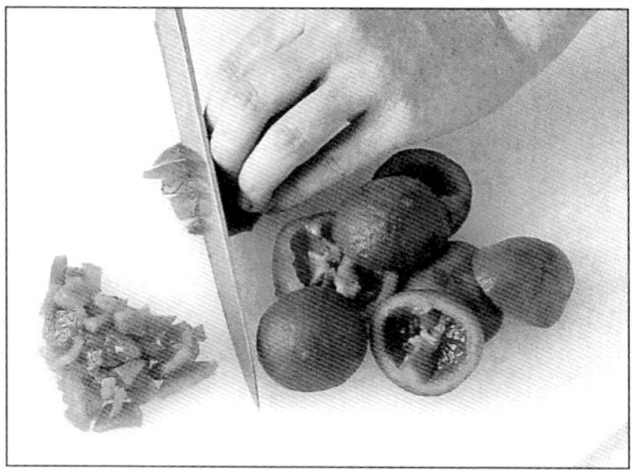

3 Use a large knife to cut the peeled tomato into strips, then chop across the strips to make dice. Use as required.

Chopping Onions

Cutting onion into uniform-size dice makes cooking easy. This method can't be beaten.

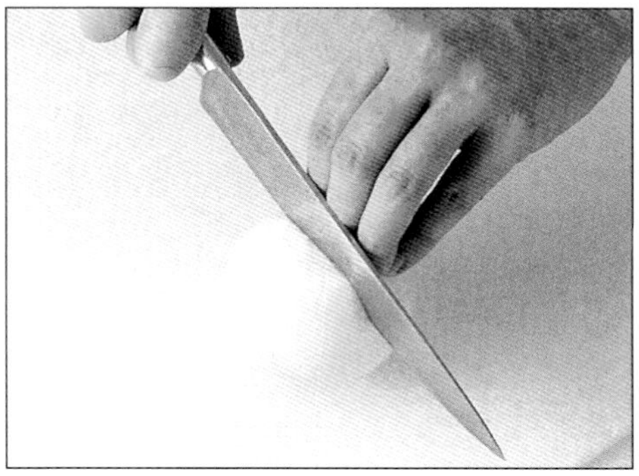

1 Peel the onion. Cut it in half with a large knife and set it cut-side down on a board. Make lengthways vertical cuts along the onion, cutting almost but not quite through to the root.

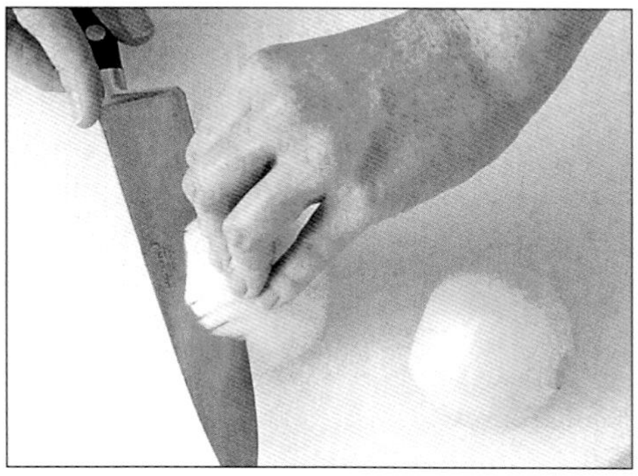

2 Make two horizontal cuts from the stalk end and towards the root, but not through it.

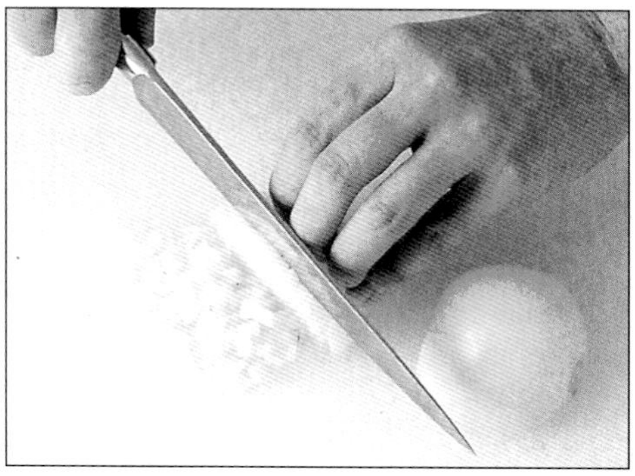

3 Cut the onion crossways to form small, even dice. Use as required.

Cook's Tip

This technique also works for shallots, but because they are smaller, you may not need to make the horizontal cuts.

Making Basic Pasta Dough on a Work Surface

The best place to make, knead and roll out pasta dough is on a wooden kitchen table – the larger the better. The surface should be warm, so marble is not suitable.

Ingredients

200g/7oz/1¾ cups plain flour
pinch of salt
2 eggs
10ml/2 tsp cold water

Serves 3–4

Variations

Tomato: add 20ml/4 tsp concentrated tomato purée to the eggs before mixing.
Spinach: add 115g/4oz frozen spinach, thawed and squeezed of excess moisture. Liquidize with the eggs, before adding to the flour.
Herb: add 45ml/3 tbsp finely chopped fresh herbs to the eggs before mixing the dough.

1 Sift the flour and salt on to a clean work surface and make a well in the centre with your hand.

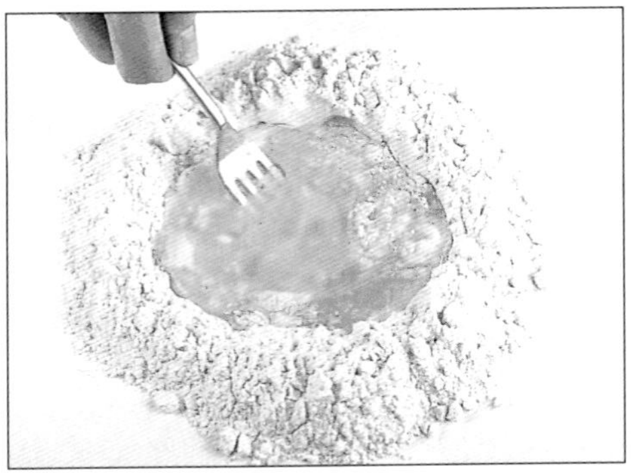

2 Put the eggs and water into the well. Using a fork, beat the eggs gently together, then gradually draw in the flour from the sides, to make a thick paste.

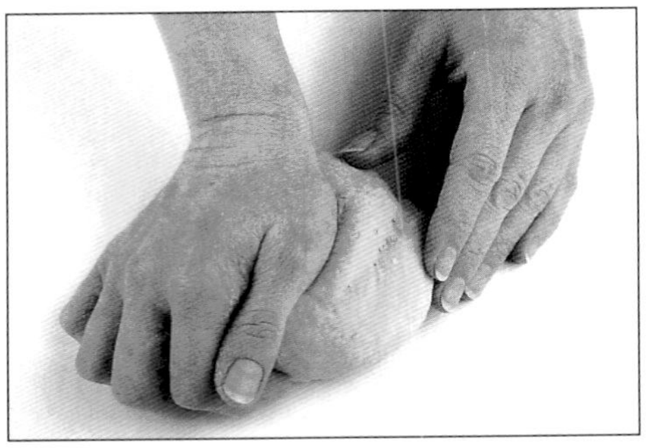

3 When the mixture becomes too stiff to use a fork, use your hands to mix to a firm dough. Knead the dough for about 5 minutes, until smooth. (This can be done in an electric food mixer fitted with a dough hook.) Wrap in clear film to prevent it drying out and leave to rest for 20–30 minutes.

Making Basic Pasta Dough in a Bowl

1 Sift the flour and salt into a glass bowl and make a well in the centre. Add the eggs and water.

2 Using a fork, beat the eggs gently together, then gradually draw in the flour from the sides, to make a thick paste.

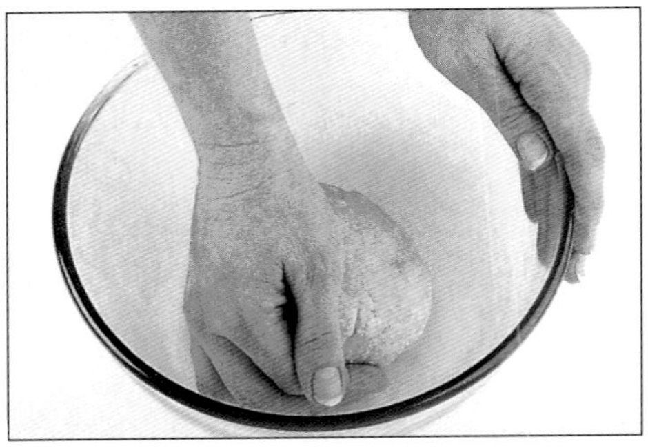

3 When the mixture becomes too stiff to use a fork, use your hands to mix to a firm dough. Knead the dough for 5 minutes until smooth. (This can be done in an electric food mixer fitted with a dough hook.) Wrap in clear film to prevent it drying out and leave for 20–30 minutes.

Rolling Out Pasta Dough by Hand

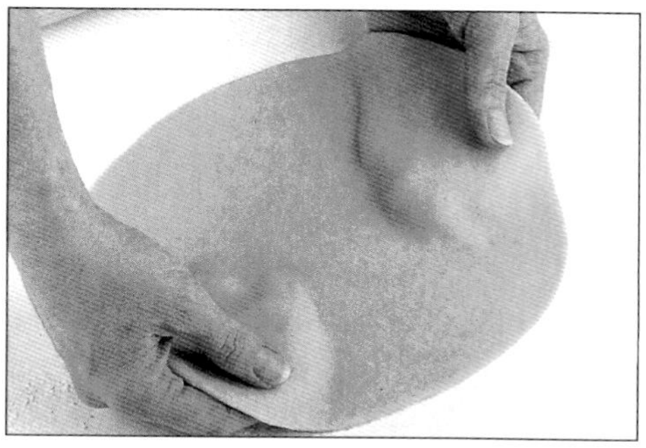

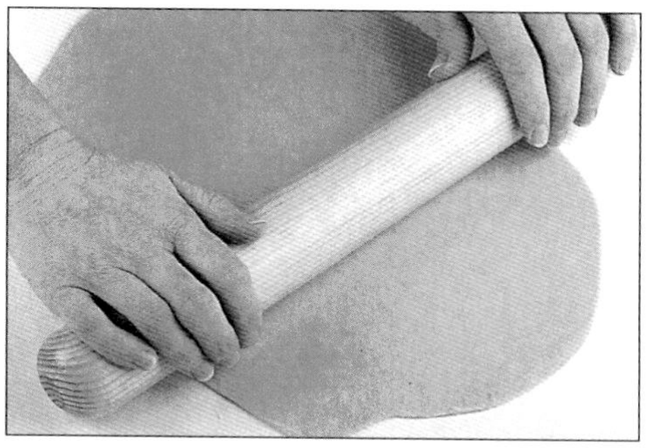

1 Cut the basic dough in quarters. Use one quarter at a time and re-wrap the rest in clear film so it does not dry out. Flatten the dough and dust liberally with flour. Start rolling out the dough, making sure you roll it evenly.

2 As the dough becomes thinner, keep on rotating it on the work surface by gently lifting the edges with your fingers and supporting it over the rolling pin. Make sure you don't tear the dough.

3 Carry on rolling out the dough until it has reached the desired thickness, about 3mm/$^{1}/_{8}$in thick.

Rolling Out Dough Using a Pasta Machine

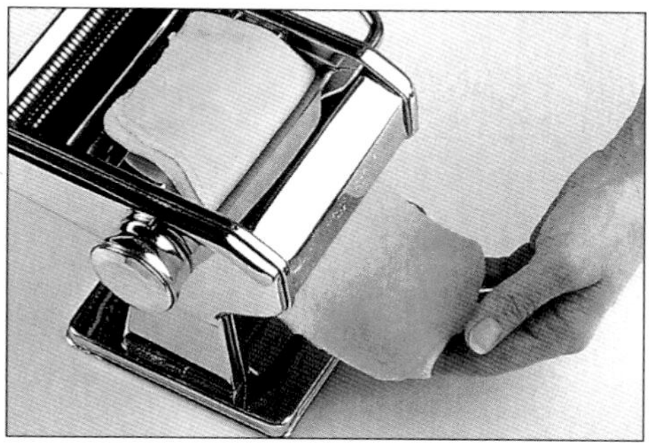

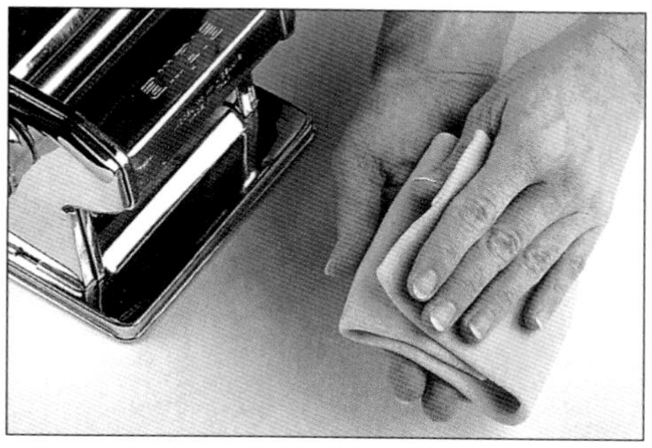

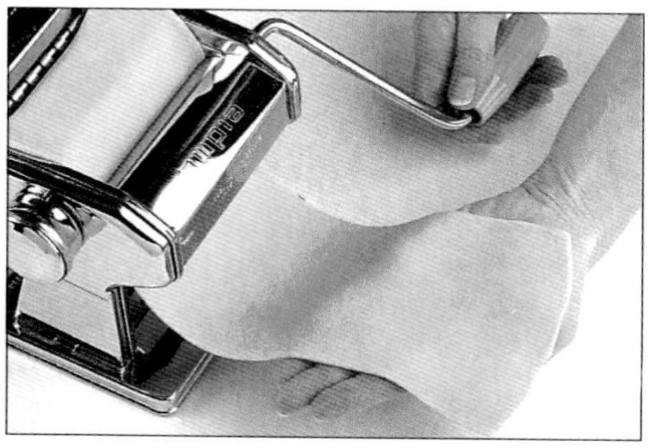

1 Cut the basic dough into quarters. Use one quarter at a time and re-wrap the rest in clear film so it does not dry out. Flatten the dough and dust liberally with flour. Start with the machine set to roll at the thickest setting. Pass the dough through the rollers several times, dusting the dough from time to time with flour until it is smooth.

2 Fold the strip of dough into three, press the joins well together and pass through the machine again. Repeat the folding and rolling several times on each setting.

3 Guide the dough through the machine but do not pull or stretch it or the dough will tear. As the dough is worked through all the settings, it will become thinner and longer. Guide the dough over your hand, as the dough is rolled out to a thin sheet. Pasta used for stuffing, such as ravioli or tortellini, should be used straightaway. Otherwise lay the rolled sheets on a clean dish towel, lightly dusted with sifted flour, and leave to dry for 10 minutes before cutting. This makes it easier to cut and prevents the strands of pasta sticking together.

Cutting Pasta Shapes

Until you are confident at handling and shaping pasta dough, it is easier to work with small quantities. Always keep the dough well wrapped in clear film to prevent it drying out, before you are ready to work with it.

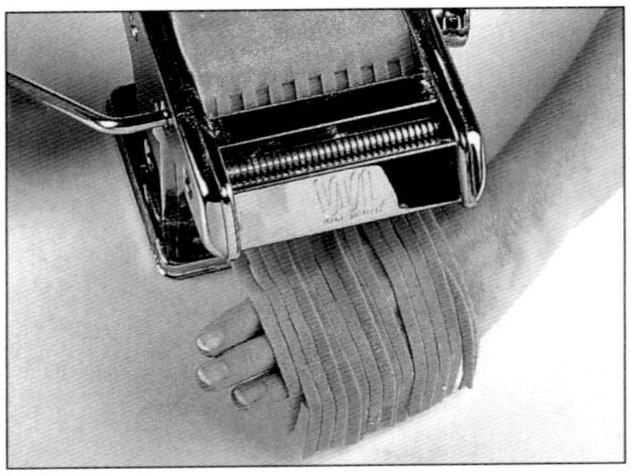

Cutting out tagliatelle

To cut tagliatelle, fit the appropriate attachment to the machine or move the handle to the appropriate slot. Cut the pasta sheets into 25cm/10in lengths and pass these through the machine as for spaghetti.

Cutting out lasagne

Take a sheet of pasta dough and cut out neat rectangles about 18 × 7.5cm/7 × 3in to make sheets of lasagne. Lay on a clean dish towel to dry.

Cutting out spaghetti

To cut spaghetti, fit the appropriate attachment to the machine or move the handle to the appropriate slot. Cut the pasta sheets into 25cm/10in lengths and pass these through the machine. Guide the strands over the back of your hand as they appear out of the machine.

Shaping Ravioli

Ravioli made in this way are not perfectly square, but they look charmingly home-made.

1 To make ravioli, place spoonfuls of filling on a sheet of dough at intervals of 5–7.5cm/2–3in, leaving a 2.5cm/1in border. Brush the dough between the spoonfuls of filling with lightly beaten egg white.

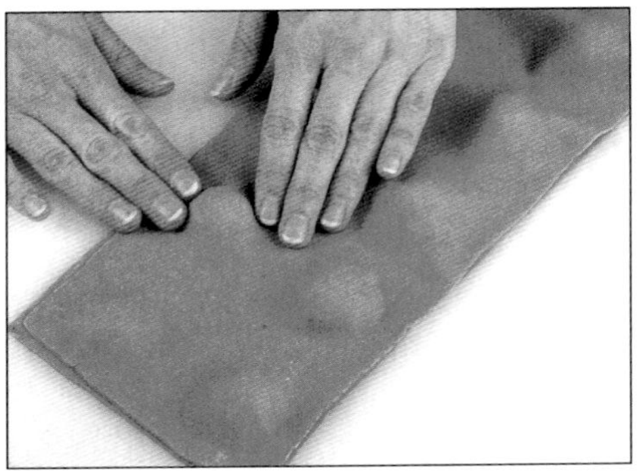

2 Lay a second sheet of pasta carefully over the top. Press around each mound of filling, excluding any air pockets.

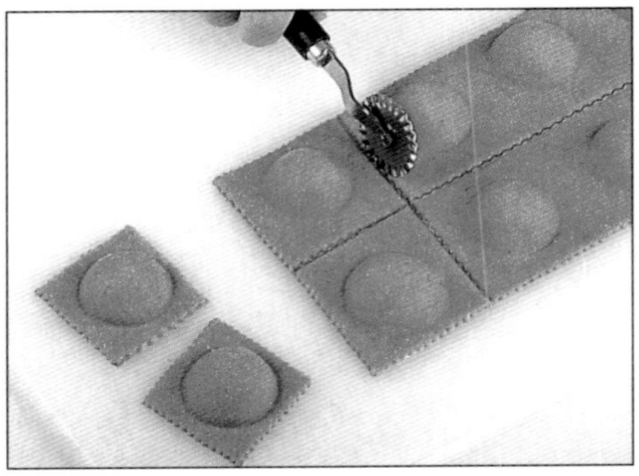

3 Using a fluted pastry wheel or a sharp knife, cut between the stuffing to make square-shaped parcels.

Making Farfalle (Pasta Bows)

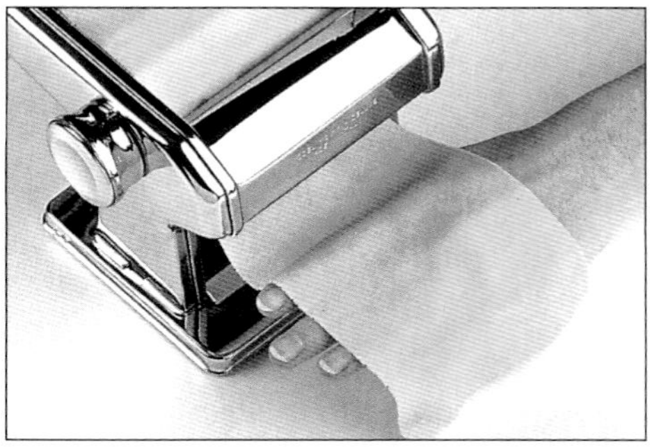

1 Roll the pasta dough through a pasta machine until the sheets are very thin. Then cut into long strips 4cm/1½in wide.

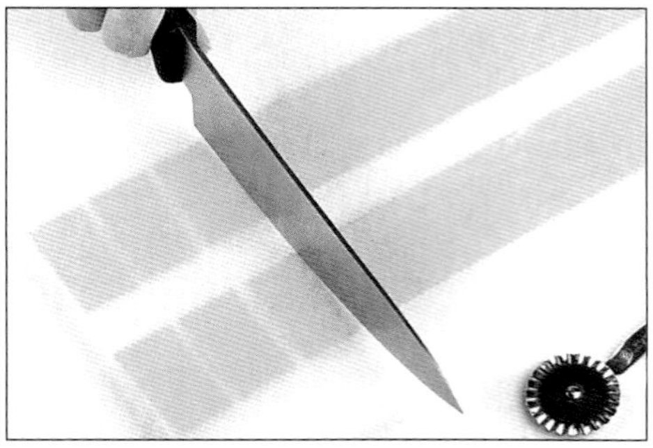

2 Cut the strips into small rectangles. Run a pastry wheel along the two shorter edges of the little rectangles – this will give the bows a decorative edge.

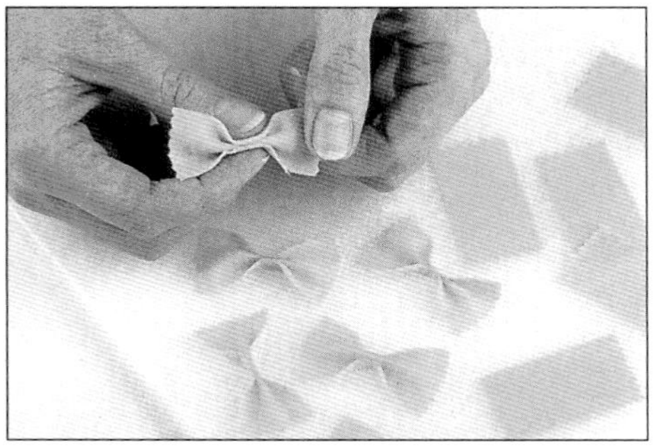

3 Moisten the centre of the strips and using a finger and thumb, gently pinch each rectangle together in the middle to make little pasta bows.

Making Tagliatelle

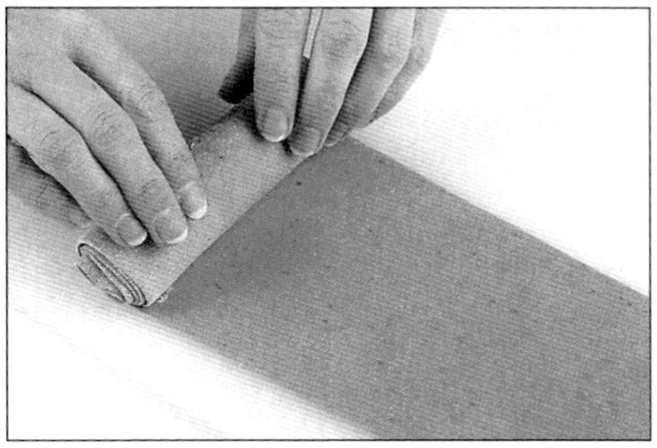

1 Lightly flour some spinach-flavoured pasta dough, cut into a rectangle 30 × 10cm/12 × 4in and roll it up.

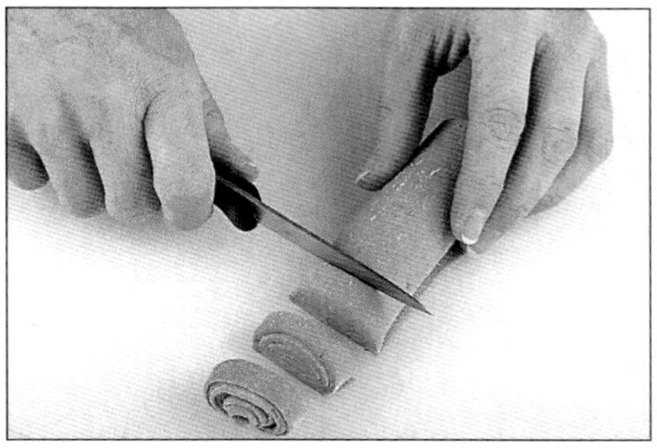

2 Using a sharp knife, cut straight across the pasta roll.

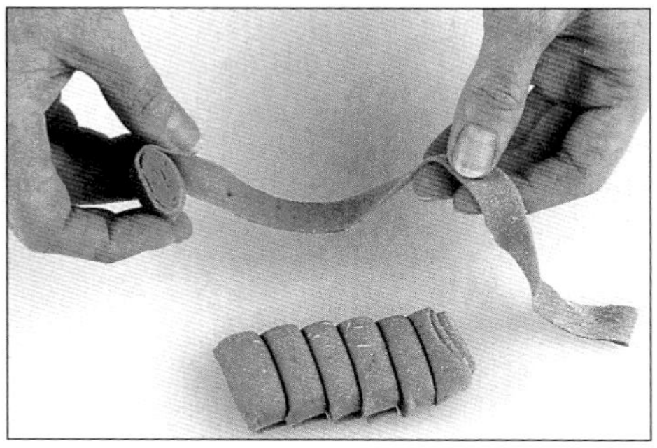

3 Carefully unravel each little roll as you cut it to make ribbons of fresh tagliatelle.

Cooking Pasta

1 Before starting to cook either sauce or pasta, read through the recipe carefully. It is important to know which needs to be cooked for the longest time – sometimes it is the pasta and sometimes the sauce, so don't always assume one or the other. The sauce can often be made ahead of time and reheated, but pasta is almost like a hot soufflé – it waits for no one.

2 There needs to be plenty of room for the pasta to move around in the large amount of water it requires, so a big pan is essential. The best type of pan is a tall, lightweight, straight-sided, stainless steel pasta cooking pot with its own in-built draining pan. Both outer and inner pans have two handles each, which ensures easy and safe lifting and draining. It is well worth investing in one of these pans.

3 Use a large quantity of water. If there is not enough water, the pasta shapes will stick together as they swell and the pan will become overcrowded. This will result in gummy-textured pasta. Before adding the pasta, the water should be at a fast rolling boil. The quickest way to do this is to boil water in the kettle, then pour it into the pasta pan, which should be set over high heat.

SOUPS

DELICIOUS *soups can be made in no time at all and they provide a* TEMPTING *start to a meal or make a complete* LIGHT *meal on their own when served with a hunk of fresh crusty* ITALIAN *bread. We include a selection of home-made* LOW-FAT *Italian soups for you to make and enjoy such as Roasted* PEPPER *Soup, Italian Vegetable Soup, Chicken and Pasta Soup and Roasted* TOMATO *and Pasta Soup.*

ITALIAN VEGETABLE SOUP

Fresh vegetables, cooked beans and pasta combine well with vegetable stock to create this tasty, virtually fat-free Italian soup.

INGREDIENTS

1 small carrot
1 baby leek
1 celery stick
50g/2oz green cabbage
900ml/1 1/2 pints/3 3/4 cups vegetable stock
1 bay leaf
115g/4oz/1 cup cooked cannellini or haricot beans
25g/1oz/1/4 cup dried soup pasta, such as tiny shells, bows, stars or elbows
salt and freshly ground black pepper
snipped fresh chives, to garnish

SERVES 4

1 Cut the carrot, leek and celery into 5cm/2in long julienne strips. Slice the cabbage very finely. Set aside. Put the stock and bay leaf into a large saucepan and bring to the boil. Add the carrot, leek and celery, cover and simmer for 6 minutes, stirring occasionally.

2 Add the cabbage, beans and pasta shapes. Stir, then simmer, uncovered, for a further 4–5 minutes, or until the vegetables and pasta are tender or *al dente*, stirring occasionally.

3 Remove the bay leaf and season with salt and pepper to taste. Ladle into soup bowls and garnish with snipped chives. Serve immediately.

NUTRITIONAL NOTES

Per portion:

Energy	63Kcals/266kJ
Total fat	0.48g
Saturated fat	0.07g
Cholesterol	0mg
Fibre	1.48g

VEGETABLE MINESTRONE

This vegetable and pasta soup makes a tasty starter or snack dish which is very low in fat.

3 Add the tomatoes, the saffron with its liquid and the frozen peas. Bring back to the boil and add the soup pasta. Simmer for 10 minutes until tender or *al dente*, stirring occasionally.

4 Season with sugar, salt and pepper to taste. Stir in the chopped herbs just before serving. Ladle into soup bowls and serve.

Ingredients

large pinch of saffron strands
1 onion, chopped
1 leek, sliced
1 celery stick, sliced
2 carrots, diced
2–3 garlic cloves, crushed
600ml/1 pint/2½ cups chicken stock
2 x 400g/14oz cans chopped tomatoes
50g/2oz/½ cup frozen peas
50g/2oz/½ cup dried soup pasta, such as anellini
5ml/1 tsp caster sugar
15ml/1 tbsp chopped fresh parsley
15ml/1 tbsp chopped fresh basil
salt and freshly ground black pepper

Serves 4

1 Soak the saffron strands in 15ml/1 tbsp boiling water in a small bowl. Leave to stand for 10 minutes.

2 Meanwhile, put the onion, leek, celery, carrots and garlic into a large saucepan. Add the chicken stock, bring to the boil, cover and simmer for about 10 minutes.

Nutritional Notes

Per portion:

Energy	77Kcals/330kJ
Total fat	0.6g
Saturated fat	0.1g
Cholesterol	0mg
Fibre	2.9g

LITTLE STUFFED HATS IN BROTH

This soup is served in northern Italy on Santo Stefano (St Stephen's Day – or Boxing Day) and on New Year's Day. It makes a light change from all the celebration food the day before.

Ingredients

1.2 litres/2 pints/5 cups chicken stock
90–115g/3½–4oz/1 cup fresh or dried cappelletti
30ml/2 tbsp dry white wine (optional)
about 15ml/1 tbsp finely chopped fresh flat leaf parsley (optional)
salt and freshly ground black pepper
shredded flat leaf parsley, to garnish
15ml/1 tbsp grated fresh Parmesan cheese, to serve

Serves 4

1 Pour the chicken stock into a large saucepan and bring to the boil. Add a little salt and pepper to taste.

2 Drop in the pasta, stir well and bring back to the boil. Reduce the heat to a simmer and cook, according to the packet instructions, until the pasta is tender or *al dente*. Stir the pasta frequently during cooking to ensure that it cooks evenly.

3 Swirl in the wine and parsley, if using, then adjust the seasoning. Ladle into warmed soup bowls, then sprinkle with shredded flat leaf parsley and grated Parmesan. Serve immediately.

Nutritional Notes

Per portion:

Energy	103Kcals/436kJ
Total fat	1.7g
Saturated fat	0.8g
Cholesterol	3.7mg
Fibre	0.8g

TINY PASTA IN BROTH

In Italy this tasty pasta soup is often served with bread for a light evening supper or for a quick midday snack. You can use any other dried tiny soup pastas in place of the funghetti.

Ingredients

1.2 litres/2 pints/5 cups beef stock
75g/3oz/¾ cup dried tiny soup pasta, such as funghetti
2 pieces bottled roasted red pepper, about 50g/2oz
salt and freshly ground black pepper
25g/1oz coarsely shaved fresh Parmesan cheese, to serve

Serves 4

1 Bring the beef stock to the boil in a large saucepan. Add salt and pepper to taste, then drop in the dried soup pasta. Stir well and bring the stock back to the boil.

2 Reduce the heat to a simmer and cook for 7–8 minutes, or according to the packet instructions, until the pasta is tender or *al dente*. Stir frequently during cooking to prevent the pasta shapes from sticking together.

Nutritional Notes

Per portion:

Energy	108Kcals/457kJ
Total fat	3.7g
Saturated fat	1.5g
Cholesterol	6.2mg
Fibre	0.8g

3 Drain the pieces of roasted pepper and dice them finely. Place them in the bottom of four soup bowls. Taste the soup and adjust the seasoning. Ladle into the soup bowls and serve immediately, with shavings of Parmesan served separately.

FRESH TOMATO SOUP

Intensely flavoured sun-ripened tomatoes need little embellishment in this fresh-tasting low-fat soup. For the best flavour, choose the ripest looking tomatoes you can find.

Ingredients

1.5kg/3–3½lb ripe tomatoes
400ml/14fl oz/1⅔ cups chicken or vegetable stock
45ml/3 tbsp sun-dried tomato purée
30–45ml/2–3 tbsp balsamic vinegar
10–15ml/2–3 tsp caster sugar
small handful fresh basil leaves
salt and freshly ground black pepper
fresh basil leaves, to garnish
6 small toasted cheese croûtes, and 30ml/2 tbsp half-fat crème fraîche, to serve

Serves 6

Cook's Tip

Add the vinegar and sugar a little at a time, tasting the soup as you go, to ensure you use just the right amount of each.

1 Plunge the tomatoes into a bowl of boiling water for 30 seconds, then refresh in cold water. Drain. Peel and discard the skins and quarter the tomatoes. Put them in a large saucepan and pour over the chicken or vegetable stock. Bring to the boil, reduce the heat, cover and simmer gently for 10 minutes until the tomatoes are pulpy.

2 Stir in the tomato purée, vinegar, sugar and basil. Season with salt and pepper, then cook gently, stirring, for 2 minutes. Purée the soup in a blender or food processor, then return to the rinsed-out saucepan and reheat gently until piping hot. Serve in soup bowls topped with one or two toasted cheese croûtes and a teaspoonful of crème fraîche. Garnish with basil leaves.

Nutritional Notes

Per portion:

Energy	108Kcals/460kJ
Total fat	3.5g
Saturated fat	1.8g
Cholesterol	2.6mg
Fibre	2.7g

CHICKEN AND PASTA SOUP

Skinless cooked chicken, mushrooms and pasta combine well with a flavourful stock, to create this tasty, low-fat soup, ideal for a starter or snack.

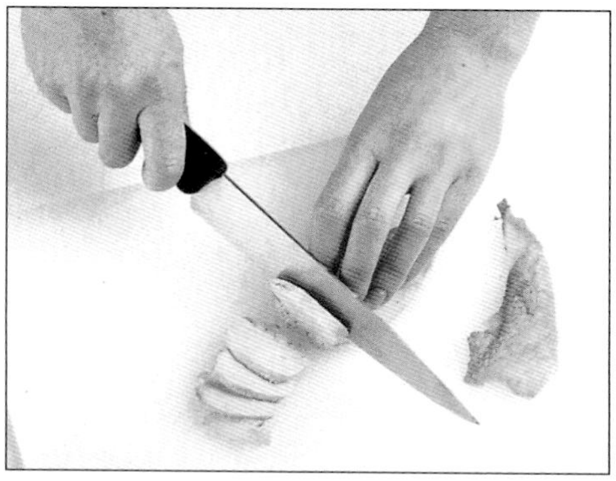

3 Remove and discard the skin from the chicken and slice the meat thinly using a sharp knife. Add to the soup and season to taste. Heat the soup through for about 2–3 minutes.

4 Stir in the pasta, bring to the boil, cover and simmer for 7–8 minutes until tender or *al dente*. Just before serving, remove and discard the bay leaf. Stir in the white wine and chopped parsley, heat through for 2–3 minutes, then adjust the seasoning and serve in soup bowls.

INGREDIENTS

900ml/1 1/2 pints/3 3/4 cups chicken stock
1 bay leaf
4 spring onions, sliced
225g/8oz/3 cups button mushrooms, sliced
115g/4oz cooked chicken breast
50g/2oz/1/2 cup dried soup pasta, such as stellette
150ml/1/4 pint/2/3 cup dry white wine
15ml/1 tbsp chopped fresh parsley
salt and freshly ground black pepper

SERVES 4–6

1 Put the stock and bay leaf into a saucepan and bring to the boil.

2 Add the spring onions and mushrooms and stir to mix.

NUTRITIONAL NOTES

Per portion:

Energy	74Kcals/312kJ
Total fat	1g
Saturated fat	0.3g
Cholesterol	8.24mg
Fibre	0.75g

TOMATO AND FRESH BASIL SOUP

A soup for late summer, when fresh plum tomatoes are at their most flavoursome, this fresh tomato soup flavoured with basil creates a tasty supper dish.

Ingredients

15ml/1 tbsp olive oil
1 onion, finely chopped
900g/2lb ripe Italian plum tomatoes, roughly chopped
1 garlic clove, roughly chopped
about 750ml/1¼ pints/3 cups chicken or vegetable stock
120ml/4fl oz/½ cup dry white wine
30ml/2 tbsp sun-dried tomato purée
30ml/2 tbsp shredded fresh basil, plus a few whole leaves to garnish
30ml/2 tbsp single cream
salt and freshly ground black pepper

Serves 4

1 Heat the olive oil in a large saucepan over a medium heat. Add the chopped onion and cook gently for about 5 minutes, stirring frequently, until it is softened but not brown.

Nutritional Notes

Per portion:

Energy	77Kcals/324kJ
Total fat	3.9g
Saturated fat	1.1g
Cholesterol	2.74mg
Fibre	1.75g

2 Stir in the chopped tomatoes and garlic, then add the stock, white wine and tomato purée, with salt and pepper to taste. Bring to the boil, then reduce the heat, half-cover the pan and simmer gently for 20 minutes, stirring the mixture occasionally to stop the tomatoes sticking to the base of the pan.

3 Purée the soup with the shredded basil in a blender or food processor until smooth, then press through a sieve into a clean pan. Discard the remaining contents of the sieve.

4 Add the cream to the soup in the pan and heat through, stirring. Do not allow the soup to boil. Check the consistency of the soup and add more hot stock if necessary, then adjust the seasoning. Pour into soup bowls and garnish with whole basil leaves. Serve at once.

FARMHOUSE SOUP

Root vegetables form the basis of this low-fat, chunky, minestrone-style soup. For a more substantial meal, serve with fresh crusty bread.

INGREDIENTS

15ml/1 tbsp olive oil
1 onion, roughly chopped
3 carrots, cut into large chunks
175–200g/6–7oz turnips, cut into large chunks
175g/6oz swede, cut into large chunks
400g/14oz can chopped Italian tomatoes
15ml/1 tbsp tomato purée
5ml/1 tsp dried mixed herbs
5ml/1 tsp dried oregano
50g/2oz/½ cup dried peppers, washed and thinly sliced (optional)
1.5 litres/2½ pints/6¼ cups vegetable stock or water
50g/2oz/½ cup dried small macaroni or conchiglie
400g/14oz can red kidney beans, rinsed and drained
30ml/2 tbsp chopped fresh flat leaf parsley
salt and freshly ground black pepper
15ml/1 tbsp grated fresh Parmesan cheese, to serve

SERVES 6

1 Heat the oil in a large saucepan, add the onion and cook over a low heat for about 5 minutes until softened. Add the prepared fresh vegetables, canned tomatoes, tomato purée, dried herbs and dried peppers, if using. Stir in salt and pepper to taste. Pour in the stock or water and bring to the boil. Stir well, cover, reduce the heat and simmer for 30 minutes, stirring occasionally.

2 Add the pasta and bring to the boil, stirring, then simmer, uncovered, for about 5 minutes or according to the packet instructions, until the pasta is just tender or *al dente*. Stir frequently.

3 Stir in the beans. Heat through for 2–3 minutes, then remove from the heat and stir in the parsley. Adjust the seasoning. Serve hot in soup bowls, sprinkled with a little grated Parmesan.

COOK'S TIP

Dried Italian peppers are piquant and firm with a "meaty" bite, which makes them ideal for adding substance to vegetarian soups.

NUTRITIONAL NOTES

Per portion:

Energy	159Kcals/671kJ
Total fat	4g
Saturated fat	0.9g
Cholesterol	2.36mg
Fibre	6.6g

ROASTED PEPPER SOUP

Grilling intensifies the flavour of red and yellow peppers and helps this soup keep its stunning colour. No added fat is used for this recipe, creating a delicious and virtually fat-free soup.

INGREDIENTS

3 red peppers
1 yellow pepper
1 onion, chopped
1 garlic clove, crushed
750ml/1¼ pints/3 cups vegetable stock
15ml/1 tbsp plain flour
salt and freshly ground black pepper
red and yellow peppers, diced, to garnish

SERVES 4

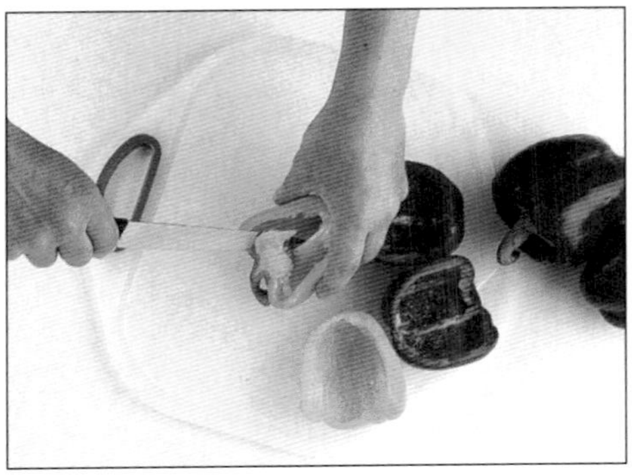

1 Preheat the grill. Halve the red and yellow peppers and cut out and discard their stalks and white pith. Scrape out and discard the seeds.

2 Line a grill pan with foil and arrange the halved peppers, skin-side up, in a single layer. Grill under a hot grill until the skins have blackened and blistered.

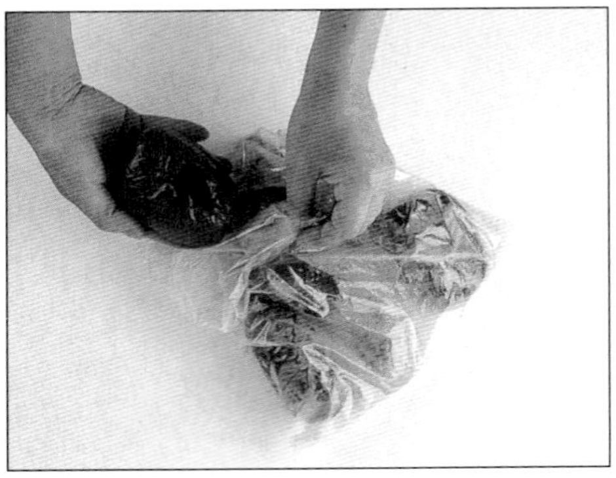

3 Transfer the grilled peppers to a plastic bag and leave for a few minutes. Once cool, gently peel away and discard their skins. Roughly chop the pepper flesh. Set aside.

4 Put the onion, garlic clove and 150ml/¼ pint/⅔ cup stock into a large saucepan. Bring to the boil and boil for about 5 minutes until most of the stock has reduced in volume. Reduce the heat and stir until the onion and garlic are softened and just beginning to colour.

NUTRITIONAL NOTES
Per portion:

Energy	28Kcals/117kJ
Total fat	0.2g
Saturated fat	0.04g
Cholesterol	0mg
Fibre	0.8g

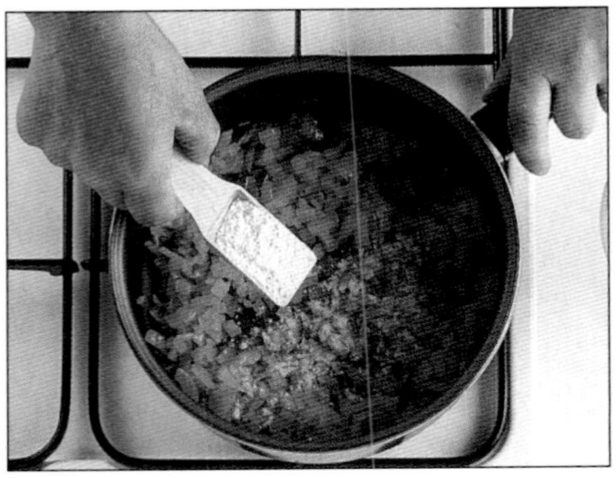

5 Sprinkle the flour over the onions, then gradually stir in the remaining stock. Add the chopped peppers and bring to the boil, stirring. Cover and allow to simmer for 5 minutes.

6 Leave to cool slightly, then purée in a blender or food processor until smooth. Season to taste. Return to the rinsed-out saucepan and reheat until piping hot. Ladle into soup bowls and garnish each portion with a sprinkling of diced peppers. Serve.

COOK'S TIP

Sautéeing onions and garlic in stock, as described in Step 4, is a very useful technique in low-fat cooking. The trick is to allow the stock to reduce almost entirely, from which point the onions and garlic will start to brown, rather than simply being boiled.

PASTA AND CHICK-PEA SOUP

A simple, country-style Italian soup, ideal for a flavourful, low-fat starter. You can use other pasta shapes, but conchiglie are ideal because they scoop up the chick-peas and beans.

INGREDIENTS
1 onion
2 carrots
2 celery sticks
15ml/1 tbsp olive oil
400g/14oz can chick-peas, rinsed and drained
200g/7oz can cannellini beans, rinsed and drained
150ml/1/4 pint/2/3 cup passata
120ml/4fl oz/1/2 cup water
1.5 litres/2 1/2 pints/6 1/4 cups vegetable or chicken stock
1 fresh or dried rosemary sprig
200g/7oz/scant 2 cups dried conchiglie
salt and freshly ground black pepper
fresh rosemary leaves, to garnish
15ml/1 tbsp grated fresh Parmesan cheese, to serve

SERVES 6

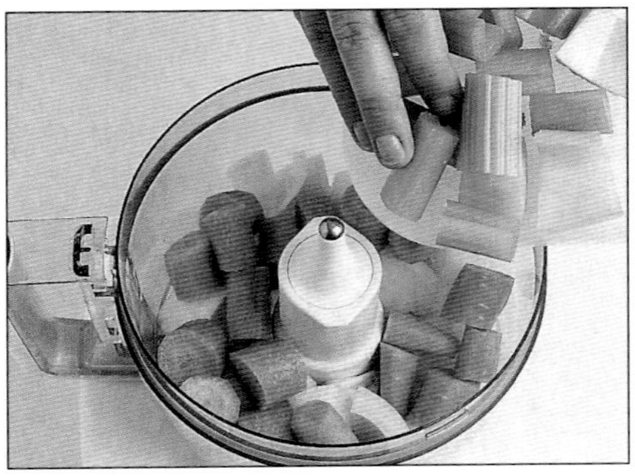

1 Chop the onion, carrots and celery sticks finely, either in a food processor or by hand.

2 Heat the olive oil in a large saucepan, add the chopped vegetables and cook over a low heat, stirring frequently, for 5–7 minutes.

3 Add the chick-peas and cannellini beans, stir well to mix, then cook for 5 minutes. Stir in the passata and water. Cook, stirring, for 2–3 minutes.

4 Add 475ml/16fl oz/2 cups of the stock, the rosemary sprig and salt and pepper to taste. Bring to the boil, cover, then simmer gently, stirring occasionally, for 1 hour.

NUTRITIONAL NOTES
Per portion:

Energy	201Kcals/849kJ
Total fat	4.5g
Saturated fat	0.9g
Cholesterol	1.84mg
Fibre	3.4g

5 Pour in the remaining stock, add the pasta and bring to the boil, stirring. Reduce the heat and simmer, stirring frequently for 7–8 minutes, or according to the packet instructions, until the pasta is tender or *al dente*. Adjust the seasoning. Remove and discard the rosemary sprig and serve the hot soup in soup bowls, topped with a few rosemary leaves and a little grated Parmesan.

LENTIL AND PASTA SOUP

This rustic Italian vegetarian soup makes a warming winter meal. It goes well with granary or crusty Italian bread to create a healthy, low-fat supper dish.

INGREDIENTS

175g/6oz/¾ cup brown lentils
3 garlic cloves
1 litre/1¾ pints/4 cups water
15ml/1 tbsp olive oil
1 onion, finely chopped
2 celery sticks, finely chopped
30ml/2 tbsp sun-dried tomato purée
1.75 litres/3 pints/7½ cups vegetable stock
a few fresh marjoram leaves
a few fresh basil leaves
leaves from 1 fresh thyme sprig
50g/2oz/½ cup dried small pasta shapes, such as tubetti
salt and freshly ground black pepper
tiny fresh herb leaves, to garnish

SERVES 6

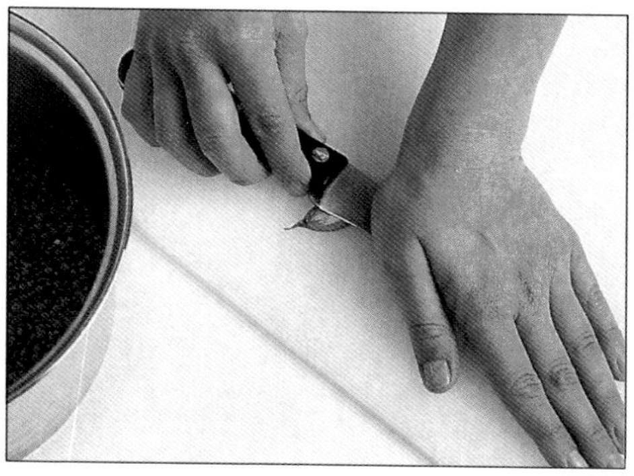

1 Put the lentils in a large saucepan. Smash 1 garlic clove (there's no need to peel it first) and add it to the lentils. Pour in the water and bring to the boil. Reduce the heat to a gentle simmer and cook, stirring occasionally, for about 20 minutes or until the lentils are just tender. Tip the lentils into a sieve, remove the garlic and set it aside. Rinse the lentils under the cold tap, then leave them to drain.

2 Heat the oil in a large saucepan. Add the onion and celery and cook over a low heat, stirring frequently, for 5–7 minutes until softened.

3 Crush the remaining garlic, then peel and mash the reserved garlic. Add to the vegetables with the tomato purée and the lentils. Stir, then add the stock, the fresh herbs and salt and pepper to taste. Bring to the boil, then simmer for 30 minutes, stirring occasionally.

4 Add the pasta and bring back to the boil, stirring. Simmer, stirring frequently for 7–8 minutes, or according to the packet instructions, until the pasta is tender or *al dente*. Adjust the seasoning. Serve hot, sprinkled with the herb leaves.

COOK'S TIP

Use green lentils instead of brown if you like, but don't use the orange or red ones as they go mushy.

NUTRITIONAL NOTES

Per portion:

Energy	145Kcals/615kJ
Total fat	3.2g
Saturated fat	0.4g
Cholesterol	0mg
Fibre	3.2g

PUGLIA-STYLE MINESTRONE

This is a tasty low-fat soup for a supper early in the week because it can be made with the leftover carcass of Sunday's roast chicken.

Ingredients

1 roast chicken carcass
1 onion, quartered lengthways
1 carrot, roughly chopped
1 celery stick, roughly chopped
a few black peppercorns
1 small handful mixed fresh herbs, such as parsley and thyme
1 chicken stock cube
50g/2oz/½ cup dried tubetti
salt and freshly ground black pepper
25g/1oz ricotta salata or feta cheese, coarsely grated or crumbled, and 30ml/2 tbsp fresh mint leaves, to serve

Serves 4

1 Break the chicken carcass into pieces and place these in a large saucepan. Add the onion, carrot, celery, peppercorns and fresh herbs, then crumble in the stock cube and add a good pinch of salt. Cover the chicken generously with cold water (you will need about 1.5 litres/2½ pints/6¼ cups) and bring to the boil over a high heat.

2 Reduce the heat, half cover the pan and simmer gently for about 1 hour. Remove the pan from the heat and leave the mixture to cool, then strain the liquid through a colander or sieve into a clean, large saucepan.

3 Remove any meat from the chicken bones, cut it into bite-size pieces and set aside. Discard the carcass and all the flavouring ingredients.

4 Bring the stock in the pan to the boil, add the pasta and simmer, stirring frequently for 5–6 minutes, or according to the packet instructions, until only just tender or *al dente*.

5 Add the chicken and heat through for a few minutes, by which time the pasta will be ready. Adjust the seasoning. Serve hot in soup bowls, sprinkled with the ricotta salata or feta cheese and mint leaves.

Nutritional Notes

Per portion:

Energy	59Kcals/250kJ
Total fat	1.5g
Saturated fat	0.9g
Cholesterol	4.38mg
Fibre	0.4g

PASTA, BEAN AND VEGETABLE SOUP

This tasty soup is a speciality from the Calabrian region of Italy. The combination of pulses, pasta and vegetables creates a filling, low-fat soup.

INGREDIENTS

75g/3oz/scant 1/2 cup brown lentils
15g/1/2oz/1/2 cup dried mushrooms
15ml/1 tbsp olive oil
1 carrot, diced
1 celery stick, diced
1 onion, finely chopped
1 garlic clove, finely chopped
a little chopped fresh flat leaf parsley
a good pinch of crushed red chillies (optional)
1.5 litres/2 1/2 pints/6 1/4 cups vegetable stock
150g/5oz/scant 1 cup each canned red kidney beans, cannellini beans and chick-peas, rinsed and drained
115g/4oz/1 cup dried small pasta shapes, such as rigatoni, penne or penne rigate
salt and freshly ground black pepper
chopped flat leaf parsley, to garnish
30ml/2 tbsp grated fresh Pecorino cheese, to serve

SERVES 6

1 Put the lentils in a medium saucepan, add 475ml/16fl oz/2 cups water and bring to the boil over a high heat. Reduce the heat to a gentle simmer and cook, stirring occasionally, for 15–20 minutes or until just tender. Meanwhile, soak the dried mushrooms in 175ml/6fl oz/3/4 cup warm water for 15–20 minutes.

2 Tip the lentils into a sieve to drain, then rinse under the cold tap. Drain the soaked mushrooms and reserve the soaking liquid. Finely chop the mushrooms and set aside.

3 Heat the oil in a large saucepan and add the carrot, celery, onion, garlic, parsley and chillies, if using. Cook over a low heat for 5–7 minutes, stirring occasionally. Add the stock, then the mushrooms and their soaking liquid.

4 Bring to the boil, then add the beans, chick-peas and lentils. Season to taste. Cover, and simmer gently for 20 minutes.

5 Add the pasta and bring the soup back to the boil, stirring. Simmer, stirring frequently for 7–8 minutes, or according to the packet instructions, until the pasta is tender or *al dente*. Check the seasoning, and serve hot, sprinkled with parsley and Pecorino.

NUTRITIONAL NOTES

Per portion:

Energy	202Kcals/855kJ
Total fat	5g
Saturated fat	1.1g
Cholesterol	3.02mg
Fibre	4.9g

ROASTED TOMATO AND PASTA SOUP

When the only tomatoes you can buy are not particularly flavoursome, make this soup. The oven-roasting compensates for any lack of flavour in the tomatoes.

INGREDIENTS

450g/1lb ripe Italian plum tomatoes, halved lengthways
1 large red pepper, quartered lengthways and deseeded
1 large red onion, quartered lengthways
2 garlic cloves, unpeeled
15ml/1 tbsp olive oil
1.2 litres/2 pints/5 cups vegetable stock or water
good pinch of sugar
90g/3½oz/scant 1 cup dried small pasta shapes, such as tubetti or small macaroni
salt and freshly ground black pepper
fresh basil leaves, to garnish

SERVES 4

1 Preheat the oven to 190°C/375°F/Gas 5. Spread out the tomatoes, red pepper, onion and garlic in a roasting tin and drizzle with the olive oil. Roast in the oven for 30–40 minutes until the vegetables are soft and charred, stirring and turning them halfway through the cooking time.

2 Tip the vegetables into a blender or food processor, add about 250ml/8fl oz/ 1 cup of the stock or water and blend until puréed. Scrape into a sieve placed over a large saucepan and press the purée through the sieve into the pan. Discard the contents of the sieve.

3 Add the remaining stock or water, the sugar and salt and pepper to taste. Bring to the boil, stirring.

4 Add the pasta and simmer, stirring frequently for 7–8 minutes, or according to the packet instructions, until the pasta is tender or *al dente*. Adjust the seasoning. Serve hot in soup bowls, garnished with fresh basil leaves.

COOK'S TIP

The soup can be frozen without the pasta. Thaw and bring to the boil before adding the pasta.

NUTRITIONAL NOTES

Per portion:

Energy	145Kcals/611kJ
Total fat	4.6g
Saturated fat	0.7g
Cholesterol	0mg
Fibre	2.4g

WILD MUSHROOM SOUP

Dried porcini mushrooms have an intense flavour so only a small quantity is needed for this delicious soup. The beef stock helps to strengthen the earthy flavour of the mushrooms.

Ingredients

25g/1oz/½ cup dried porcini mushrooms
15ml/1 tbsp olive oil
2 leeks, thinly sliced
2 shallots, roughly chopped
1 garlic clove, roughly chopped
225g/8oz/3 cups fresh wild mushrooms
about 1.2 litres/2 pints/5 cups beef stock
2.5ml/½ tsp dried thyme
30ml/2 tbsp single cream
salt and freshly ground black pepper
fresh thyme sprigs, to garnish

Serves 4

1 Put the dried porcini in a bowl, add 250ml/8fl oz/1 cup warm water and leave to soak for 20–30 minutes. Lift out of the liquid and squeeze over the bowl to remove as much of the soaking liquid as possible. Strain all the liquid and reserve to use later. Finely chop the porcini and set aside.

2 Heat the olive oil in a large saucepan. Add the leeks, shallots and garlic and cook gently for about 5 minutes, stirring the mixture frequently, until softened but not coloured.

3 Chop or slice the fresh mushrooms and add to the pan. Stir over a medium heat for a few minutes until they begin to soften. Pour in the beef stock and bring to the boil. Add the chopped porcini, reserved soaking liquid, dried thyme and salt and pepper. Reduce the heat, half cover the pan and simmer gently for 30 minutes, stirring occasionally.

4 Pour about three-quarters of the soup into a blender or food processor and blend until smooth. Return to the soup remaining in the pan, stir in the cream and heat through gently. Check the consistency and add more stock if the soup is too thick. Adjust the seasoning. Serve hot in soup bowls, garnished with fresh thyme sprigs.

Nutritional Notes

Per portion:

Energy	66Kcals/276kJ
Total fat	4.7g
Saturated fat	1.2g
Cholesterol	3.32mg
Fibre	1.2g

FRESH TOMATO AND ONION SOUP

This delicious wholesome soup is full of flavour and is low in fat too. Serve with slices of wholemeal or granary bread for a more substantial snack.

INGREDIENTS

10ml/2 tsp sunflower oil
1 large onion, chopped
2 celery sticks, chopped
175g/6oz/¾ cup split red lentils
2 large tomatoes, skinned and roughly chopped
900ml/1½ pints/3¾ cups vegetable stock
10ml/2 tsp mixed dried Italian herbs, such as oregano and thyme
salt and freshly ground black pepper
chopped fresh parsley, to garnish

SERVES 4

1 Heat the oil in a large saucepan. Add the chopped onion and celery and cook for 5 minutes, stirring occasionally. Add the lentils and cook for 1 minute.

2 Stir in the tomatoes, stock, herbs and seasoning. Cover, bring to the boil and simmer for about 20 minutes, stirring occasionally, until the lentils and vegetables are cooked and tender. Remove the pan from the heat and set the soup aside to cool slightly.

3 Purée the soup in a blender or food processor until smooth. Adjust the seasoning, return to the rinsed-out saucepan and reheat gently until piping hot. Serve garnished with chopped parsley.

NUTRITIONAL NOTES

Per portion:

Energy	117Kcals/493kJ
Total fat	2.0g
Saturated fat	0.3g
Cholesterol	1mg
Fibre	1.9g

MIXED VEGETABLE SOUP WITH CONCHIGLIETTE

Lean smoked bacon rashers add delicious flavour to this Italian-style low-fat vegetable and pasta soup.

3 Add the milk and season with salt and pepper. Purée half of the soup in a blender or food processor until smooth, then return to the pan with the pasta shells. Bring to the boil and simmer for 10 minutes, stirring occasionally.

4 Meanwhile, fry the bacon rashers quickly in a non-stick frying pan for 2–3 minutes until the meat is cooked, stirring frequently. Stir into the soup and ladle into soup bowls to serve. Serve with breadsticks, if you like.

INGREDIENTS

1 small green pepper
450g/1lb potatoes, peeled and diced
350g/12oz/2 cups canned or frozen sweetcorn
1 onion, chopped
1 celery stick, chopped
1 bouquet garni (bay leaf, parsley stalks and thyme)
600ml/1 pint/2½ cups chicken stock
300ml/½ pint/1¼ cups skimmed milk
50g/2oz small dried pasta shells (conchigliette)
115g/4oz lean smoked back bacon rashers, diced
breadsticks, to serve (optional)
salt and freshly ground black pepper

SERVES 6

1 Halve the green pepper and remove and discard the stalk and seeds. Cut the flesh into small dice. Place in a bowl, cover with boiling water and leave to stand for 2 minutes. Rinse and drain.

2 Put the green pepper into a saucepan with the diced potatoes, sweetcorn, onion, celery, bouquet garni and chicken stock. Bring to the boil, cover and simmer for 20 minutes until the vegetables are tender, stirring occasionally.

NUTRITIONAL NOTES

Per portion:

Energy	177Kcals/748kJ
Total fat	3.6g
Saturated fat	1.2g
Cholesterol	10.82mg
Fibre	1.8g

LENTIL SOUP WITH TOMATOES

This classic rustic Italian soup is low in fat and flavoured with rosemary, and is delicious served with crusty bread or low-fat garlic bread.

INGREDIENTS

225g/8oz/1 cup dried green or brown lentils
10ml/2 tsp extra virgin olive oil
2 rindless lean back bacon rashers, cut into small dice
1 onion, finely chopped
2 celery sticks, finely chopped
2 carrots, finely diced
2 fresh rosemary sprigs, finely chopped
2 bay leaves
400g/14oz can chopped plum tomatoes
1.75 litres/3 pints/7½ cups vegetable stock
salt and freshly ground black pepper
fresh bay leaves and rosemary sprigs, to garnish

SERVES 4

1 Place the lentils in a bowl and cover with cold water. Leave to soak for 2 hours. Rinse and drain well.

2 Heat the oil in a large saucepan. Add the bacon and cook for about 3 minutes, then stir in the chopped onion and cook for 5 minutes until softened, stirring occasionally. Stir in the celery, carrots, chopped rosemary, bay leaves and lentils.

3 Add the tomatoes and stock and bring to the boil. Reduce the heat, half cover the pan, and simmer for about 1 hour, or until the lentils are perfectly tender, stirring occasionally.

4 Remove and discard the bay leaves, add salt and pepper to taste and serve garnished with bay leaves and rosemary.

NUTRITIONAL NOTES

Per portion:

Energy	235Kcals/995kJ
Total fat	4.9g
Saturated fat	0.9g
Cholesterol	3.48mg
Fibre	6.9g

SPINACH AND RICE SOUP

Use very fresh, young spinach leaves to prepare this light and fresh-tasting low-fat Italian soup.

INGREDIENTS

675g/1½lb fresh spinach, washed
15ml/1 tbsp extra virgin olive oil
1 small onion, finely chopped
2 garlic cloves, finely chopped
1 small fresh red chilli, deseeded and finely chopped
115g/4oz/generous ½ cup risotto rice
1.2 litres/2 pints/5 cups vegetable stock
salt and freshly ground black pepper
20ml/4 tsp grated fresh Pecorino cheese, to serve

SERVES 4

1 Place the spinach in a large saucepan with just the water clinging to the leaves. Add a large pinch of salt and heat gently until wilted. Remove from the heat and drain, reserving any liquid.

2 Either chop the spinach finely or place in a food processor and blend to a purée.

3 Heat the oil in a saucepan and cook the onion, garlic and chilli for 4–5 minutes, stirring occasionally. Stir in the rice, then the stock and spinach liquid. Boil, then simmer for 10 minutes. Add the spinach and seasoning and cook for 5–7 minutes. Serve with the Pecorino cheese.

NUTRITIONAL NOTES

Per portion:

Energy	235Kcals/995kJ
Total fat	4.9g
Saturated fat	0.9g
Cholesterol	3.48mg
Fibre	6.9g

RIBOLLITA

Ribollita is rather like minestrone, but includes beans instead of pasta. In Italy it is traditionally served ladled over bread and a rich green vegetable, making it a delicious and wholesome soup.

INGREDIENTS

15ml/1 tbsp olive oil
2 onions, chopped
2 carrots, sliced
4 garlic cloves, crushed
2 celery sticks, thinly sliced
1 fennel bulb, trimmed and chopped
2 large courgettes, thinly sliced
400g/14oz can chopped tomatoes
15ml/1 tbsp home-made or bought pesto
900ml/1½ pints/3¾ cups vegetable stock
400g/14oz can haricot or borlotti beans, drained
salt and freshly ground black pepper

TO FINISH

450g/1lb young spinach or other dark greens, such as chard or cabbage
10ml/2 tsp extra virgin olive oil
8 small slices white bread
15ml/1 tbsp shaved fresh Parmesan cheese (optional)

SERVES 8

1 Heat the oil in a large saucepan. Add the onions, carrots, garlic, celery and fennel and fry gently for 10 minutes, stirring occasionally. Add the courgettes and fry for a further 2 minutes.

2 Add the chopped tomatoes, pesto, stock and beans and bring to the boil. Reduce the heat, cover and simmer gently for 25–30 minutes, until the vegetables are completely tender, stirring occasionally. Season with salt and pepper to taste.

3 To serve, fry the spinach or greens in the oil for 2 minutes or until wilted. Spoon over the bread in soup bowls, then ladle the soup over the top and serve. Serve with Parmesan cheese shavings sprinkled on top, if you like.

NUTRITIONAL NOTES

Per portion:

Energy	181Kcals/761kJ
Total fat	4.85g
Saturated fat	0.75g
Cholesterol	0mg
Fibre	6.1g

CLAM AND PASTA SOUP

This recipe uses store-cupboard ingredients to create a delicious and filling low-fat soup. Serve it with hot focaccia or ciabatta for an informal supper with friends.

INGREDIENTS

15ml/1 tbsp olive oil
1 large onion, finely chopped
2 garlic cloves, crushed
400g/14oz can chopped tomatoes
15ml/1 tbsp sun-dried tomato purée
5ml/1 tsp sugar
5ml/1 tsp dried mixed Italian herbs
about 750ml/1¼ pints/3 cups fish or vegetable stock
150ml/¼ pint/⅔ cup red wine
50g/2oz/½ cup small dried pasta shapes
150g/5oz jar or can clams in natural juice
30ml/2 tbsp finely chopped fresh flat leaf parsley, plus a few whole leaves, to garnish
salt and freshly ground black pepper

SERVES 4

1 Heat the oil in a large saucepan. Cook the onion gently for 5 minutes, stirring frequently, until softened.

2 Add the garlic, tomatoes, tomato purée, sugar, herbs, stock and wine, and salt and pepper to taste. Bring the mixture to the boil. Reduce the heat, half cover the pan and simmer for 10 minutes, stirring the mixture occasionally.

3 Add the pasta and continue simmering, uncovered, for 10 minutes or until the pasta is tender or *al dente*. Stir occasionally.

4 Add the clams and their juice to the soup and heat through for 3–4 minutes, adding more stock if required. Do not let it boil or the clams will be tough. Remove from the heat, stir in the chopped parsley and adjust the seasoning. Serve hot, ladled into soup bowls and sprinkled with coarsely ground black pepper and parsley leaves, to garnish.

NUTRITIONAL NOTES

Per portion:

Energy	165Kcals/695kJ
Total fat	3.4g
Saturated fat	0.4g
Cholesterol	0mg
Fibre	1.5g

CONSOMMÉ WITH AGNOLOTTI

A flavourful Italian pasta soup, ideal for a tasty starter or snack.

Ingredients

75g/3oz cooked, peeled prawns
75g/3oz canned crab meat, drained
5ml/1 tsp fresh root ginger, peeled and finely grated
15ml/1 tbsp fresh white breadcrumbs
5ml/1 tsp light soy sauce
1 spring onion, finely chopped
1 garlic clove, crushed
1 quantity of basic pasta dough (see Techniques section)
egg white, beaten
400g/14oz can chicken or fish consommé
30ml/2 tbsp sherry or vermouth
salt and freshly ground black pepper
50g/2oz cooked, peeled prawns and fresh coriander leaves, to garnish

Serves 6

1 Put the prawns, crab meat, ginger, breadcrumbs, soy sauce, onion, garlic and seasoning into a blender or food processor and blend until smooth. Set aside.

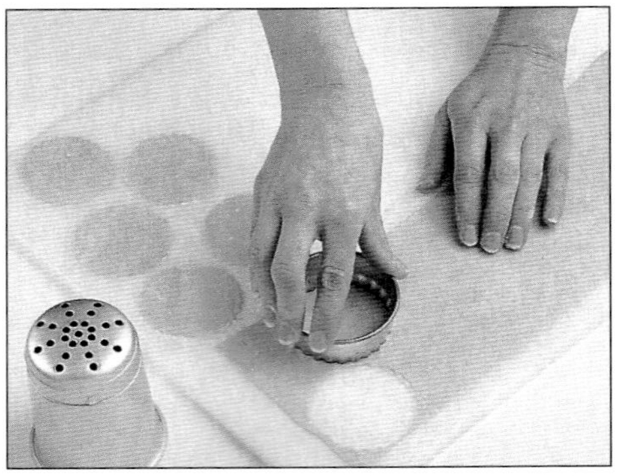

2 Roll the pasta into thin sheets. Stamp out 32 rounds 5cm/2in in diameter, with a fluted pastry cutter.

3 Place a small teaspoon of the puréed filling in the centre of half the pasta rounds. Brush the edges of each round with egg white and sandwich together by placing a second pasta round on top. Pinch the edges together firmly to stop the filling seeping out.

4 Cook the pasta in a large saucepan of boiling, salted water for 5 minutes (cook in batches to stop them sticking together). Remove from the pan and drop into a bowl of cold water for 5 seconds before removing and placing on a tray.

5 Heat the chicken or fish consommé in a saucepan with the sherry or vermouth. When piping hot, add the cooked pasta shapes and simmer for 1–2 minutes.

6 Serve the cooked pasta in shallow soup bowls covered with hot consommé. Garnish with prawns and coriander.

Nutritional Notes

Per portion:

Energy	177Kcals/747kJ
Total fat	2.7g
Saturated fat	0.7g
Cholesterol	89.66mg
Fibre	1g

Cook's Tip

You can make these pasta shapes a day in advance. Cover with clear film and store in the fridge.

STARTERS, SALADS AND SNACKS

This APPETIZING *array of low-fat Italian recipes provides tempting dishes to launch a meal,* HEALTHY *and* REFRESHING *salads and tasty low-fat snacks to enjoy at any time of the day. Choose from* ITALIAN *dishes such as Aubergine, Garlic and* PEPPER *Pâté,* ROCKET, *Pear and Parmesan Salad, Tomato Pesto Toasties and* PARMA HAM *and Pepper Pizzas.*

AUBERGINE SUNFLOWER PÂTÉ

This delicious grilled aubergine pâté, flavoured with sunflower seeds and fresh herbs, makes a tempting low-fat starter or snack.

INGREDIENTS

1 large aubergine
1 garlic clove, crushed
15ml/1 tbsp lemon juice
30ml/2 tbsp sunflower seeds
45ml/3 tbsp low-fat natural yogurt
handful of fresh coriander or parsley, plus extra to garnish
ground black pepper
vegetable sticks, to serve

SERVES 4

1 Cut the aubergine in half and place, cut side down, on a baking sheet. Place under a hot grill for 15–20 minutes, until the skin is blackened and the flesh is soft.

2 Leave for a few minutes to cool slightly, then scoop the flesh into a blender or food processor. Discard the skin. Add the garlic, lemon juice, sunflower seeds and yogurt to the processor. Blend together until smooth.

3 Roughly chop the fresh coriander or parsley and mix into the aubergine mixture. Season with black pepper, then spoon into a serving dish. Garnish with coriander or parsley and serve with vegetable sticks.

NUTRITIONAL NOTES

Per portion:

Energy	59Kcals/245kJ
Total fat	4g
Saturated fat	0.5g
Cholesterol	0.44mg
Fibre	1.5g

PEPPER DIPS WITH CRUDITÉS

Make one or both of these colourful Italian vegetable dips – if you have time to make both they look spectacular together and are both low-fat too!

INGREDIENTS

2 red peppers, halved and deseeded
2 yellow peppers, halved and deseeded
2 garlic cloves
30ml/2 tbsp lemon juice
20ml/4 tsp olive oil
50g/2oz/1 cup fresh white breadcrumbs
salt and freshly ground black pepper
prepared fresh vegetables, for dipping

SERVES 6

1 Place the peppers in two separate saucepans with a peeled clove of garlic. Add just enough water to cover.

2 Bring to the boil, then cover and simmer for 15 minutes until tender. Drain, cool, then purée the peppers separately in a blender or food processor, adding half the lemon juice and olive oil to each purée.

3 Stir half the breadcrumbs into each purée and season to taste with salt and pepper. Spoon the dips into serving dishes, garnish with a grinding of black pepper and serve with a selection of fresh vegetables for dipping.

NUTRITIONAL NOTES

Per portion:

Energy	60Kcals/253kJ
Total fat	3g
Saturated fat	0.5g
Cholesterol	0mg
Fibre	1.1g

AUBERGINE, GARLIC AND PEPPER PÂTÉ

Serve this Italian-style chunky, garlicky pâté of smoky baked aubergine and red peppers on a bed of salad, accompanied by crispbreads.

INGREDIENTS

3 aubergines
2 red peppers
5 garlic cloves
7.5ml/1½ tsp pink peppercorns in brine, drained and crushed
30ml/2 tbsp chopped fresh coriander

SERVES 4

NUTRITIONAL NOTES

Per portion:

Energy	15Kcals/64kJ
Total fat	0.4g
Saturated fat	0.1g
Cholesterol	0mg
Fibre	1.8g

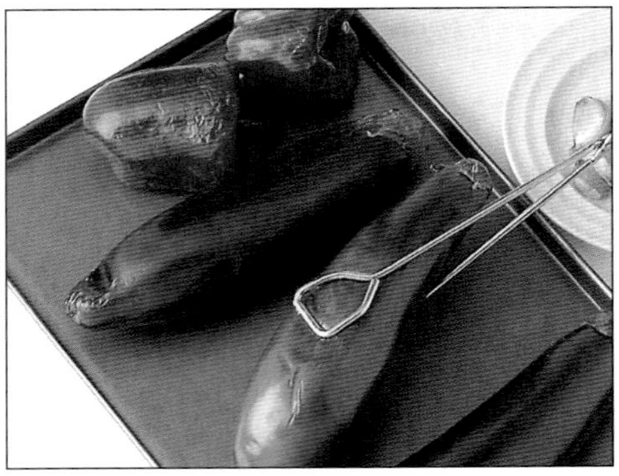

1 Preheat the oven to 200°C/400°F/Gas 6. Arrange the whole aubergines, peppers and garlic cloves on a baking sheet and place in the oven. After 10 minutes remove the garlic cloves. Turn over the aubergines and peppers and return to the oven.

2 Carefully peel the garlic cloves and place them in the bowl of a blender or food processor.

3 After a further 20 minutes remove the blistered and charred peppers from the oven and place in a plastic bag. Leave to cool.

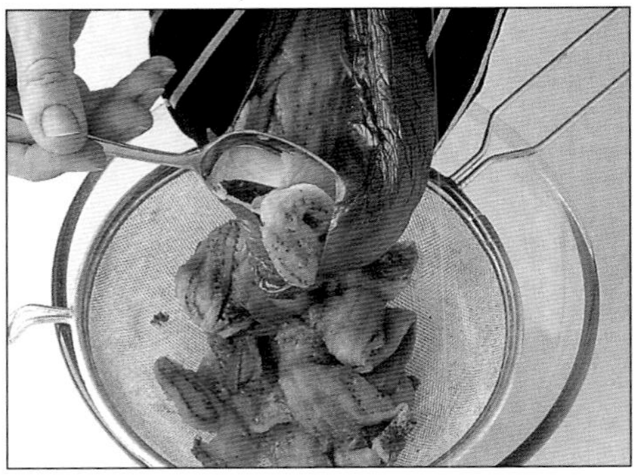

4 After a further 10 minutes remove the aubergines from the oven. Split in half and scoop the flesh into a sieve placed over a bowl. Discard the skin. Press the flesh with a spoon to remove the bitter juices. Discard the juices.

5 Add the aubergine flesh to the garlic in the blender or food processor and blend until smooth. Place in a large bowl.

6 Peel and chop the red peppers and stir into the aubergine mixture. Mix in the peppercorns and fresh coriander, spoon into a serving dish and serve at once.

CANNELLINI BEAN PURÉE WITH GRILLED CHICORY

The slightly bitter flavours of the chicory and radicchio make a wonderful marriage with the creamy bean purée to create this low-fat starter or snack.

3 Cut each radicchio head into eight wedges. Preheat the grill.

4 Lay out the chicory and radicchio on a baking tray and brush lightly with the walnut oil. Grill for 2–3 minutes. Serve with the bean purée and scatter over the orange shreds to garnish, if using.

INGREDIENTS

400g/14oz can cannellini beans
45ml/3 tbsp low-fat fromage frais
finely grated rind and juice of 1 large orange
15ml/1 tbsp finely chopped fresh rosemary
4 heads of chicory
2 heads of radicchio
10ml/2 tsp walnut oil
longer shreds of orange rind, to garnish (optional)

SERVES 4

COOK'S TIP

Other suitable pulses to use are haricot, mung or broad beans.

1 Drain the beans, rinse, and drain them again. Purée the beans in a blender or food processor with the fromage frais, orange rind and juice and rosemary. Set aside.

2 Cut the heads of chicory in half along the length.

NUTRITIONAL NOTES

Per portion:

Energy	142Kcals/602kJ
Total fat	3.4g
Saturated fat	0.5g
Cholesterol	0.11mg
Fibre	1.1g

ROASTED PLUM TOMATOES WITH GARLIC

A very typical Italian dish, these roast tomatoes flavoured with garlic are so simple to prepare, yet taste absolutely wonderful. A shallow earthenware dish will allow the tomatoes to char.

Ingredients

8 plum tomatoes
12 garlic cloves
20ml/4 tsp extra virgin olive oil
3 bay leaves
salt and freshly ground black pepper
45ml/3 tbsp fresh oregano leaves, to garnish

Serves 4

1 Preheat the oven to 230°C/450°F/Gas 8. Cut the plum tomatoes in half, leaving a small part of the green stem intact for the final decoration.

2 Select an ovenproof dish that will hold all the tomatoes snugly together in a single layer. Place them in the dish with the cut side facing upwards, and push each of the whole, unpeeled garlic cloves among them.

3 Lightly brush the tomatoes with the oil, add the bay leaves and sprinkle black pepper over the top.

4 Bake in the oven for about 35–45 minutes until the tomatoes have softened and are sizzling in the dish. They should be charred around the edges. Season with salt and a little more black pepper, if needed. Garnish with the fresh oregano leaves and serve immediately.

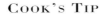

Cook's Tip

Select ripe, juicy tomatoes without any blemishes to get the best flavour.

Variation

For a sweet alternative, use halved and seeded red or yellow peppers instead of the tomatoes.

Nutritional Notes

Per portion:

Energy	57Kcals/238kJ
Total fat	4.0g
Saturated fat	0.6g
Cholesterol	0mg
Fibre	1.1g

ARTICHOKE SALAD WITH SALSA AGRODOLCE

Agrodolce is an Italian sweet-and-sour sauce which makes an ideal accompaniment for this artichoke and bean salad.

INGREDIENTS

6 small globe artichokes
juice of 1 lemon
15ml/1 tbsp olive oil
2 onions, roughly chopped
175g/6oz/1 cup fresh or frozen broad beans (shelled weight)
175g/6oz/1 1/2 cups fresh or frozen peas (shelled weight)
salt and freshly ground black pepper
fresh mint leaves, to garnish

FOR THE SALSA AGRODOLCE

120ml/4fl oz/1/2 cup white wine vinegar
15ml/1 tbsp caster sugar
handful of fresh mint leaves, roughly torn

SERVES 4–6

1 Peel and discard the outer leaves from the artichokes and cut into quarters. Place the artichokes in a bowl of water with the lemon juice.

2 Heat the oil in a large saucepan and add the onions. Cook until the onions are golden, stirring occasionally. Add the broad beans and stir, then drain the artichokes and add to the pan. Pour in about 300ml/1/2 pint/1 1/4 cups of water, bring to the boil, then cook, covered, for 10–15 minutes.

3 Add the peas, season with salt and pepper and cook for a further 5 minutes, stirring occasionally, until the vegetables are tender. Strain through a sieve, discard the liquid, then place all the vegetables in a bowl, leave to cool, cover and chill.

4 To make the salsa agrodolce, mix all the ingredients in a saucepan. Heat gently for 2–3 minutes until the sugar has dissolved. Simmer for 5 minutes, stirring occasionally. Remove from the heat and let cool. To serve, drizzle the salsa over the vegetables and garnish with mint leaves.

NUTRITIONAL NOTES

Per portion:

Energy	182Kcals/759kJ
Total fat	4g
Saturated fat	0.6g
Cholesterol	0mg
Fibre	5.5g

GARLIC BAKED TOMATOES

For the best results, use Italian plum tomatoes, which have a warm, slightly sweet flavour. Serve this tasty dish with fresh Italian bread or crispbreads.

INGREDIENTS

25g/1oz/2 tbsp unsalted butter
1 large garlic clove, crushed
5ml/1 tsp finely grated orange rind
4 firm plum tomatoes, or 2 large beef tomatoes
salt and freshly ground black pepper
fresh basil leaves, to garnish

SERVES 4

1 Soften the butter in a small bowl and blend with the crushed garlic, orange rind, and seasoning. Chill for a few minutes.

2 Preheat the oven to 200°C/400°F/Gas 6. Halve the tomatoes crossways and trim the bases so they stand upright.

3 Place the tomatoes in an ovenproof dish and spread the butter equally over each.

4 Bake the tomatoes in the oven for 15–25 minutes, depending on the size of the tomato halves, until just tender. Serve sprinkled with the fresh basil leaves.

NUTRITIONAL NOTES

Per portion:

Energy	49Kcals/204kJ
Total fat	5g
Saturated fat	3.3g
Cholesterol	13.88mg
Fibre	0.3g

LEMON CARROT SALAD

This tangy, colourful and refreshing salad creates an ideal low-fat snack or accompaniment.

INGREDIENTS

450g/1lb small, young carrots
finely grated rind and juice of 1/2 lemon
15ml/1 tbsp soft light brown sugar
30ml/2 tbsp sunflower oil
5ml/1 tsp hazelnut or sesame oil
5ml/1 tsp chopped fresh oregano
salt and freshly ground black pepper

SERVES 6

NUTRITIONAL NOTES

Per portion:

Energy	76Kcals/318kJ
Total fat	4.7g
Saturated fat	0.6g
Cholesterol	0mg
Fibre	1.8g

1 Finely grate the carrots and place them in a large bowl. Stir in the lemon rind and 15–30ml/1–2 tbsp of the lemon juice.

VARIATION

Experiment with different herbs. Tarragon goes well with carrots.

2 Add the sugar, sunflower and hazelnut or sesame oils, and mix well. Add more lemon juice and seasoning to taste, then sprinkle on the oregano and toss lightly to mix. Leave the salad for 1 hour before serving, garnished with a sprig of oregano.

ROCKET, PEAR AND PARMESAN SALAD

For a sophisticated start to a meal with friends, try this simple Italian salad of fresh, ripe pears, tasty Parmesan and aromatic leaves of rocket. Serve with fresh Italian bread or crispbreads.

Ingredients

3 ripe pears, such as Williams or Packhams
10ml/2 tsp lemon juice
15ml/1 tbsp hazelnut or walnut oil
115g/4oz rocket
25g/1oz fresh Parmesan cheese
ground black pepper

Serves 4

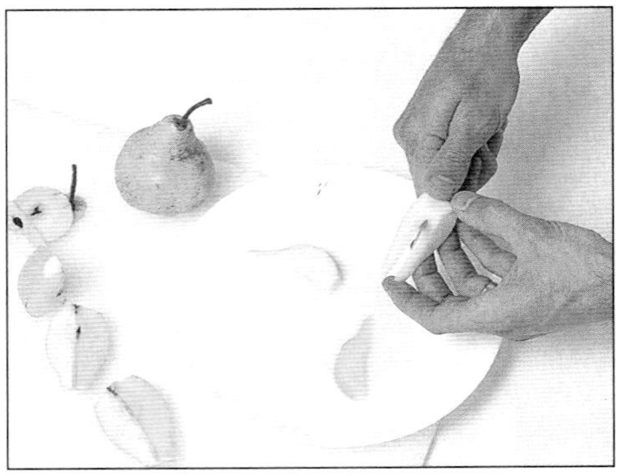

1 Peel and core the pears and slice thickly. Place in a bowl and moisten with lemon juice to keep the flesh white.

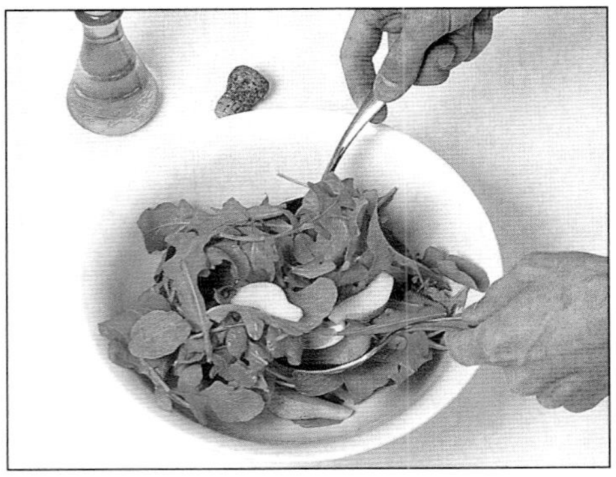

2 Combine the nut oil with the pears. Add the rocket leaves and toss to mix.

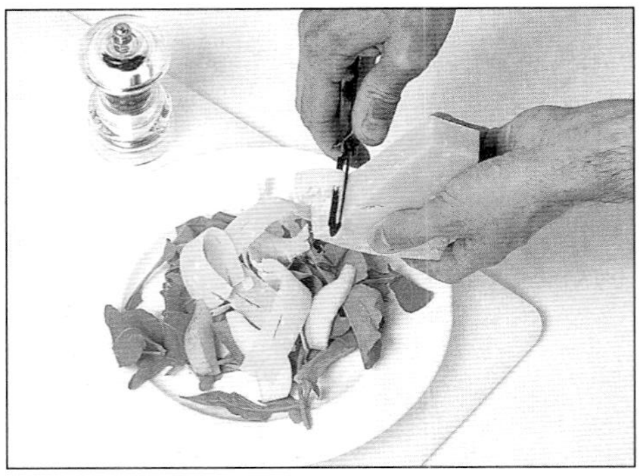

3 Divide the salad among four small plates and top each portion with shavings of Parmesan cheese. Season with ground black pepper and serve.

Cook's Tip

You can grow your own rocket from early spring to late summer. You can also use watercress instead.

Nutritional Notes

Per portion:

Energy	102Kcals/424kJ
Total fat	5g
Saturated fat	1.6g
Cholesterol	6.24mg
Fibre	2.6g

MELON, PARMA HAM AND STRAWBERRY SALAD

Sections of cool fragrant melon wrapped with thin slices of air-dried Italian ham make this delicious Italian salad starter or snack.

INGREDIENTS

1 large melon, cantaloupe, Galia or Charentais
115g/4oz Parma or Serrano ham, thinly sliced

FOR THE SALSA

225g/8oz strawberries
5ml/1 tsp caster sugar
20ml/4 tsp groundnut or sunflower oil
15ml/1 tbsp unsweetened orange juice
2.5ml/½ tsp finely grated orange rind
2.5ml/½ tsp finely grated fresh root ginger
salt and freshly ground black pepper

SERVES 4

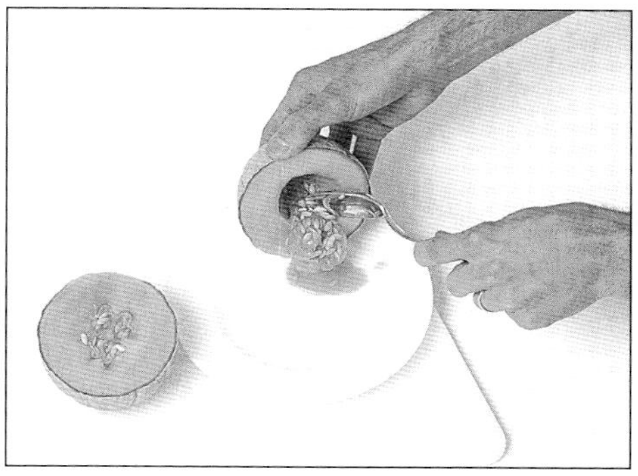

1 Halve the melon and take the seeds out with a spoon. Cut the rind away with a paring knife. Discard the seeds and rind, then slice the melon flesh thickly. Chill until ready to serve.

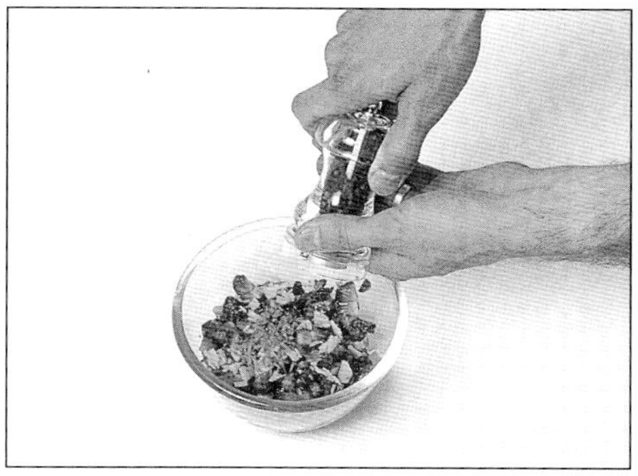

2 To make the salsa, hull the strawberries and cut them into large dice. Place in a small mixing bowl with the sugar and crush lightly to release the juices. Add the oil, orange juice, orange rind and ginger. Season with salt and a generous twist of black pepper.

3 Arrange the melon on a serving plate, lay the ham over the top and serve with the bowl of salsa alongside.

NUTRITIONAL NOTES

Per portion:

Energy	89Kcals/369kJ
Total fat	4.9g
Saturated fat	0.8g
Cholesterol	13.66mg
Fibre	0.8g

COOK'S TIP

Melon has a very subtle flavour. To enjoy it at its best, do not over-chill it.

THREE-COLOUR SALAD

This classic Italian dish, *insalata tricolore*, creates an appetizing and colourful starter or snack. Use plum or vine-ripened tomatoes for the best flavour.

Ingredients

1 small red onion, thinly sliced
6 large full-flavoured tomatoes
50g/2oz/1 small bunch rocket or watercress, roughly chopped
115g/4oz reduced-fat mozzarella cheese, thinly sliced or grated
20ml/4 tsp extra virgin olive oil
30ml/2 tbsp pine nuts (optional)
salt and freshly ground black pepper

Serves 6

1 Soak the onion slices in a bowl of cold water for 30 minutes, then drain and pat dry.

2 Prepare the tomatoes for skinning by slashing them with a sharp knife and dipping briefly in boiling water.

3 Peel off the skins and then slice each tomato using a sharp knife.

4 Arrange half the tomato slices on a large platter, or divide them among six small plates if you prefer.

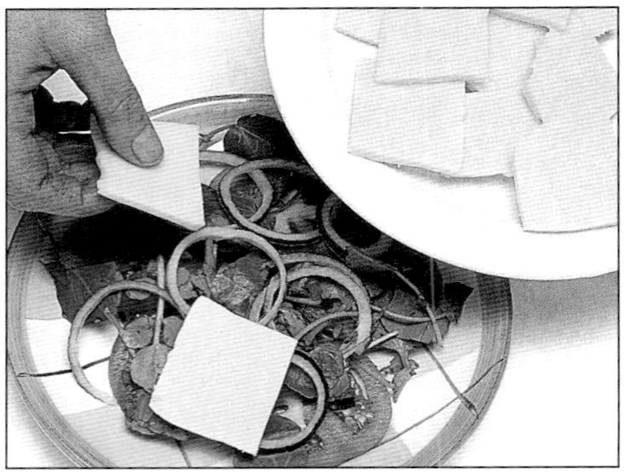

5 Layer with half the chopped rocket or watercress and half the onion slices, seasoning well. Add half the cheese, sprinkling over a little more seasoning as you go.

6 Repeat with the remaining tomato and onion slices, salad leaves and cheese.

7 Season well to finish and sprinkle the oil over the salad. Scatter the pine nuts over the top, if using. Cover the salad and chill for at least 2 hours before serving.

Variations

Instead of the fresh rocket or watercress, use chopped fresh basil, which goes particularly well with the flavour of ripe tomatoes. To reduce the fat content even further, omit the oil and sprinkle the salad with a fat-free vinaigrette dressing.

Nutritional Notes

Per portion:

Energy	75Kcals/314kJ
Total fat	5g
Saturated fat	2g
Cholesterol	7.36mg
Fibre	0.6g

ROASTED PEPPER AND TOMATO SALAD

This recipe brings together perfectly the colours, flavours and textures of southern Italian food. Serve this low-fat dish at room temperature with a green salad.

INGREDIENTS

3 red peppers
6 large plum tomatoes
2.5ml/½ tsp dried red chilli flakes
1 red onion, thinly sliced
3 garlic cloves, finely chopped
finely grated rind and juice of 1 lemon
45ml/3 tbsp chopped fresh flat leaf parsley
20ml/4 tsp extra virgin olive oil
salt and freshly ground black pepper
25g/1oz black and green olives and extra chopped fresh flat leaf parsley, to garnish

SERVES 4

1 Preheat the oven to 220°C/425°F/Gas 7. Place the peppers on a baking sheet and roast in the oven, turning occasionally, for 10 minutes or until the skins are almost blackened. Add the tomatoes to the baking sheet and bake for a further 5 minutes.

2 Place the peppers in a plastic bag, close the top loosely, trapping in the steam, and then set them aside with the tomatoes until they are cool enough to handle.

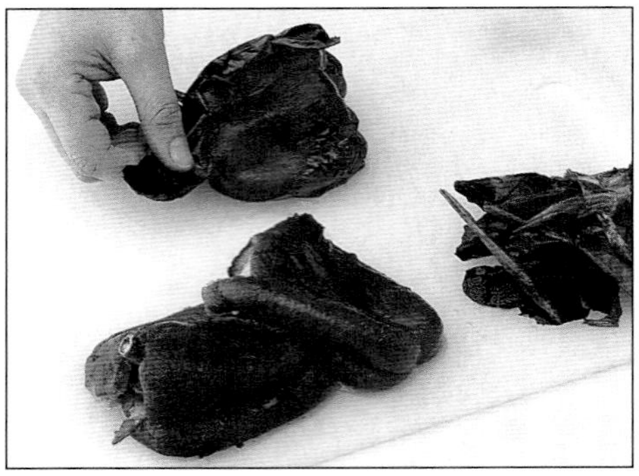

3 Carefully pull off and discard the skin from the peppers. Remove and discard the seeds, then chop the peppers and tomatoes roughly and place them together in a mixing bowl.

4 Add the chilli flakes, onion, garlic, lemon rind and juice. Sprinkle over the parsley. Mix well, then transfer to a serving dish. Sprinkle with a little salt and pepper, drizzle over the olive oil and scatter the olives and extra parsley over the top to garnish. Serve the salad at room temperature.

NUTRITIONAL NOTES

Per portion:

Energy	78Kcals/323kJ
Total fat	4.9g
Saturated fat	0.8g
Cholesterol	0mg
Fibre	2.1g

MARINATED COURGETTES

This is a simple vegetable dish which is prepared all over Italy using the best of the season's courgettes. It can be eaten hot or cold and creates a delicious accompaniment to a main course.

INGREDIENTS

4 courgettes
40ml/8 tsp extra virgin olive oil
30ml/2 tbsp chopped fresh mint, plus whole leaves, to garnish
30ml/2 tbsp white wine vinegar
salt and freshly ground black pepper

SERVES 6

1 Cut the courgettes into thin slices. Heat 20ml/4 tsp of the oil in a wide heavy-based saucepan.

2 Fry the courgettes in batches, for 4–6 minutes, until tender and brown around the edges. Transfer the courgettes to a bowl. Season well.

NUTRITIONAL NOTES

Per portion:

Energy	50Kcals/206KJ
Total fat	5.0g
Saturated fat	0.7g
Cholesterol	0mg
Fibre	0.3g

3 Heat the remaining oil, then add the mint and vinegar and let bubble for a few seconds. Stir into the courgettes. Marinate for 1 hour, then serve with mint leaves.

DUCK BREAST SALAD

Succulent duck breasts are grilled, then sliced and tossed together with pasta and fruit in a delicious virtually fat-free dressing to create this tempting salad.

INGREDIENTS

2 duck breasts, boned
5ml/1 tsp coriander seeds, crushed
350g/12oz dried rigatoni
150ml/¼ pint/⅔ cup fresh orange juice
15ml/1 tbsp lemon juice
10ml/2 tsp clear honey
1 shallot, finely chopped
1 garlic clove, crushed
1 celery stick, chopped
75g/3oz dried cherries
45ml/3 tbsp port or red wine
15ml/1 tbsp chopped fresh mint, plus extra to garnish
30ml/2 tbsp chopped fresh coriander, plus extra to garnish
1 eating apple, cored and diced
2 oranges, segmented
salt and freshly ground black pepper

SERVES 6

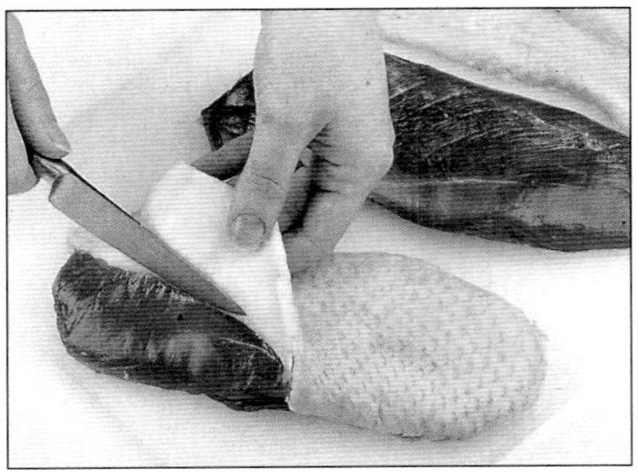

1 Remove and discard the skin and fat from the duck breasts and season with salt and pepper. Rub the duck breasts all over with crushed coriander seeds. Preheat the grill, then grill the duck for 7–10 minutes depending on size. Wrap in foil and set aside for about 20 minutes.

2 Meanwhile, cook the pasta in a large saucepan of boiling, salted water until tender or *al dente*. Drain thoroughly and rinse under cold running water, then drain again. Leave to cool.

3 In the meantime, make the dressing. Put the orange juice, lemon juice, honey, shallot, garlic, celery, cherries, port or red wine, chopped mint and coriander into a bowl, whisk together then set aside for 20–30 minutes.

NUTRITIONAL NOTES

Per portion:

Energy	298Kcals/1266kJ
Total fat	2.3g
Saturated fat	0.5g
Cholesterol	27.5mg
Fibre	3g

4 Slice the duck very thinly. (It should be pink in the centre.)

5 Put the pasta into a bowl, add the duck, dressing, diced apple and segments of orange. Toss well to mix. Transfer the salad to a serving plate and garnish with the extra mint and coriander. Serve.

COOK'S TIP

To skin the duck breasts, slide your fingers between the skin and breast and gently pull to separate. Use a sharp knife to loosen any stubborn parts.

VARIATION

Other shapes of pasta may be substituted for the rigatoni. Penne work well, although long varieties, such as tagliatelle, are also good.

WARM CHICKEN SALAD

Succulent cooked chicken pieces are combined with vegetables and rice in a light chilli dressing to create this appetizing lunch or supper salad.

INGREDIENTS

50g/2oz mixed salad leaves
50g/2oz baby spinach leaves
50g/2oz watercress
30ml/2 tbsp chilli sauce
30ml/2 tbsp dry sherry
15ml/1 tbsp light soy sauce
15ml/1 tbsp tomato ketchup
10ml/2 tsp olive oil
8 shallots, finely chopped
1 garlic clove, crushed
350g/12oz skinless, boneless chicken breasts, cut into thin strips
1 red pepper, deseeded and sliced
175g/6oz mangetouts, trimmed
400g/14oz can baby sweetcorn, drained and halved lengthways
275g/10oz can brown rice
salt and freshly ground black pepper
fresh parsley sprig, to garnish

SERVES 6

1 Arrange the mixed salad leaves and the spinach leaves on a serving dish, tearing up any large ones. Add the watercress and toss to mix. Set aside.

2 In a small bowl, mix together the chilli sauce, sherry, soy sauce and tomato ketchup and set aside.

3 Heat the oil in a large non-stick frying pan or wok. Add the shallots and garlic and stir-fry for 1 minute over a medium heat. Add the chicken and stir-fry for 3–4 minutes.

4 Add the pepper, mangetouts, sweetcorn and rice and stir-fry for 2–3 minutes.

5 Pour in the chilli sauce mixture and stir-fry for 2–3 minutes, until hot and bubbling. Season to taste with salt and pepper. Spoon the chicken mixture over the salad leaves, toss together to mix and serve immediately, garnished with a fresh parsley sprig.

NUTRITIONAL NOTES

Per portion:

Energy	191Kcals/804kJ
Total fat	4g
Saturated fat	1g
Cholesterol	25mg
Fibre	2.6g

CRAB PASTA SALAD WITH SPICY DRESSING

White crab meat and fusilli pasta are tossed together in a spicy dressing to create this flavourful Italian-style salad which is very low in fat.

INGREDIENTS

350g/12oz dried fusilli
1 small red pepper, deseeded and finely chopped
2 x 175g/6oz cans white crab meat
115g/4oz cherry tomatoes, halved
1/4 cucumber, halved, deseeded and sliced into crescents
15ml/1 tbsp lemon juice
300ml/1/2 pint/1 1/4 cups low-fat natural yogurt
2 celery sticks, finely chopped
10ml/2 tsp horseradish sauce
2.5ml/1/2 tsp ground paprika
2.5ml/1/2 tsp Dijon mustard
30ml/2 tbsp sweet tomato pickle or chutney
salt and freshly ground black pepper
fresh basil, to garnish

SERVES 6

1 Cook the pasta in a large saucepan of boiling salted water, according to the packet instructions, until tender or *al dente*. Drain and rinse the pasta thoroughly under cold water. Drain again and set aside.

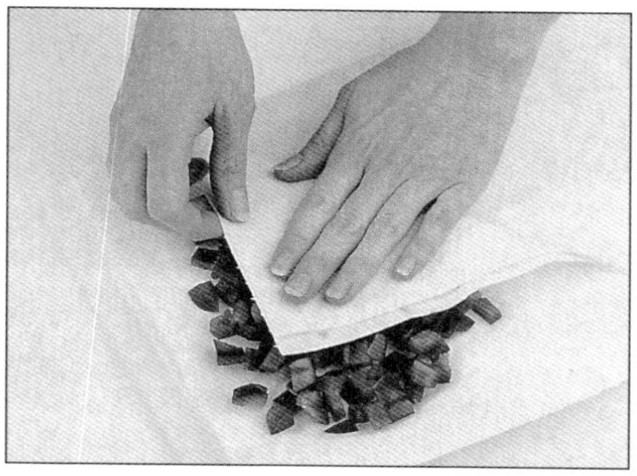

2 Put the red pepper in a bowl and cover with boiling water. Stand for 1 minute. Drain and rinse under cold water. Pat dry on kitchen paper and set aside.

3 Drain the crab meat and pick over carefully. Discard any pieces of shell. Put the crab meat into a bowl with the tomatoes and cucumber. Season with salt and pepper and sprinkle with lemon juice. Set aside.

4 To make the dressing, put the yogurt in a bowl and add the red pepper, celery, horseradish, paprika, mustard and sweet tomato pickle or chutney. Mix the pasta with the crab mixture and dressing and transfer to a serving dish. Garnish with fresh basil and serve.

NUTRITIONAL NOTES

Per portion:

Energy	293Kcals/1244kJ
Total fat	2.3g
Saturated fat	0.5g
Cholesterol	45mg
Fibre	2.4g

SPICY CHICKEN SALAD

This tasty Italian-style low-fat chicken and pasta salad creates an ideal lunch or supper dish for family or friends.

INGREDIENTS

5ml/1 tsp ground cumin seeds
5ml/1 tsp ground paprika
5ml/1 tsp ground turmeric
1–2 garlic cloves, crushed
45–60ml/3–4 tbsp fresh lime juice
4 small chicken breasts, boned and skinned
225g/8oz dried rigatoni
1 red pepper, deseeded and chopped
2 celery sticks, thinly sliced
1 shallot or small onion, finely chopped
15g/½oz stuffed green olives, halved
30ml/2 tbsp clear honey
10ml/2 tsp wholegrain mustard
salt and freshly ground black pepper
mixed salad leaves, to serve

SERVES 6

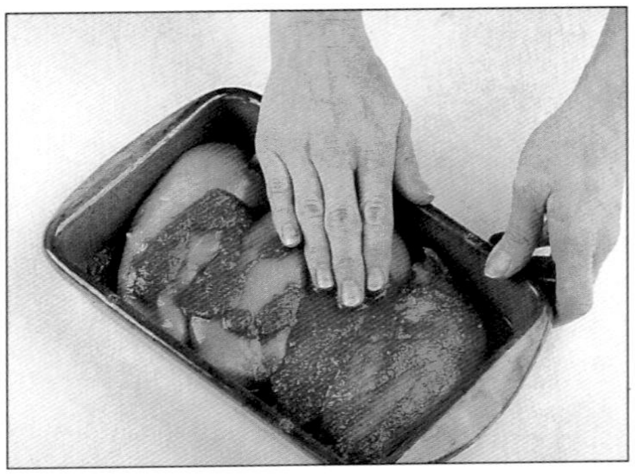

1 Mix the cumin, paprika, turmeric, garlic, seasoning and 30ml/2 tbsp lime juice in a bowl. Lay the chicken in a shallow non-metallic dish and rub the mixture over the chicken breasts. Cover with clear film and leave in a cool place for about 3 hours or overnight.

2 Preheat the oven to 200°C/400°F/Gas 6. Put the chicken on a grill rack in a single layer and bake in the oven for 20 minutes until cooked. (Alternatively, grill for 8–10 minutes on each side.)

3 Meanwhile, cook the rigatoni in a large saucepan of boiling, salted water until tender or *al dente*. Drain and rinse under cold water. Leave to drain thoroughly.

4 Put the red pepper, celery, shallot or onion and olives into a large bowl with the pasta and toss to mix.

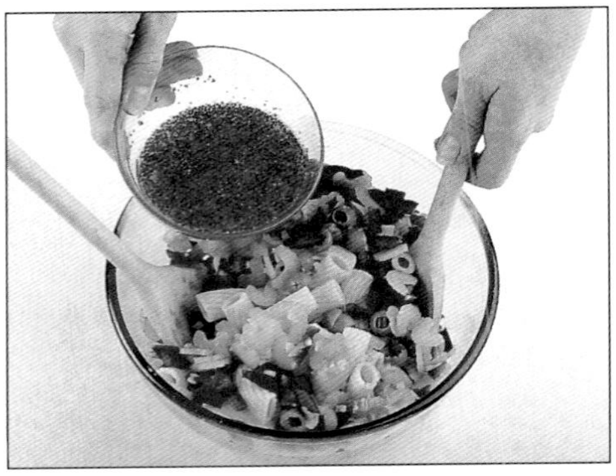

5 Mix the honey, mustard and remaining lime juice together in a bowl and pour over the pasta. Toss to mix well.

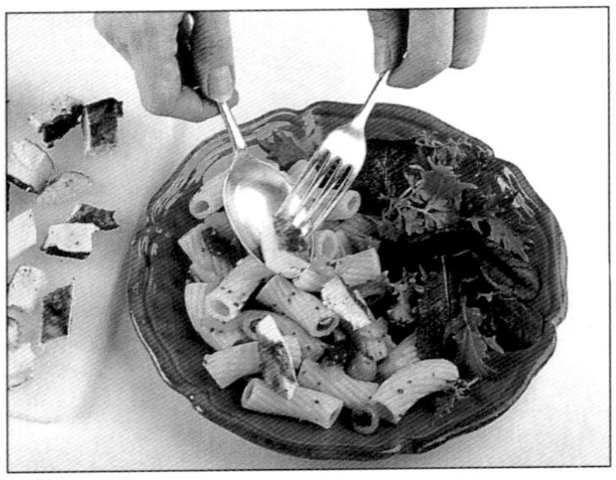

6 Cut the chicken into bite-size pieces. Arrange the mixed salad leaves on a serving dish, spoon the pasta mixture in the centre of the leaves and top with the spicy chicken pieces.

NUTRITIONAL NOTES

Per portion:

Energy	234Kcals/993kJ
Total fat	4g
Saturated fat	1.1g
Cholesterol	37.88mg
Fibre	1.6g

FARFALLE SALAD WITH PIQUANT PEPPERS

Peppers, pasta and fresh coriander add delicious flavour to this quick and easy Italian starter or supper dish.

Ingredients

1 red, 1 yellow and 1 orange pepper
1 garlic clove, crushed
30ml/2 tbsp capers
30ml/2 tbsp raisins
5ml/1 tsp wholegrain mustard
finely grated rind and juice of 1 lime
5ml/1 tsp clear honey
30ml/2 tbsp chopped fresh coriander
225g/8oz dried farfalle
salt and freshly ground black pepper
shaved fresh Parmesan cheese, to serve (optional)

Serves 8

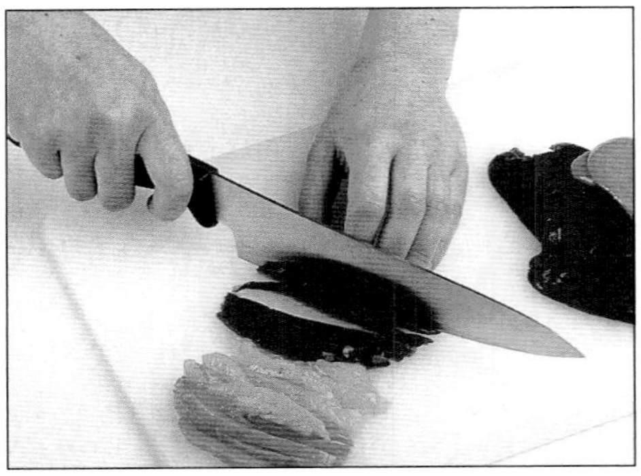

1 Quarter the peppers and remove and discard the stalk and seeds. Put into a saucepan of boiling water and cook for 10–15 minutes until tender. Drain and rinse under cold water. Drain again. Peel away and discard the skin and cut the flesh into strips lengthways. Set aside.

Nutritional Notes

Per portion:

Energy	160Kcals/681kJ
Total fat	1g
Saturated fat	0.2g
Cholesterol	0mg
Fibre	1.9g

2 Put the garlic, capers, raisins, mustard, lime rind and juice, honey, coriander and seasoning into a bowl and whisk together. Set aside.

Variation

If you prefer, make this salad with only one colour of pepper. The green ones are too bitter, however, and are not suitable.

3 Cook the pasta in a large saucepan of boiling, salted water for 10–12 minutes until tender or *al dente*. Drain.

4 Return the pasta to the pan, add the reserved peppers and dressing. Heat gently and toss to mix. Transfer to a warm serving bowl and serve. Serve sprinkled with a few shavings of Parmesan cheese, if using.

LEMON AND HERB RISOTTO CAKE

This unusual Italian rice dish can be served as a low-fat main course with salad, or as a satisfying side dish. It is also good served cold, and packs well for picnics.

INGREDIENTS

1 small leek, thinly sliced
600ml/1 pint/2½ cups chicken stock
225g/8oz/1 cup short grain rice
finely grated rind of 1 lemon
30ml/2 tbsp chopped fresh chives
30ml/2 tbsp chopped fresh parsley
75g/3oz/¾ cup grated reduced-fat mozzarella cheese
salt and freshly ground black pepper
fresh parsley sprigs and lemon wedges, to garnish

SERVES 6

1 Preheat the oven to 200ºC/400ºF/Gas 6. Lightly oil a 21cm/8½in round, loose-based cake tin. Set aside.

2 Cook the leek in a large saucepan with 45ml/3 tbsp stock, stirring over a moderate heat, to soften.

3 Add the rice and the remaining stock. Bring to the boil. Cover and simmer, stirring occasionally, for about 20 minutes, or until all the liquid is absorbed.

4 Remove the pan from the heat, stir in the lemon rind, chopped herbs, cheese and seasoning and mix well. Spoon the mixture into the prepared tin, level the surface, cover with foil.

5 Bake in the oven for 30–35 minutes or until lightly browned. Turn out on to a serving plate and serve hot or cold in slices, garnished with parsley sprigs and lemon wedges.

NUTRITIONAL NOTES

Per portion:

Energy	165Kcals/698kJ
Total fat	3g
Saturated fat	1.4g
Cholesterol	4.94mg
Fibre	0.4g

VARIATION

The best type of rice to choose for this recipe is the Italian round grain arborio rice, but if it is not available, use pudding rice instead.

TOMATO PESTO TOASTIES

Ready-made pesto is high in fat but, as its flavour is so powerful, it can be used in very small amounts with good effect, as in these tasty low-fat toasties.

Ingredients

2 thick slices of crusty bread
45ml/3 tbsp skimmed milk soft cheese or low-fat fromage frais
10ml/2 tsp red or green pesto
1 beef tomato
1 red onion
salt and freshly ground black pepper

Serves 2

1 Toast the bread slices under a hot grill until golden brown on both sides, turning once. Leave to cool.

2 Mix together the soft cheese or fromage frais and pesto in a small bowl until well blended, then spread thickly on to the toasted bread.

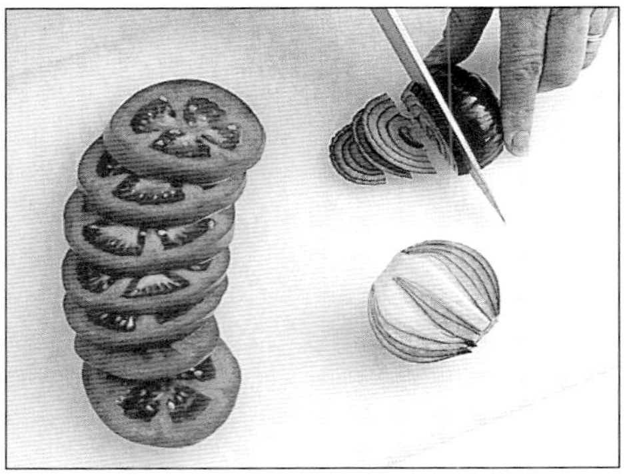

3 Cut the tomato and onion, crossways, into thin slices using a large sharp knife.

4 Arrange the tomato and onion slices, overlapping, on top of the toast and season. Cook under a hot grill until heated through, then serve, garnished with a sprig of thyme.

Cook's Tip

Almost any type of crusty bread can be used, but Italian ciabatta and French bread give the best flavour.

Nutritional Notes

Per portion:

Energy	149Kcals/629kJ
Total fat	4g
Saturated fat	1g
Cholesterol	2.57mg
Fibre	1.2g

PARMA HAM AND PEPPER PIZZAS

The delicious flavours of these quick and easy Italian pizza snacks are hard to beat. Serve with mixed salad leaves and sliced plum tomatoes.

INGREDIENTS

½ loaf of ciabatta bread
1 red pepper, roasted, peeled and deseeded
1 yellow pepper, roasted, peeled and deseeded
4 thin slices Parma ham, cut into thick strips
50g/2oz reduced-fat mozzarella cheese
ground black pepper
tiny fresh basil leaves, to garnish

MAKES 4

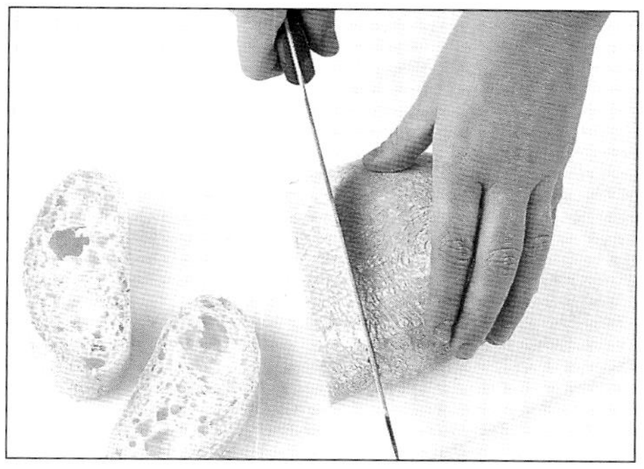

1 Cut the bread into four thick slices and toast until golden.

2 Cut the roasted peppers into thick strips and arrange on the toasted bread with the strips of Parma ham. Preheat the grill.

3 Thinly slice the mozzarella and arrange on top, then grind over plenty of black pepper. Grill for 2–3 minutes until the cheese is bubbling.

NUTRITIONAL NOTES

Per portion:

Energy	213Kcals/903kJ
Total fat	3.9g
Saturated fat	1.67g
Cholesterol	8.76mg
Fibre	1.5

4 Scatter the basil leaves on top to garnish and serve immediately.

MEAT, POULTRY AND FISH DISHES

WHITE FISH *is naturally low in fat and by choosing* LEAN CUTS *of meat and poultry these foods can be* ENJOYED *as part of a* HEALTHY *low-fat diet. Choose from this nourishing collection of low-fat Italian* MAIN COURSE *meat, poultry and fish dishes including* PANCETTA *and Broad Bean* RISOTTO, *Tuscan Chicken and Roast Monkfish with* GARLIC *and Fennel.*

FILLET OF BEEF WITH HERBY TAGLIATELLE

This Italian-style fillet of beef served with herby pasta creates a delicious low-fat main course or supper dish.

INGREDIENTS
450g/1lb lean beef fillet
450g/1lb fresh tagliatelle made with sun-dried tomatoes and herbs
115g/4oz cherry tomatoes
1/2 cucumber

FOR THE MARINADE
15ml/1 tbsp soy sauce
15ml/1 tbsp sherry
5ml/1 tsp fresh root ginger, peeled and grated
1 garlic clove, crushed

FOR THE HERB DRESSING
150ml/1/4 pint/2/3 cup low-fat natural yogurt
1 garlic clove, crushed
30–45ml/2–3 tbsp chopped fresh herbs (chives, parsley, thyme)
salt and freshly ground black pepper

SERVES 6

1 Mix all the marinade ingredients together in a shallow non-metallic dish, put the beef in and turn it over to coat it. Cover with clear film and leave for 30 minutes to allow the flavours to penetrate the meat.

2 Preheat the grill. Lift the fillet out of the marinade and pat it dry with kitchen paper. Grill on a grill rack for 8 minutes on each side, basting with the marinade.

3 Transfer to a plate, cover with foil and leave to stand for 20 minutes.

4 Mix the dressing ingredients thoroughly. Cook the pasta in a large saucepan of lightly salted boiling water, according to the packet instructions, until tender or *al dente*. Drain thoroughly, rinse under cold water and drain again.

5 Cut the cherry tomatoes in half. Cut the cucumber in half lengthways, scoop out and discard the seeds with a teaspoon and slice the flesh thinly into crescents.

6 Put the pasta, cherry tomatoes, cucumber and dressing into a bowl and toss to mix well. Slice the beef thinly and arrange on serving plates with the pasta salad served alongside.

NUTRITIONAL NOTES
Per portion:

Energy	201Kcals/848kJ
Total fat	4.3g
Saturated fat	1.7g
Cholesterol	45.25mg
Fibre	1.2g

BEEF STEW WITH TOMATOES, WINE AND PEAS

This is a traditional Italian recipe known as spezzatino which is perfect for a winter lunch or dinner. Serve it with boiled or mashed potatoes to soak up the delicious sauce.

INGREDIENTS

30ml/2 tbsp plain flour
10ml/2 tsp chopped fresh thyme or 5ml/1 tsp dried thyme
450g/1lb lean braising or stewing steak, cut into cubes
10ml/2 tsp olive oil
2 onions, roughly chopped
450g/1lb jar sugocasa or passata
250ml/8fl oz/1 cup beef stock
250ml/8fl oz/1 cup red wine
2 garlic cloves, crushed
30ml/2 tbsp tomato purée
275g/10oz/2½ cups shelled fresh peas
5ml/1 tsp sugar
salt and freshly ground black pepper
fresh thyme sprigs, to garnish

SERVES 6

1 Preheat the oven to 160°C/325°F/Gas 3. Put the flour in a shallow dish and season with the chopped thyme and salt and pepper. Add the beef cubes and turn to coat evenly with the flour.

VARIATION

Use thawed frozen peas instead of fresh. Add them 10 minutes before the end of cooking.

2 Heat the oil in a large flameproof casserole, add the beef and seal on all sides over a medium heat. Remove with a slotted spoon and place on a plate.

3 Add the onion to the pan, scraping the base of the pan to mix in any sediment. Cook gently for 3 minutes, stirring frequently, then stir in the sugocasa or passata, stock, wine, garlic and tomato purée. Bring to the boil, stirring. Return the beef to the pan and stir well to coat with the sauce. Cover and cook in the oven for 1½ hours.

4 Stir in the peas and sugar. Re-cover, return the casserole to the oven and cook for a further 30 minutes, or until the beef is tender. Adjust the seasoning to taste. Garnish with fresh thyme sprigs and serve immediately.

NUTRITIONAL NOTES

Per portion:

Energy	183Kcals/768kJ
Total fat	4.9g
Saturated fat	1.5g
Cholesterol	38.3mg
Fibre	2.8g

CALF'S LIVER WITH BALSAMIC VINEGAR

This delicious sweet-and-sour liver dish is a speciality of Venice. Serve it very simply, with green beans sprinkled with toasted fresh breadcrumbs, for an appetizing supper dish.

INGREDIENTS

15ml/1 tbsp plain flour
2.5ml/½ tsp finely chopped fresh sage
4 thin slices calf's liver, cut into serving pieces
15ml/1 tbsp olive oil
2 small red onions, sliced and separated into rings
150ml/¼ pint/⅔ cup dry white wine
45ml/3 tbsp balsamic vinegar
pinch of sugar
salt and freshly ground black pepper
fresh sage sprigs, to garnish

SERVES 4

1 Spread out the flour in a shallow bowl. Season it with the chopped sage and plenty of salt and pepper. Add the liver and turn it in the flour until well coated.

2 Heat the oil in a wide, heavy-based saucepan or frying pan. Add the onion rings and cook gently, stirring frequently, for about 5 minutes until softened but not coloured. Remove with a fish slice, place on a plate and set aside.

3 Add the coated liver to the juices in the pan and cook over a medium heat for 2–3 minutes on each side. Transfer to warmed serving plates and keep hot.

4 Add the wine and vinegar to the pan and stir to mix with the pan juices and any sediment. Add the onions and sugar and heat through until hot and bubbling, stirring. Spoon the sauce over the liver, garnish with fresh sage sprigs and serve at once.

NUTRITIONAL NOTES

Per portion:

Energy	110Kcals/457kJ
Total fat	4.9g
Saturated fat	1g
Cholesterol	102.85mg
Fibre	0.3g

VEAL WITH TOMATOES AND WHITE WINE

This famous Milanese dish is delicious and hearty and creates an ideal main course meal for special occasions. It goes very well with a green salad.

INGREDIENTS

30ml/2 tbsp plain flour
4 pieces of lean veal shank
2 small onions
10ml/2 tsp olive oil
1 large celery stick, finely chopped
1 carrot, finely chopped
2 garlic cloves, finely chopped
400g/14oz can chopped tomatoes
300ml/½ pint/1¼ cups dry white wine
300ml/½ pint/1¼ cups chicken or veal stock
1 strip of thinly pared lemon rind
2 bay leaves, plus extra for garnishing
salt and freshly ground black pepper

FOR THE GREMOLATA

30ml/2 tbsp finely chopped fresh flat leaf parsley
finely grated rind of 1 lemon
1 garlic clove, finely chopped

SERVES 4

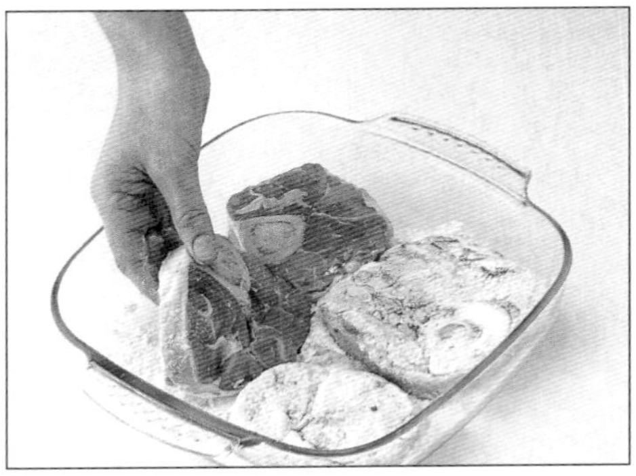

1 Preheat the oven to 160°C/325°F/Gas 3. Season the flour with salt and pepper and spread it out in a shallow bowl. Add the pieces of veal and turn them in the flour until they are evenly coated. Shake off any excess flour.

2 Slice one of the onions into rings. Heat the olive oil in a large flameproof casserole, then add the veal pieces, with the onion rings, and brown the veal on both sides over a medium heat. Remove the veal with tongs, place on a plate and set aside to drain.

3 Chop the remaining onion and add to the pan with the celery, carrot and garlic. Stir the bottom of the pan to mix in the juices and sediment. Cook gently, stirring frequently, for about 5 minutes until the vegetables soften slightly.

4 Add the tomatoes, wine, stock, lemon rind and bay leaves, then season to taste with salt and pepper. Bring the mixture to the boil, stirring.

5 Return the veal pieces to the pan and stir to coat thoroughly with the sauce. Cover and cook in the oven for 2 hours or until the veal feels tender when pierced with a fork.

6 Meanwhile, make the gremolata. Mix together the parsley, lemon rind and garlic in a small bowl. Remove the casserole from the oven and discard the lemon rind and bay leaves. Adjust the seasoning. Serve hot, sprinkled with the gremolata and garnished with bay leaves.

NUTRITIONAL NOTES

Per portion:

Energy	219Kcals/919kJ
Total fat	4.8g
Saturated fat	1.2g
Cholesterol	84.8mg
Fibre	1.3g

PANCETTA AND BROAD BEAN RISOTTO

This delicious Italian risotto makes a healthy and filling low-fat meal, served with cooked fresh seasonal vegetables or a mixed green salad.

INGREDIENTS

10ml/2 tsp olive oil
1 onion, chopped
2 garlic cloves, finely chopped
115g/4oz smoked pancetta or smoked lean back bacon, diced
350g/12oz/1¾ cups risotto rice
1.5 litres/2½ pints/6¼ cups simmering chicken stock
225g/8oz/1⅓ cups frozen baby broad beans
30ml/2 tbsp chopped fresh mixed herbs, such as parsley, thyme and oregano
salt and freshly ground black pepper
shaved fresh Parmesan cheese, to serve (optional)

SERVES 6

1 Heat the oil in a large saucepan. Add the onion, garlic and pancetta or bacon and cook gently for about 5 minutes, stirring occasionally. Do not allow the onion and garlic to brown.

2 Add the rice and cook for 1 minute, stirring. Add a ladleful of stock and cook, stirring, until absorbed.

3 Add more ladlefuls of stock until the rice is tender and almost all the liquid absorbed. This will take 30–35 minutes. Meanwhile, cook the broad beans in salted, boiling water for about 3 minutes. Drain and stir into the risotto, with the herbs. Season to taste. Sprinkle with shavings of Parmesan cheese, if using.

NUTRITIONAL NOTES

Per portion:

Energy	294Kcals/1250kJ
Total fat	5g
Saturated fat	1.6g
Cholesterol	8.5mg
Fibre	2.7g

HUNTER'S CHICKEN

This traditional Italian dish combines chicken in a flavourful tomato, mushroom and herb sauce to create a tempting main course, ideal served with mashed potatoes or cooked polenta.

Ingredients

15g/½oz/¼ cup dried porcini mushrooms
10ml/2 tsp olive oil
4 small chicken portions, on the bone, skinned
1 large onion, thinly sliced
400g/14oz can chopped tomatoes
150ml/¼ pint/⅔ cup red wine
1 garlic clove, crushed
leaves of 1 sprig of fresh rosemary, finely chopped
115g/4oz/1¾ cups fresh field mushrooms, thinly sliced
salt and freshly ground black pepper
fresh rosemary sprigs, to garnish

Serves 4

1 Put the porcini in a bowl, add 250ml/8fl oz/1 cup warm water and leave to soak for 20–30 minutes. Remove from the liquid and squeeze over the bowl. Strain the liquid and reserve. Finely chop the porcini.

2 Heat the oil in a large flameproof casserole. Add the chicken. Sauté over a medium heat for 5 minutes, or until golden. Remove and drain on absorbent kitchen paper.

3 Add the onion and chopped porcini mushrooms to the pan. Cook gently, stirring frequently, for about 3 minutes until the onion has softened but not browned. Stir in the chopped tomatoes, wine and reserved mushroom soaking liquid, then add the crushed garlic and chopped rosemary, with salt and pepper to taste. Bring to the boil, stirring all the time.

4 Return the chicken to the pan and turn to coat it with the sauce. Cover and simmer gently for 30 minutes.

5 Add the fresh mushrooms and stir well to mix into the sauce. Continue simmering gently for 10 minutes or until the chicken is tender. Adjust the seasoning to taste. Serve hot, garnished with fresh rosemary sprigs.

Nutritional Notes

Per portion:

Energy	190Kcals/801kJ
Total fat	5g
Saturated fat	1.3g
Cholesterol	44.12mg
Fibre	1.2g

TUSCAN CHICKEN

This simple Italian peasant casserole has all the flavours of traditional Tuscan ingredients and creates a delicious, low-fat supper dish.

INGREDIENTS

8 chicken thighs, skinned
5ml/1 tsp olive oil
1 onion, thinly sliced
2 red peppers, deseeded and sliced
1 garlic clove, crushed
300ml/½ pint/1¼ cups passata
150ml/¼ pint/⅔ cup dry white wine
a large sprig of fresh oregano, chopped, or 5ml/1 tsp dried oregano
400g/14oz can cannellini beans, drained
45ml/3 tbsp fresh breadcrumbs
salt and freshly ground black pepper
fresh oregano sprigs, to garnish

SERVES 6

1 Fry the chicken in the oil in a non-stick or heavy pan until golden brown all over. Remove from the pan, place on a plate and keep hot. Add the onion and peppers to the pan and gently sauté until softened, but not brown. Add the garlic.

2 Add the chicken, passata, wine and oregano and stir. Season well and bring to the boil, stirring, then cover the pan tightly.

3 Lower the heat and simmer gently, stirring occasionally, for 30–35 minutes or until the chicken is tender and the juices run clear, not pink, when pierced with the point of a knife.

4 Stir in the cannellini beans and simmer for a further 5 minutes until heated through. Sprinkle with the breadcrumbs and cook under a hot grill until golden brown. Serve immediately, garnished with fresh oregano sprigs.

NUTRITIONAL NOTES

Per portion:

Energy	256Kcals/1083kJ
Total fat	4.8g
Saturated fat	1.3g
Cholesterol	49.3mg
Fibre	1.1g

CHICKEN IN A SALT CRUST

Cooking food in a casing of salt gives a deliciously moist, tender flavour that, surprisingly, is not too salty. Serve with a selection of cooked fresh seasonal vegetables.

Ingredients

1.75kg/4–4½lb chicken
about 2.25kg/5¼lb coarse sea salt

Serves 6

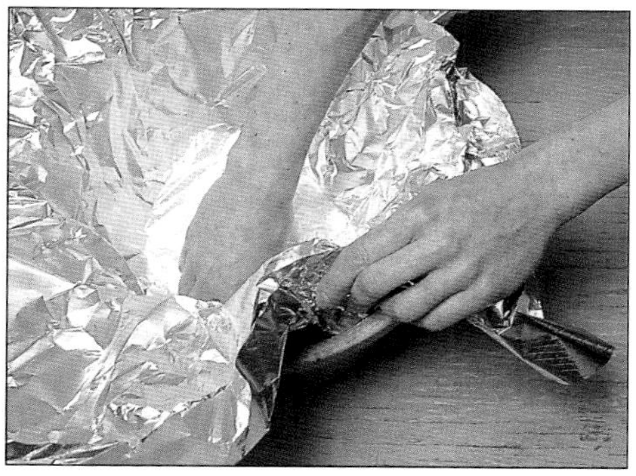

1 Preheat the oven to 220°C/425°F/Gas 7. Choose a deep ovenproof dish into which the whole chicken will fit snugly. Line the dish with a double thickness of heavy foil, allowing plenty of foil to overhang it.

2 Truss the chicken tightly so that the salt cannot fall into the cavity. Place the chicken on a thin layer of salt in the dish.

Cook's Tip

This recipe makes a stunning and unusual main course. Garnish the salt-encrusted chicken with fresh mixed herbs and take to the table. Scrape away the salt and transfer to a clean plate to carve.

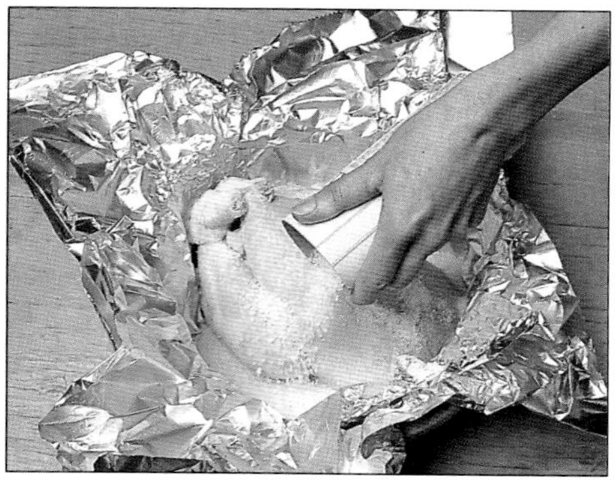

3 Pour the remaining salt all around and over the top of the chicken until it is completely encased. Sprinkle the top with a little water.

4 Cover tightly with the foil and bake the chicken on the lower shelf in the oven for 1¾ hours until the chicken is cooked and tender.

5 To serve the chicken, open out the foil and ease it out of the dish. Place on a large serving platter. Crack open the salt crust on the chicken and brush away the salt. Remove and discard the skin from the chicken and carve the meat into slices. Serve.

Nutritional Notes

Per portion:

Energy	156Kcals/659kJ
Total fat	4.4g
Saturated fat	1.3g
Cholesterol	61.6mg
Fibre	0g

PRAWNS IN FRESH TOMATO SAUCE

Fresh prawns are cooked and served in a fresh tomato sauce to create this appetizing Italian-style low-fat dish.

Ingredients

20ml/4 tsp olive oil
1 onion, finely chopped
1 celery stick, finely chopped
1 small red pepper, deseeded and chopped
120ml/4fl oz/½ cup red wine
15ml/1 tbsp wine vinegar
400g/14oz can plum tomatoes, chopped, with their juice
1kg/2¼lb uncooked prawns, in their shells
2–3 garlic cloves, finely chopped
45ml/3 tbsp finely chopped fresh parsley
1 dried chilli, crumbled or chopped (optional)
salt and freshly ground black pepper

Serves 6

1 Heat half the oil in a heavy-based saucepan. Add the onion and cook over a low heat until soft, stirring occasionally. Stir in the chopped celery and pepper and cook for 5 minutes. Increase the heat and add the wine, vinegar and tomatoes. Bring the mixture to the boil and cook for 5 minutes, stirring occasionally. Reduce the heat, cover the pan and simmer for about 30 minutes, until the vegetables are soft, stirring occasionally.

Nutritional Notes

Per portion:

Energy	114Kcals/476kJ
Total fat	3.2g
Saturated fat	0.6g
Cholesterol	49.2mg
Fibre	0.8g

2 Remove the pan from the heat and allow the vegetable mixture to cool a little, then purée through a food mill to make a tomato sauce. Set aside.

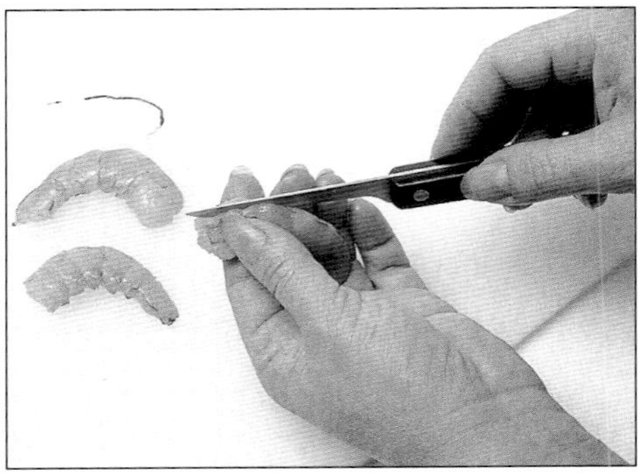

3 Shell the prawns. Make a shallow incision with a small, sharp knife along the back of each prawn and remove the long, black vein. Set the prawns aside.

4 Heat the remaining oil in a clean, heavy-based saucepan. Stir in the garlic and parsley, plus the chilli, if using. Cook over a medium heat, stirring, until the garlic is golden. Stir in the prepared tomato sauce and bring to the boil.

5 Stir in the prepared prawns. Bring the sauce back to the boil. Reduce the heat slightly and simmer, stirring occasionally, until the prawns are pink and stiff: this will take about 6–8 minutes, depending on their size. Season to taste and serve.

MEDITERRANEAN FISH CUTLETS

These low-fat fish cutlets are ideal served with boiled potatoes, broccoli and carrots for a delicious Italian supper.

INGREDIENTS

4 white fish cutlets, about 150g/5oz each
about 150ml/¼ pint/⅔ cup fish stock or dry white wine (or a mixture of the two), for poaching
1 bay leaf, a few black peppercorns and a strip of pared lemon rind, for flavouring
chopped fresh parsley, to garnish

FOR THE TOMATO SAUCE

400g/14oz can chopped tomatoes
1 garlic clove, crushed
15ml/1 tbsp pastis or other aniseed-flavoured liqueur
15ml/1 tbsp drained capers
12–16 stoned black olives
salt and freshly ground black pepper

SERVES 4

1 To make the tomato sauce, place the chopped tomatoes, garlic, pastis or other liqueur, capers and olives in a saucepan. Season to taste with salt and pepper and cook over a low heat for about 15 minutes, stirring occasionally.

2 Meanwhile, place the fish in a frying pan, pour over the stock and/or wine and add the bay leaf, peppercorns and lemon rind. Cover and simmer for 10 minutes or until the fish is cooked and the flesh flakes easily.

3 Using a slotted spoon, transfer the fish to a heated serving dish. Strain the fish stock into the tomato sauce and boil to reduce slightly. Season the sauce, pour it over the fish and serve immediately, sprinkled with the chopped fresh parsley to garnish.

COOK'S TIP

Remove the skin from the fish cutlets and use fewer olives to reduce calories and fat even further. Use 450g/1lb fresh tomatoes, skinned and chopped, in place of canned.

NUTRITIONAL NOTES

Per portion:

Energy	165Kcals/685kJ
Total fat	3.55g
Saturated fat	0.5g
Cholesterol	69mg
Fibre	0.8g

ITALIAN FISH PARCELS

Fresh sea bass fillets are topped with mixed Italian vegetables, then barbecued or oven-baked to create this tasty dish, ideal for eating *al fresco*.

Ingredients

4 pieces skinless sea bass fillet or 4 whole small sea bass
10ml/2 tsp olive oil for brushing
2 shallots, thinly sliced
1 garlic clove, chopped
15ml/1 tbsp capers
6 sun-dried tomatoes, finely chopped
4 black olives, pitted and thinly sliced
finely grated rind and juice of 1 lemon
5ml/1 tsp paprika
salt and freshly ground black pepper

Serves 4

1 If you are using whole fish, gut them, taking care not to insert the knife too far. Use a teaspoon or your fingers to scrape out the contents. Leave the scales on as they will hold the fragile fish together during cooking.

2 Wash the cavity and the outside of the fish thoroughly with cold water.

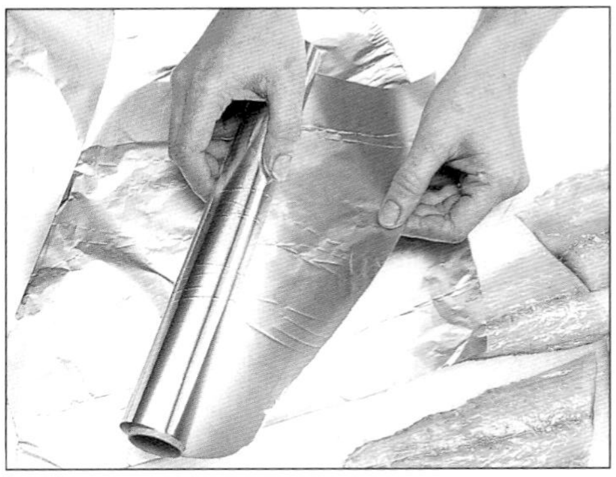

3 Cut four large squares of double-thickness foil, large enough to enclose the fish. Brush each square with a little olive oil.

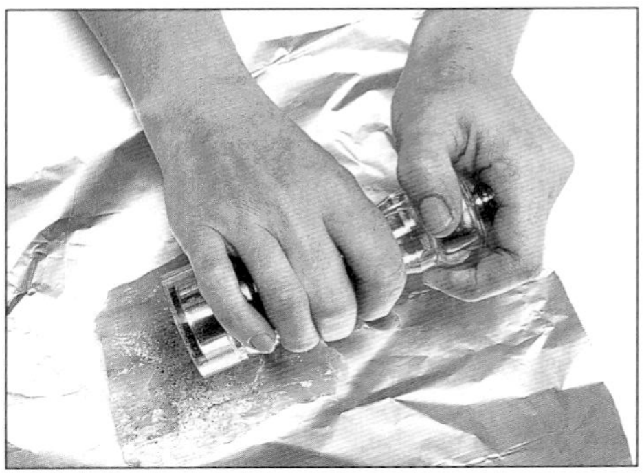

4 Place a piece of fish in the centre of each piece of foil and season well with salt and pepper.

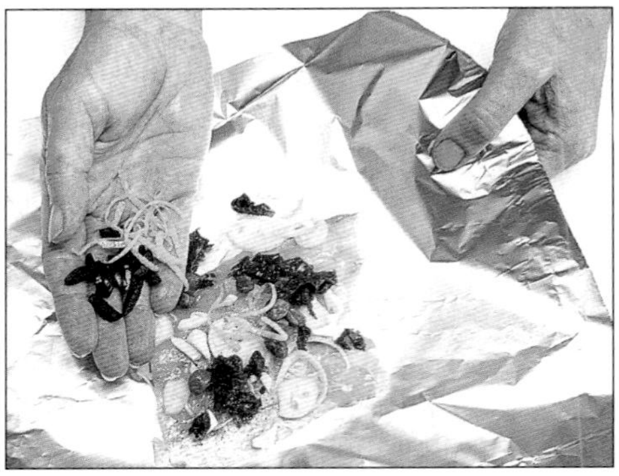

5 Scatter over the shallots, garlic, capers, sun-dried tomatoes, olives and grated lemon rind. Sprinkle with the lemon juice and paprika.

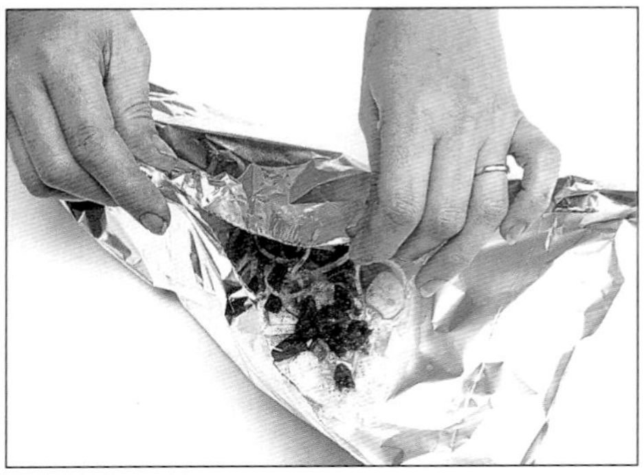

6 Fold the foil over to enclose the fish loosely, sealing the edges firmly so none of the juices can escape.

7 Place on a moderately hot barbecue and cook for 8–10 minutes. Then open up the tops of the parcels and serve.

Cook's Tips

• When choosing fish, look for bright, slightly bulging eyes and shiny, faintly slimy skin. Open up the gills to check that they are clear red or dark pink and prod the fish lightly to check that the flesh is springy. All fish should have only a faint, pleasant smell; you can tell a stale fish a mile off by its disagreeable odour.

• Sea bass are prized for their delicate white flesh, and these slim, elegant fish are almost always sold whole. They don't have any irritating small bones, and as a result are never cheap.

Nutritional Notes

Per portion:

Energy	117Kcals/492kJ
Total fat	4.5g
Saturated fat	0.6g
Cholesterol	50.2mg
Fibre	0.1g

Variations

• These parcels can also be baked in the oven: place them on a baking sheet and cook at 200°C/400°F/Gas 6 for 15–20 minutes.

• Sea bass is good for this recipe, but you could also use small whole trout, or white fish fillet such as cod or haddock.

ROAST MONKFISH WITH GARLIC AND FENNEL

Fresh monkfish quickly roasted with garlic and fennel is delicious served with boiled new potatoes for a summertime Italian meal.

Ingredients

1.2kg/2½lb monkfish tail
8 garlic cloves
15ml/1 tbsp olive oil
2 fennel bulbs, sliced
juice and zest of 1 lemon
1 bay leaf, plus extra to garnish
salt and freshly ground black pepper

Serves 6

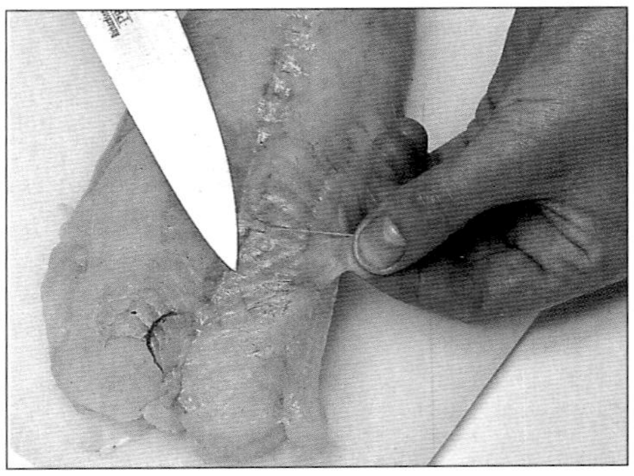

1 Preheat the oven to 220°C/425°F/Gas 7. With a sharp filleting knife, carefully cut away the thin membrane covering the outside of the monkfish; keep the knife flat against the fish to avoid cutting too much of the flesh away. When finished, discard the membrane.

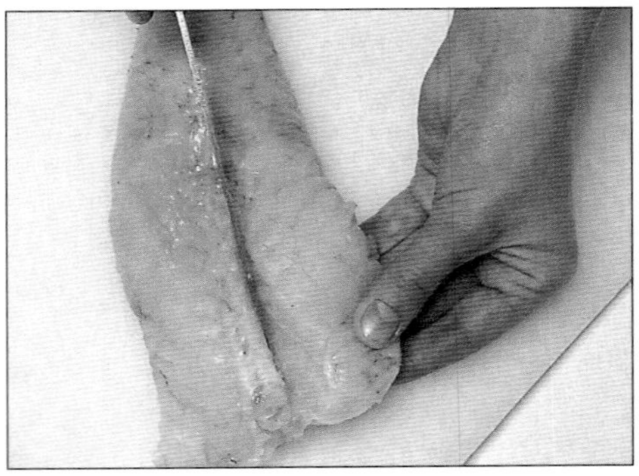

2 Cut along one side of the central bone to remove the fillet. Repeat on the other side. Discard the bone.

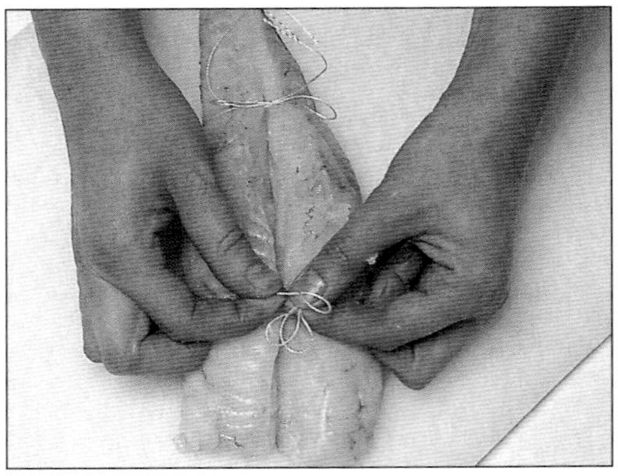

3 Tie the separated fillets together with string to reshape as a tailpiece.

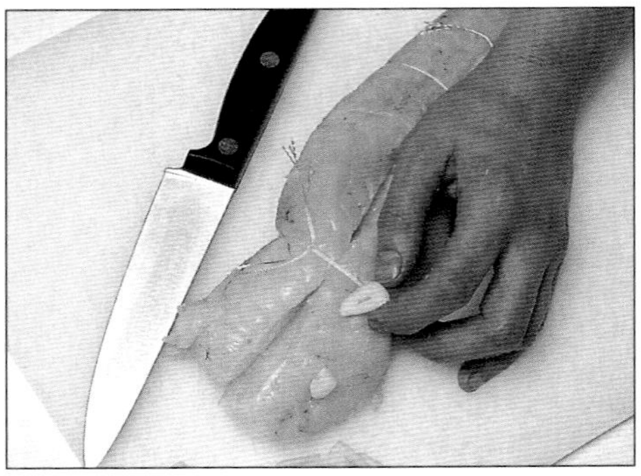

4 Peel and slice the garlic cloves and cut incisions into the fish flesh. Place the garlic slices in the incisions.

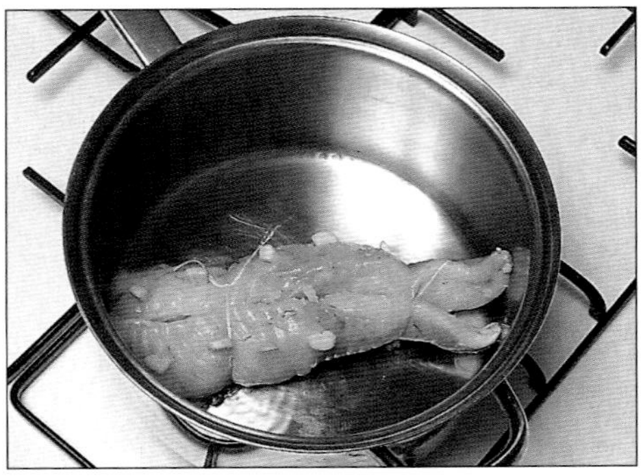

5 Heat the oil in a large, heavy-based saucepan and cook the fish until sealed on all sides.

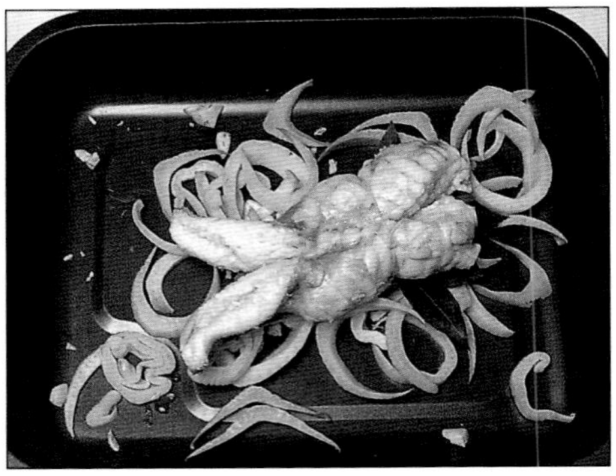

6 Place the fish in a roasting dish together with the fennel slices, lemon juice, bay leaf and seasoning.

7 Roast in the oven for about 20 minutes, until tender and cooked through. Serve immediately, garnished with bay leaves and lemon zest.

Cook's Tips

- Monkfish is usually available all the year round, but if it is not available then you could substitute another firm white fish, such as huss.
- The aniseed-like flavour of fennel goes particularly well with fish. The leaves can be used as a garnish if you like.

Nutritional Notes

Per portion:

Energy	234Kcals/988kJ
Total fat	4.7g
Saturated fat	0.6g
Cholesterol	123.5mg
Fibre	1.2g

MONKFISH WITH PEPPERED CITRUS MARINADE

A fresh citrus fruit marinade adds delicious flavour to monkfish fillets and creates a low-fat, appetizing dish ideal for cooking and eating *al fresco*.

Ingredients

2 monkfish tails, about 350g/12oz each
1 lime
1 lemon
2 oranges
a handful of fresh thyme sprigs
20ml/4 tsp olive oil
15ml/1 tbsp mixed peppercorns, roughly crushed
salt and freshly ground black pepper

Serves 4

1 Remove and discard any skin from the monkfish tails.

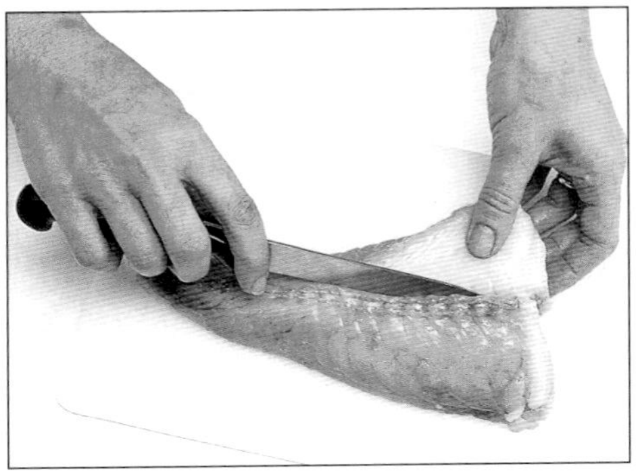

2 Cut carefully down one side of the backbone, sliding the knife between the bone and flesh, to remove the fillet on one side. (You can ask your fishmonger to do this for you.)

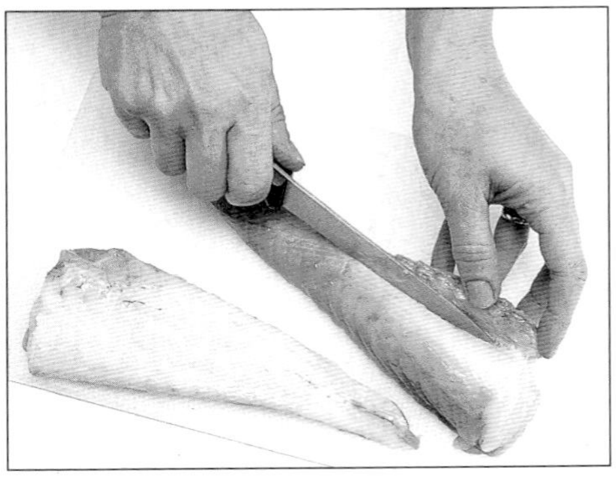

3 Turn the fish and repeat on the other side. Repeat on the second tail. Discard the bones. Lay the fillets out flat.

4 Cut two slices from each of the citrus fruits and arrange over two fillets. Add a few sprigs of thyme and season. Finely grate the rind from the remaining fruit and sprinkle over the fish.

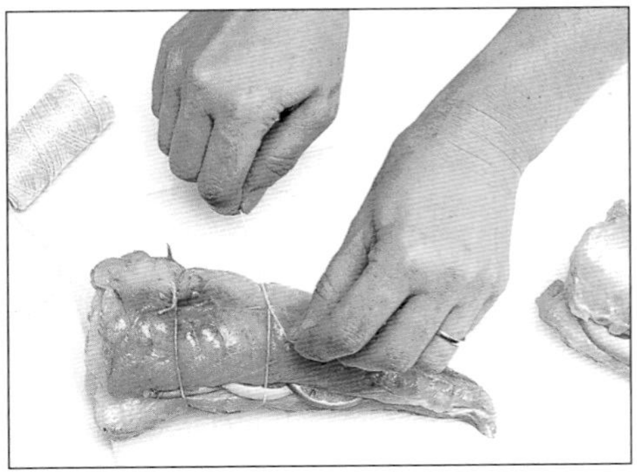

5 Lay the other two fillets on top and tie them firmly at intervals, with fine cotton string, to hold them in shape. Place in a wide, shallow, non-metallic dish.

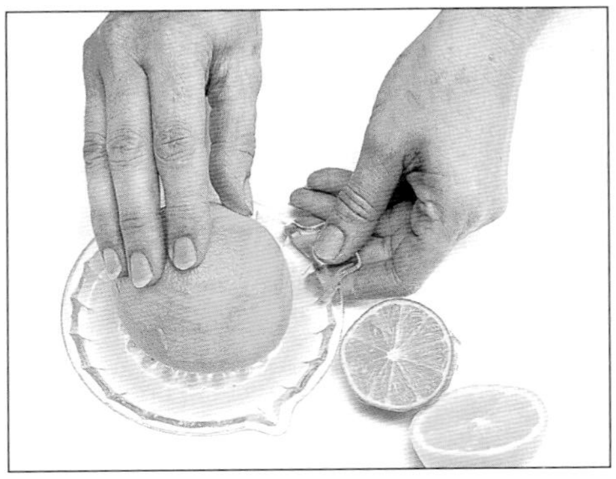

6 Squeeze the juice from the citrus fruits and mix it with the oil and more salt and black pepper.

7 Spoon the juice mixture over the fish. Cover and leave to marinate for about an hour, turning occasionally and spooning the marinade over it.

8 Drain the monkfish, reserving the marinade, and sprinkle with the crushed peppercorns. Cook on a medium hot barbecue for 15–20 minutes, basting the fish with the marinade and turning it occasionally, until it is evenly cooked. Serve immediately.

Nutritional Notes

Per portion:

Energy	176Kcals/741kJ
Total fat	5g
Saturated fat	0.7g
Cholesterol	80.6mg
Fibre	0g

Variation

You can also use this marinade for monkfish kebabs.

BAKED PLAICE WITH ITALIAN VEGETABLE SAUCE

Fresh plaice fillets are oven-baked in an Italian mixed vegetable sauce to create a very low-fat meal for family or friends.

Ingredients

4 large plaice fillets
2 small red onions
120ml/4fl oz/½ cup vegetable stock
60ml/4 tbsp dry red wine
1 garlic clove, crushed
2 courgettes, sliced
1 yellow pepper, deseeded and sliced
400g/14oz can chopped tomatoes
15ml/1 tbsp chopped fresh thyme
salt and freshly ground black pepper
fresh thyme sprigs, to garnish
potato gratin, to serve

Serves 4

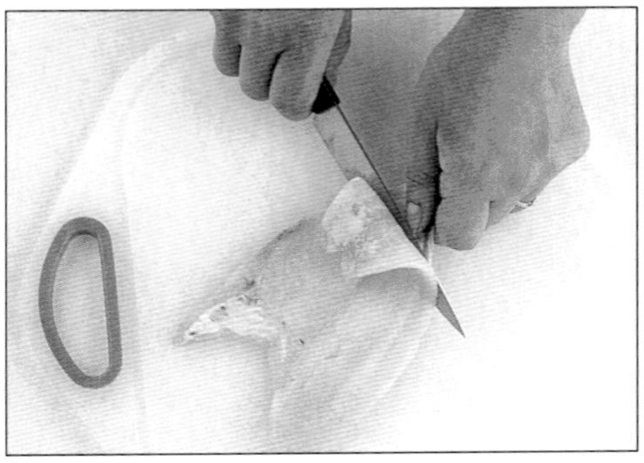

1 Preheat the oven to 180ºC/350ºF/Gas 4. Lay the fillets skin-side down and, holding the tail end, push a sharp knife between the skin and flesh in a sawing movement. Hold the knife at a slight angle with the blade towards the skin. Discard the skin and set the fish aside.

2 Cut each onion into eight wedges. Put into a heavy-based saucepan with the vegetable stock. Cover, bring to the boil and simmer for 5 minutes. Uncover and continue to cook, stirring occasionally, until the stock has reduced entirely. Add the red wine and crushed garlic to the pan and continue to cook until the onions are soft, stirring occasionally.

3 Stir in the courgettes, yellow pepper, tomatoes and chopped thyme and season to taste. Simmer for 3 minutes. Spoon the sauce into a large casserole.

4 Fold each plaice fillet in half and put on top of the vegetable sauce. Cover and cook in the oven for 15–20 minutes, until the fish is opaque and flakes easily. Garnish with fresh thyme sprigs and serve with a potato gratin.

Cook's Tip

Skinless white fish fillets such as plaice are low in fat and make an ideal tasty and nutritious basis for many low-fat recipes such as this one.

Nutritional Notes

Per portion:

Energy	144Kcals/612kJ
Total fat	2.7g
Saturated fat	0.4g
Cholesterol	46.2mg
Fibre	1.5g

BAKED COD WITH TOMATOES

For the very best flavour, use firm sun-ripened tomatoes for this Italian tomato sauce and make sure it is fairly thick before spooning it over the cod. Serve with boiled new potatoes and a salad.

INGREDIENTS

10ml/2 tsp olive oil
1 onion, chopped
2 garlic cloves, finely chopped
450g/1lb tomatoes, peeled, deseeded and chopped
5ml/1 tsp tomato purée
60ml/4 tbsp dry white wine
60ml/4 tbsp chopped fresh flat leaf parsley
4 cod cutlets
30ml/2 tbsp dried breadcrumbs
salt and freshly ground black pepper
boiled new potatoes and mixed green salad, to serve

SERVES 4

1 Preheat the oven to 190°C/375°F/Gas 5. Heat the oil in a frying pan and fry the onion for about 5 minutes, stirring occasionally. Add the garlic, tomatoes, tomato purée, wine and seasoning and stir to mix.

2 Bring the sauce just to the boil, then reduce the heat slightly and cook, uncovered, for 15–20 minutes until thick, stirring occasionally. Stir in the parsley.

3 Lightly grease an ovenproof dish, put in the cod cutlets and spoon an equal quantity of the tomato sauce on to each. Sprinkle the breadcrumbs over the top.

4 Bake in the oven for 20–30 minutes, basting occasionally with the sauce, until the fish is cooked through, and the breadcrumbs are golden. Serve hot with new potatoes and a mixed green salad.

COOK'S TIP

For extra speed, use a 400g/14oz can of chopped tomatoes in place of the fresh tomatoes and 5–10ml/1–2 tsp ready-minced garlic in place of the garlic cloves.

NUTRITIONAL NOTES

Per portion:

Energy	151Kcals/647kJ
Total fat	1.5g
Saturated fat	0.2g
Cholesterol	55.2mg
Fibre	2.42g

ITALIAN FISH STEW

The different regions of Italy have their own variations of this low-fat dish. Buy some of the fish whole so you can simmer them, then remove the cooked flesh and strain the juices for the stock.

INGREDIENTS

900g/2lb mixture of fish fillets or steaks, such as monkfish, cod, haddock, halibut or hake
900g/2lb mixture of conger eel, red or grey mullet, snapper or small white fish
1 onion, halved
1 celery stick, roughly chopped
225g/8oz squid
225g/8oz fresh mussels
675g/1 1/2lb ripe tomatoes
15ml/1 tbsp olive oil
1 large onion, thinly sliced
3 garlic cloves, crushed
5ml/1 tsp saffron strands
150ml/1/4 pint/2/3 cup dry white wine
90ml/6 tbsp chopped fresh parsley
salt and freshly ground black pepper
croûtons, to serve (optional)

SERVES 6

1 Remove and discard any skin and bones from the fish fillets or steaks, cut the fish into large pieces and reserve. Place the bones in a saucepan with all the remaining fish.

2 Add the onion and celery and cover with water. Bring almost to the boil, then reduce the heat and simmer for about 30 minutes. Lift out the fish and remove the flesh from the bones. Reserve the flesh and discard the bones. Strain and reserve the stock and discard the contents of the sieve.

3 To prepare the squid, twist the head and tentacles away from the body. Cut the head from the tentacles. Discard the body contents and peel the skin. Wash the tentacles and bodies and dry on kitchen paper. Scrub the mussels, discarding any that are damaged or open ones that do not close when tapped.

4 Plunge the tomatoes into a bowl of boiling water for 30 seconds, then refresh in cold water. Peel away and discard the skins and chop the tomatoes roughly.

5 Heat the oil in a large saucepan or sauté pan. Add the onion and garlic and fry gently for 3 minutes. Add the squid and the reserved uncooked white fish, and fry quickly on all sides, stirring frequently. Remove from the pan, and drain.

6 Add 475ml/16fl oz/2 cups reserved fish stock, the tomatoes and saffron to the pan. Pour in the wine. Bring to the boil, then reduce the heat and simmer for about 5 minutes. Add the mussels, cover, and cook for 3–4 minutes until the mussels have opened. Discard any that remain closed. Season the sauce and add all the fish. Cook gently for 5 minutes until hot, stirring occasionally. Scatter with the parsley and serve with croûtons, if using.

NUTRITIONAL NOTES

Per portion:

Energy	321Kcals/1355kJ
Total fat	5g
Saturated fat	0.7g
Cholesterol	136.8mg
Fibre	1g

MONKFISH WITH TOMATO AND OLIVE SAUCE

This low-fat Italian dish comes from the coast of Calabria in southern Italy. Serve with garlic-flavoured mashed potatoes for an ideal family meal.

Ingredients

450g/1lb fresh mussels in their shells, scrubbed
a few fresh basil sprigs
2 garlic cloves, roughly chopped
300ml/½ pint/1¼ cups dry white wine
15ml/1 tbsp olive oil
900g/2lb monkfish fillets, skinned and cut into large chunks
1 onion, finely chopped
500g/1¼lb jar sugocasa or passata
15ml/1 tbsp sun-dried tomato purée
50g/2oz/½ cup stoned black olives
salt and freshly ground black pepper
extra fresh basil leaves, to garnish

Serves 4

1 Put the mussels in a flameproof casserole with some of the basil leaves, the garlic and wine. Cover and bring to the boil. Lower the heat and simmer for 5 minutes, shaking the pan frequently. Remove the mussels, discarding any that fail to open. Strain and reserve the cooking liquid.

2 Heat the oil in a flameproof casserole, add the monkfish pieces and sauté over a medium heat until they just change colour. Remove the fish from the pan, place on a plate and set aside.

3 Add the onion to the juices in the casserole and cook gently for about 5 minutes, stirring frequently, until softened. Add the sugocasa or passata, the reserved cooking liquid from the mussels and the tomato purée. Season to taste with salt and pepper. Bring to the boil, stirring, then reduce the heat, cover and allow to simmer for 20 minutes, stirring occasionally.

Nutritional Notes

Per portion:

Energy	221Kcals/931kJ
Total fat	4.6g
Saturated fat	0.7g
Cholesterol	81.9mg
Fibre	1.1g

4 Pull off and discard the top shells from the cooked mussels and set them aside. Add the monkfish pieces to the tomato sauce and cook gently for 5 minutes. Gently stir in the olives and remaining basil, then adjust the seasoning to taste. Place the mussels in their half shells on top of the sauce, cover the pan and heat the mussels through for 1–2 minutes. Serve at once, garnished with basil leaves.

TROUT AND PARMA HAM RISOTTO ROLLS

This makes a delicious and elegant low-fat meal. The risotto – made with porcini or chanterelle mushrooms and prawns – is an ideal accompaniment for the flavourful trout rolls.

INGREDIENTS

4 trout fillets, skinned
4 thin slices of Parma ham
capers, to garnish

FOR THE RISOTTO

10ml/2 tsp olive oil
8 large raw prawns, peeled and deveined
1 onion, chopped
225g/8oz/generous 1 cup risotto rice
about 105ml/7 tbsp white wine
about 750ml/1 1/4 pints/3 cups simmering fish or chicken stock
15g/1/2oz/2 tbsp dried porcini or chanterelle mushrooms, soaked for 10 minutes in warm water to cover
salt and freshly ground black pepper

SERVES 4

1 First make the risotto. Heat the oil in a heavy-based saucepan or deep frying pan and fry the prawns very briefly until flecked with pink, stirring. Lift out using a slotted spoon and transfer to a plate. Set aside.

COOK'S TIP

Make sure you use proper risotto rice, such as arborio or carnaroli, for this recipe. Short grain rice will not give the right consistency.

2 Add the onion to the oil in the pan. Fry over a low heat for 3–4 minutes until soft, stirring occasionally. Add the rice and stir for 3–4 minutes until the grains are evenly coated in oil. Add 75ml/5 tbsp of the wine and then the stock, a little at a time, stirring over a gentle heat and allowing the rice to absorb the liquid before adding more.

3 Drain the mushrooms, reserving the liquid, and cut the larger ones in half. Towards the end of cooking, stir the mushrooms into the risotto with 15ml/1 tbsp of the reserved mushroom liquid. If the rice is not yet *al dente*, add a little more stock or mushroom liquid and cook for 2–3 minutes more. Season to taste with salt and pepper.

4 Remove the pan from the heat and stir in the prawns. Preheat the oven to 190°C/375°F/Gas 5.

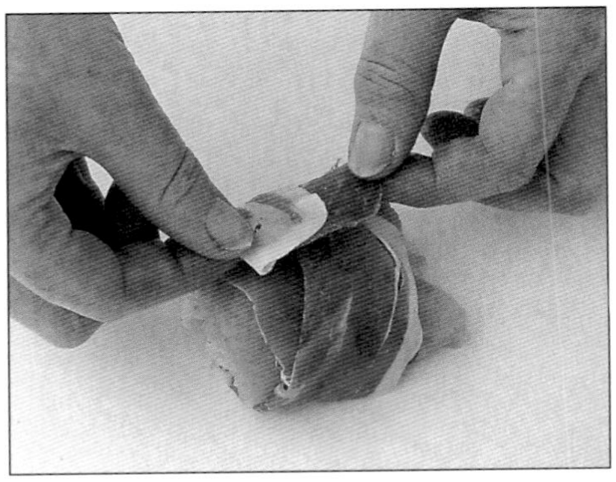

5 Take a trout fillet, place a spoonful of risotto at one end and roll up. Wrap each fillet in a slice of Parma ham and place in a lightly greased ovenproof dish.

6 Spoon any remaining risotto around the fish fillets and sprinkle over the rest of the wine. Bake the rolls in the oven for 15–20 minutes until the fish is cooked and tender. Spoon the risotto on to a platter, top with the trout rolls and garnish with some fat capers. Serve at once.

NUTRITIONAL NOTES

Per portion:

Energy	245Kcals/1035kJ
Total fat	5g
Saturated fat	1.1g
Cholesterol	63.8mg
Fibre	0.3g

VEGETARIAN DISHES AND VEGETABLES

VEGETARIAN *dishes and vegetables play an important part in a* LOW-FAT *diet, providing nutritious and filling dishes made from* FRESH INGREDIENTS *that all the family will enjoy. Many of the dishes are* SIMPLE *but substantial and provide an enticing menu, including* HERB POLENTA *with Grilled Tomatoes, Red Pepper Risotto, Stuffed Aubergines and* CAPONATA.

HERB POLENTA WITH GRILLED TOMATOES

Golden polenta flavoured with fresh summer herbs and served with sweet grilled tomatoes creates this tasty Italian dish, ideal for lunch or supper.

INGREDIENTS

175g/6oz/1 1/2 cups polenta
750ml/1 1/4 pints/3 cups stock or water
5ml/1 tsp salt
15g/1/2oz/1 tbsp butter
75ml/5 tbsp mixed chopped fresh parsley, chives and basil, plus extra to garnish
10ml/2 tsp olive oil
4 large plum or beef tomatoes, halved
salt and freshly ground black pepper

SERVES 6

1 Prepare the polenta in advance: place the stock or water in a saucepan with the salt, and bring to the boil.

2 Reduce the heat and gradually add the polenta, stirring all the time to ensure that it doesn't form any lumps.

3 Stir constantly over a moderate heat for 5 minutes, until the polenta begins to thicken and comes away from the sides of the pan.

4 Remove the pan from the heat and stir in the butter, herbs and black pepper.

5 Tip the polenta mixture into a wide, lightly greased dish or tin and spread it out evenly. Leave until it is completely cool and has set.

6 Turn the polenta out on to a board and cut it into squares or stamp out rounds with a large biscuit cutter. Lightly brush the squares or rounds with oil.

7 Lightly brush the tomatoes with oil and sprinkle with salt and pepper.

8 Cook the tomatoes and polenta on a medium hot barbecue for 5 minutes, turning once. Serve hot, garnished with fresh herbs.

NUTRITIONAL NOTES

Per portion:

Energy	185Kcals/773kJ
Total fat	4.7g
Saturated fat	2g
Cholesterol	7mg
Fibre	0.4g

VARIATION

Any mixture of fresh herbs can be used, or try using just basil or chives alone, for a really distinctive flavour.

POLENTA WITH MUSHROOMS

This low-fat Italian dish is delicious made with a mixture of fresh wild and cultivated mushrooms. Serve with a mixed leaf salad for a delicious meal.

INGREDIENTS

10g/¼oz/2 tbsp dried porcini mushrooms (omit if using wild mushrooms)
20ml/4 tsp olive oil
1 small onion, finely chopped
675g/1½lb mushrooms, wild or cultivated, or a combination of both
2 garlic cloves, finely chopped
45ml/3 tbsp chopped fresh parsley
3 tomatoes, skinned and diced
15ml/1 tbsp tomato purée
175ml/6fl oz/¾ cup warm water
1.5ml/¼ tsp fresh thyme leaves, or 1 large pinch of dried thyme
1 bay leaf
350g/12oz/3 cups polenta
salt and freshly ground black pepper
fresh parsley sprigs, to garnish

SERVES 6

1 Soak the dried mushrooms, if using, in a small bowl of warm water for about 20 minutes. Remove the mushrooms with a slotted spoon and rinse them well in several changes of cold water. Set aside. Filter the soaking water through a layer of absorbent kitchen paper placed in a sieve and reserve.

2 In a large frying pan, heat the oil and sauté the onion over a low heat until soft and golden.

3 Clean the fresh mushrooms by wiping them with a damp cloth. Cut into slices. When the onion is soft, add the mushrooms to the pan. Stir over a medium to high heat until they give up their liquid. Add the garlic, parsley and diced tomatoes. Cook for 4–5 minutes, stirring occasionally.

4 Soften the tomato purée in the warm water (use only 120ml/4fl oz/½ cup water if using dried mushrooms). Add the purée to the pan with the herbs. Add the dried mushrooms and soaking liquid, if using, and season with salt and pepper.

5 Reduce the heat to low and cook for 15–20 minutes, stirring occasionally. Remove the pan from the heat and set the sauce aside.

6 Bring 1.5 litres/2½ pints/6¼ cups water to the boil in a large, heavy-based saucepan. Add 15ml/1 tbsp salt.

7 Reduce the heat to a simmer and begin to add the polenta in a fine rain. Stir with a whisk until the polenta has all been incorporated.

8 Switch to a long-handled wooden spoon and continue to stir the polenta over a low to medium heat until it is a thick mass and pulls away from the sides of the pan. This may take 25–50 minutes, depending on the type of polenta used. For best results, never stop stirring the polenta until you remove it from the heat.

9 When the polenta has almost finished cooking, gently reheat the mushroom sauce until piping hot.

10 To serve, spoon the polenta on to a warmed serving platter. Make a well in the centre. Spoon some of the mushroom sauce into the well, and garnish with fresh parsley sprigs.

11 Serve at once, handing round the remaining mushroom sauce in a separate bowl.

NUTRITIONAL NOTES

Per portion:

Energy	244Kcals/1019kJ
Total fat	3.5g
Saturated fat	0.6g
Cholesterol	0mg
Fibre	1.5g

BAKED CHEESE POLENTA WITH TOMATO SAUCE

Polenta, or cornmeal, is a staple food in Italy. It is cooked in a similar way to porridge, and eaten soft, or set, cut into shapes, then baked or grilled. Serve with crusty Italian bread.

INGREDIENTS

5ml/1 tsp salt
250g/9oz/2¼ cups quick-cook polenta
5ml/1 tsp paprika
2.5ml/½ tsp ground nutmeg
5ml/1 tsp olive oil
1 large onion, finely chopped
2 garlic cloves, crushed
2 x 400g/14oz cans chopped tomatoes
15ml/1 tbsp tomato purée
5ml/1 tsp sugar
salt and freshly ground black pepper
50g/2oz/½ cup Gruyère, grated

SERVES 6

1 Preheat the oven to 200°C/400°F/Gas 6. Line a baking tin (28 × 18cm/11 × 7in) with clear film. Bring 1 litre/1¾ pints/4 cups water to the boil in a saucepan with the salt.

2 Pour in the polenta in a steady stream and cook for 5 minutes, stirring continuously. Beat in the paprika and nutmeg, then pour the mixture into the prepared tin and smooth the surface. Leave to cool.

3 Heat the oil in a non-stick saucepan and cook the onion and garlic until soft, stirring occasionally. Stir in the tomatoes, tomato purée, sugar and seasoning. Bring to the boil, reduce the heat and simmer for 20 minutes, stirring occasionally.

NUTRITIONAL NOTES

Per portion:

Energy	219Kcals/918kJ
Total fat	5g
Saturated fat	2g
Cholesterol	0mg
Fibre	1g

4 Turn the cooled polenta out on to a chopping board, and cut evenly into 5cm/2in squares.

5 Place half the polenta squares in a greased ovenproof dish. Spoon over half the tomato sauce, and sprinkle half the cheese over the top. Repeat the layers. Bake in the oven for about 25 minutes, until golden. Serve.

RED PEPPER RISOTTO

This delicious Italian risotto creates a flavourful and low-fat supper or main-course dish, ideally served with fresh Italian bread.

INGREDIENTS

3 large red peppers
10ml/2 tsp olive oil
3 large garlic cloves, thinly sliced
1½ x 400g/14oz cans chopped tomatoes
2 bay leaves
1.2–1.5 litres/2–2½ pints/5–6¼ cups vegetable stock
450g/1lb/2½ cups arborio rice or brown rice
6 fresh basil leaves, snipped
salt and freshly ground black pepper

SERVES 4

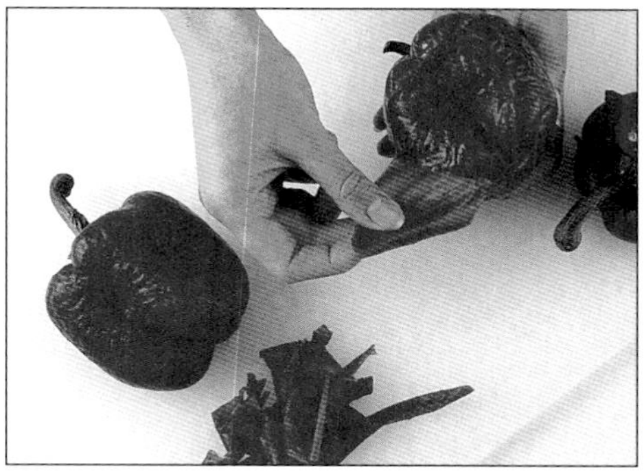

1 Preheat the grill. Put the peppers in a grill pan and grill until the skins are blackened and blistered all over. Put the peppers in a bowl, cover with several layers of damp absorbent kitchen paper and leave for 10 minutes. Peel off and discard the skins, then slice the peppers, discarding the cores and seeds. Set aside.

2 Heat the oil in a wide, shallow saucepan. Add the garlic and tomatoes and cook over a gentle heat for 5 minutes, stirring occasionally, then add the prepared pepper slices and the bay leaves. Stir well and cook gently for 15 minutes, stirring occasionally.

3 Pour the vegetable stock into a separate large, heavy-based saucepan and heat it to simmering point. Stir the rice into the vegetable mixture and cook for about 2 minutes, then add two or three ladlefuls of the hot stock. Cook, stirring occasionally, until all the stock has been absorbed into the rice.

4 Continue to add stock in this way, making sure each addition has been absorbed before adding the next. When the rice is tender, season with salt and pepper. Remove the pan from the heat, cover and leave to stand for 10 minutes. Remove and discard the bay leaves, then stir in the basil. Serve.

NUTRITIONAL NOTES

Per portion:

Energy	306Kcals/1298kJ
Total fat	3.7g
Saturated fat	0.7g
Cholesterol	0mg
Fibre	2.7g

MILANESE RISOTTO

This traditional Italian risotto is deliciously flavoured with garlic, shavings of Parmesan and fresh parsley to create a filling and flavourful low-fat dish.

INGREDIENTS

2 garlic cloves, crushed
60ml/4 tbsp chopped fresh parsley
finely grated rind of 1 lemon

FOR THE RISOTTO

5ml/1 tsp (or 1 sachet) saffron strands
15g/½oz butter
1 large onion, finely chopped
275g/10oz/1½ cups arborio rice
150ml/¼ pint/⅔ cup dry white wine
1 litre/1¾ pints/4 cups hot vegetable stock
salt and freshly ground black pepper
15g/½oz shaved fresh Parmesan cheese, to serve

SERVES 4

1 Mix together the garlic, parsley and lemon rind in a bowl. Set aside.

2 To make the risotto, put the saffron in a small bowl with 15ml/1 tbsp boiling water and leave to stand while the saffron infuses. Melt the butter in a heavy-based saucepan and gently fry the onion for 5 minutes, until softened and golden, stirring occasionally.

3 Stir in the rice and cook it for about 2 minutes until it becomes translucent. Add the wine and saffron mixture and cook, stirring, for several minutes until all the wine is absorbed.

4 Add 600ml/1 pint/2½ cups of the stock and simmer gently until the stock is absorbed, stirring frequently.

5 Gradually add more stock, a ladleful at a time, until the rice is tender, stirring frequently. (The rice might be tender and creamy before you've added all the stock, so add it slowly towards the end.)

6 Season the risotto with salt and pepper and transfer to a serving dish. Serve, scattered with shavings of Parmesan cheese and the garlic and parsley mixture.

NUTRITIONAL NOTES

Per portion:

Energy	258Kcals/1090kJ
Total fat	5g
Saturated fat	2.6g
Cholesterol	9.9mg
Fibre	1.3g

RISOTTO WITH MUSHROOMS AND PARMESAN

A classic Italian risotto of mixed mushrooms, herbs and fresh Parmesan cheese, made using long grain brown rice. Serve simply, with a mixed leaf salad tossed in a fat-free dressing.

INGREDIENTS

10ml/2 tsp olive oil
4 shallots, finely chopped
2 garlic cloves, crushed
15g/½oz/2 tbsp dried porcini mushrooms, soaked in 150ml/¼ pint/⅔ cup hot water for 20 minutes
250g/9oz/1⅓ cups long grain brown rice
900ml/1½ pints/3¾ cups well-flavoured vegetable stock
450g/1lb/6 cups mixed mushrooms, such as closed cup, chestnut and field mushrooms, sliced if large
30–45ml/2–3 tbsp chopped fresh flat leaf parsley
25g/1oz grated fresh Parmesan cheese
salt and freshly ground black pepper

SERVES 4

1 Heat the oil in a large saucepan, add the shallots and garlic and cook gently for 5 minutes, stirring. Drain the porcini, reserving their liquid, and chop roughly. Set aside. Add the brown rice to the shallot mixture and stir to coat the grains in oil.

2 Stir the stock and the porcini liquid into the rice mixture. Bring to the boil, reduce the heat and simmer, uncovered, for about 20 minutes or until most of the liquid is absorbed, stirring frequently.

3 Add the porcini and fresh mushrooms, stir, and cook for a further 10–15 minutes until the rice is tender and the liquid absorbed, stirring frequently.

4 Season with salt and pepper to taste, stir in the chopped parsley and grated Parmesan and serve at once.

NUTRITIONAL NOTES

Per portion:

Energy	233Kcals/985kJ
Total fat	4.8g
Saturated fat	1.5g
Cholesterol	4mg
Fibre	1.9g

STUFFED AUBERGINES

This typical dish from the Ligurian region of Italy is spiked with paprika and allspice, a legacy from the days when spices from the East came into northern Italy via the port of Genoa.

Ingredients

2 aubergines, about 225g/8oz each, stalks removed
275g/10oz potatoes, peeled and diced
15ml/1 tbsp olive oil
1 small onion, finely chopped
1 garlic clove, finely chopped
good pinch of ground allspice and paprika
30ml/2 tbsp skimmed milk
25g/1oz grated fresh Parmesan cheese
15ml/1 tbsp fresh white breadcrumbs
salt and freshly ground black pepper
fresh mint sprigs, to garnish
salad leaves, to serve

Serves 6

1 Bring a large saucepan of lightly salted water to the boil. Add the whole aubergines and cook for 5 minutes, turning frequently. Remove with a slotted spoon and set aside. Add the diced potatoes to the pan and boil for about 15 minutes or until cooked.

2 Meanwhile, cut the aubergines in half lengthways and gently scoop out the flesh with a small sharp knife and a spoon, leaving 5mm/¼in of the shell intact. Select a baking dish that will hold the aubergine shells snugly in a single layer. Brush it lightly with oil. Put the shells in the baking dish and chop the aubergine flesh roughly. Set aside.

3 Heat the oil in a frying pan, add the onion and cook gently, stirring frequently, until softened. Add the chopped aubergine flesh and the garlic. Cook, stirring frequently, for 6–8 minutes. Tip into a bowl and set aside. Preheat the oven to 190°C/375°F/Gas 5.

4 Drain and mash the potatoes. Add to the aubergine mixture with the ground spices and milk. Set aside 15ml/1 tbsp of the Parmesan cheese and add the rest to the aubergine mixture, stirring in salt and pepper to taste.

Nutritional Notes

Per portion:

Energy	130Kcals/549kJ
Total fat	5g
Saturated fat	1.5g
Cholesterol	5.1mg
Fibre	3.3g

5 Spoon the mixture into the aubergine shells. Mix the breadcrumbs with the reserved Parmesan cheese and sprinkle the mixture evenly over the aubergines. Bake in the oven for 30–40 minutes until the topping is crisp. Garnish with mint sprigs and serve with salad leaves.

ITALIAN STUFFED PEPPERS

These flavourful Italian stuffed peppers are easy to make for a light and healthy lunch or supper.

INGREDIENTS

10ml/2 tsp olive oil
1 red onion, sliced
1 courgette, diced
115g/4oz mushrooms, sliced
1 garlic clove, crushed
400g/14oz can chopped tomatoes
15ml/1 tbsp tomato purée
25g/1oz pine nuts (optional)
30ml/2 tbsp chopped fresh basil
4 large yellow peppers
25g/1oz/1/4 cup finely grated fresh Parmesan or Fontina cheese (optional)
salt and freshly ground black pepper
fresh basil leaves, to garnish

SERVES 4

1 Preheat the oven to 180°C/350°F/Gas 4. Heat the oil in a saucepan, add the onion, courgette, mushrooms and garlic and cook gently for 3 minutes, stirring the mixture occasionally.

2 Stir in the tomatoes and tomato purée, then bring to the boil and simmer, uncovered, for 10–15 minutes, stirring occasionally, until thickened slightly. Remove the pan from the heat and stir in the pine nuts, if using, chopped basil and seasoning. Set aside.

3 Cut the peppers in half lengthways and deseed them. Blanch the pepper halves in a saucepan of boiling water for about 3 minutes. Drain.

4 Place the peppers cut-side up in a shallow ovenproof dish and fill with the vegetable mixture.

5 Cover the dish with foil and bake in the oven for 20 minutes. Uncover, sprinkle each pepper half with a little grated cheese, if using, and bake, uncovered, for a further 5–10 minutes. Garnish with fresh basil leaves and serve.

NUTRITIONAL NOTES

Per portion:

Energy	70Kcals/293kJ
Total fat	2.5g
Saturated fat	0.4g
Cholesterol	0mg
Fibre	2.4g

MEDITERRANEAN VEGETABLES WITH CHICK-PEAS

The flavours of the Mediterranean are captured in this delicious low-fat vegetable dish, ideal for a starter or lunchtime snack, served with fresh crusty bread.

INGREDIENTS

1 onion, sliced
2 leeks, sliced
2 garlic cloves, crushed
1 red pepper, deseeded and sliced
1 green pepper, deseeded and sliced
1 yellow pepper, deseeded and sliced
350g/12oz courgettes, sliced
225g/8oz/3 cups mushrooms, sliced
400g/14oz can chopped tomatoes
30ml/2 tbsp ruby port or red wine
30ml/2 tbsp tomato purée
15ml/1 tbsp tomato ketchup (optional)
400g/14oz can chick-peas
115g/4oz/1 cup stoned black olives
45ml/3 tbsp chopped fresh mixed herbs
salt and freshly ground black pepper
chopped fresh mixed herbs, to garnish

SERVES 6

1 Put the onion, leeks, garlic, red, yellow and green peppers, courgettes and mushrooms into a large saucepan.

COOK'S TIP

For the best Mediterranean flavour, try to include fresh basil and oregano in the mixed herbs used in this recipe.

2 Add the tomatoes, port or red wine, tomato purée and tomato ketchup, if using, to the saucepan and mix all the ingredients together well.

3 Rinse and drain the chick-peas and add to the pan. Stir to mix.

4 Cover, bring to the boil then reduce the heat and simmer the mixture gently for 20–30 minutes, until the vegetables are cooked and tender but not overcooked, stirring occasionally.

5 Remove the lid of the saucepan and increase the heat slightly for the last 10 minutes of the cooking time, to thicken the sauce, if you like.

6 Stir in the olives, herbs and seasoning. Serve either hot or cold, garnished with chopped mixed herbs.

NUTRITIONAL NOTES

Per portion:

Energy	55Kcals/654kJ
Total fat	4.56g
Saturated fat	0.67g
Cholesterol	0mg
Fibre	6.98g

HABITAT
JAPAN

ROSEMARY ROASTIES

These tasty Italian-style roast potatoes use far less fat than traditional roast potatoes, and because they still have their skins they not only absorb less oil but also have more flavour.

Ingredients

1kg/2¼lb small red potatoes
10ml/2 tsp walnut or sunflower oil
30ml/2 tbsp fresh rosemary leaves
salt and paprika

Serves 4

1 Preheat the oven to 240°C/475°F/Gas 9. Leave the potatoes whole with the peel on or, if large, cut in half. Place the potatoes in a large saucepan of cold water and bring to the boil. Drain well.

2 Drizzle the walnut or sunflower oil over the potatoes and shake the pan to coat them evenly.

3 Tip the potatoes into a shallow roasting tin. Sprinkle with rosemary, salt and paprika. Roast in the oven for 30 minutes or until cooked and crisp. Serve hot.

Nutritional Notes

Per portion:

Energy	205Kcals/865kJ
Total fat	2.22g
Saturated fat	0.19g
Cholesterol	0mg
Fibre	3.25g

BAKED COURGETTES IN PASSATA

Sliced courgettes, oven-baked with onions, passata and fresh thyme, make a delicious, virtually fat-free vegetable dish.

Ingredients

5ml/1 tsp olive oil
3 large courgettes, thinly sliced
½ small red onion, finely chopped
300ml/½ pint/1¼ cups passata
30ml/2 tbsp chopped fresh thyme
garlic salt and freshly ground black pepper
fresh thyme sprigs, to garnish

Serves 4

Nutritional Notes

Per portion:

Energy	49Kcals/205kJ
Total fat	1.43g
Saturated fat	0.22g
Cholesterol	0mg
Fibre	1.73g

1 Preheat the oven to 190°C/375°F/Gas 5. Brush an ovenproof dish with the olive oil.

2 Arrange half the courgettes and onion in the dish.

3 Spoon half the passata over the vegetables and sprinkle with some of the fresh thyme, then season to taste with garlic salt and pepper.

4 Arrange the remaining courgettes and onion in the dish on top of the passata, then season to taste with more garlic salt and pepper. Spoon over the remaining passata and spread evenly.

5 Cover the dish with foil, then bake in the oven for 40–45 minutes, or until the courgettes are tender. Garnish with sprigs of fresh thyme and serve hot.

ROASTED MEDITERRANEAN VEGETABLES

Mixed Mediterranean vegetables are oven-roasted in olive oil with garlic and rosemary in this really colourful and appetizing low-fat dish. The flavour is also wonderfully intense.

INGREDIENTS

1 red pepper
1 yellow pepper
2 Spanish onions
2 large courgettes
1 large aubergine or 4 baby aubergines, trimmed
1 fennel bulb, thickly sliced
2 beef tomatoes
8 fat garlic cloves
25ml/1½ tbsp olive oil
fresh rosemary sprigs
freshly ground black pepper
lemon wedges and black olives, to garnish (optional)

SERVES 6

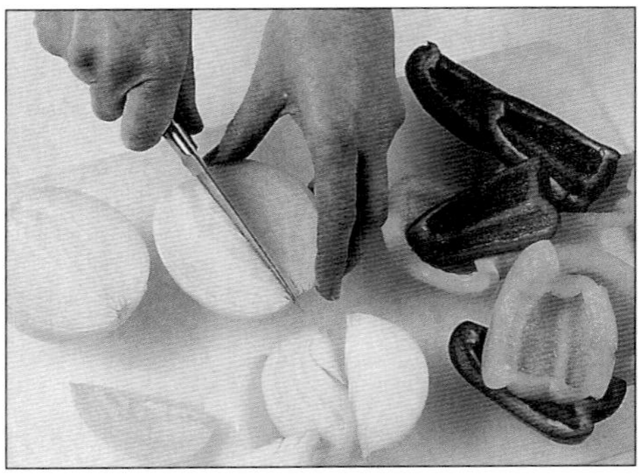

1 Halve and seed the peppers, then cut them into large chunks. Peel the onions and cut into thick wedges.

2 Cut the courgettes and aubergine(s) into large chunks.

3 Preheat the oven to 220°C/425°F/Gas 7. Spread the peppers, onions, courgettes, aubergines and fennel in a lightly greased shallow ovenproof dish or roasting pan or, if you like, arrange in rows to make a colourful design.

4 Cut each tomato in half and place, cut-side up, with the vegetables.

5 Tuck the garlic cloves in among the vegetables, then brush all the vegetables with the olive oil. Place some sprigs of rosemary among the vegetables and grind over some black pepper, particularly on the tomatoes.

6 Roast in the oven for 20–25 minutes, turning the vegetables halfway through the cooking time. Serve from the dish or on a flat platter, garnished with lemon wedges. Scatter a few black olives over the top just before serving, if you like.

NUTRITIONAL NOTES

Per portion:

Energy	72Kcals/299kJ
Total fat	4g
Saturated fat	0.6g
Cholesterol	0mg
Fibre	2.3g

PEPPER GRATIN

Serve this simple but delicious Italian dish as a low-fat starter or snack with a small mixed leaf or rocket salad and some good crusty bread to mop up the juices from the peppers.

INGREDIENTS

2 red peppers
15ml/1 tbsp extra virgin olive oil
1 garlic clove, finely chopped
5ml/1 tsp drained bottled capers
8 stoned black olives, roughly chopped
15ml/1 tbsp chopped fresh oregano
15ml/1 tbsp chopped fresh flat leaf parsley
60ml/4 tbsp fresh white breadcrumbs
salt and freshly ground black pepper
fresh herbs, to garnish

SERVES 4

1 Preheat the oven to 200°C/400°F/Gas 6. Place the peppers on a grill rack and cook under a hot grill. Turn occasionally until they are blackened and blistered all over. Remove from the heat and place in a plastic bag. Seal and leave to cool.

2 When cool, peel the peppers. (Don't skin them under the tap as the water would wash away some of the delicious smoky flavour.) Halve and remove and discard the seeds, then cut the flesh into large strips.

3 Use a little of the olive oil to grease a small baking dish. Arrange the pepper strips in the dish.

4 Scatter the garlic, capers, olives and chopped herbs on top. Season with salt and pepper. Scatter over the fresh white breadcrumbs and drizzle with the remaining olive oil. Bake in the oven for about 20 minutes until the breadcrumbs have browned. Garnish with fresh herbs and serve immediately.

NUTRITIONAL NOTES

Per portion:

Energy	72Kcals/303kJ
Total fat	3.4g
Saturated fat	0.5g
Cholesterol	0mg
Fibre	0.9g

FENNEL GRATIN

This is one of the best ways to eat fresh fennel as a snack or vegetable accompaniment.

Ingredients

2 fennel bulbs, about 675g/1½lb total
300ml/½ pint/1¼ cups semi-skimmed milk
15g/½oz/1 tbsp butter
15ml/1 tbsp plain flour
25g/1oz/scant ½ cup dry white breadcrumbs
40g/1½oz Gruyère, grated
salt and freshly ground black pepper

Serves 6

1 Preheat the oven to 240°C/475°F/Gas 9. Discard the stalks and root ends from the fennel. Slice the fennel into quarters and place in a large saucepan. Pour over the milk, bring to the boil, then simmer for 10–15 minutes until tender.

2 Grease a small baking dish. Remove the fennel pieces with a slotted spoon, reserving the milk. Arrange the fennel pieces in the dish.

3 Melt the butter in a small saucepan and add the flour. Stir well, then gradually whisk in the reserved milk. Cook the sauce until thickened, stirring.

4 Pour the sauce over the fennel pieces, sprinkle with the breadcrumbs and Gruyère. Season and bake in the oven for about 20 minutes until browned. Serve.

Variation

Instead of the Gruyère, Parmesan, Pecorino, mature Cheddar or any other strong cheese would work perfectly.

Nutritional Notes

Per portion:

Energy	89Kcals/371kJ
Total fat	4.8g
Saturated fat	2.9g
Cholesterol	8.24mg
Fibre	2.5g

ITALIAN SWEET-AND-SOUR ONIONS

Onions are naturally sweet, and when they are cooked at a high temperature the sweetness intensifies. Serve these delicious onions with cooked lean meat or cooked fresh vegetables.

Ingredients

25g/1oz/2 tbsp butter
75ml/5 tbsp sugar
120ml/4fl oz/½ cup white wine vinegar
30ml/2 tbsp balsamic vinegar
675g/1½lb small pickling onions, peeled
salt and freshly ground black pepper

Serves 6

Cook's Tip

This recipe also looks delicious when made with either yellow or red onions, cut into slices. Cooking times vary, depending on the size of the pieces.

1 Melt the butter in a large saucepan over a gentle heat. Add the sugar and cook until it begins to dissolve, stirring constantly.

2 Add the vinegars to the pan with the onions and heat gently. Season, cover and cook over a moderate heat for 20–25 minutes, stirring occasionally, until the onions are soft when pierced with a knife. Serve hot.

Nutritional Notes

Per portion:

Energy	106Kcals/447kJ
Total fat	3.6g
Saturated fat	2.2g
Cholesterol	9.5mg
Fibre	1.3g

COURGETTE AND ASPARAGUS PARCELS

To appreciate the aroma, these Italian-style courgette and asparagus-filled paper parcels should be broken open at the table. They make a tasty and low-fat vegetable accompaniment.

INGREDIENTS

2 courgettes
1 leek
225g/8oz young asparagus, trimmed
4 tarragon sprigs
4 whole garlic cloves, unpeeled
1 egg, beaten, to glaze
salt and freshly ground black pepper

SERVES 4

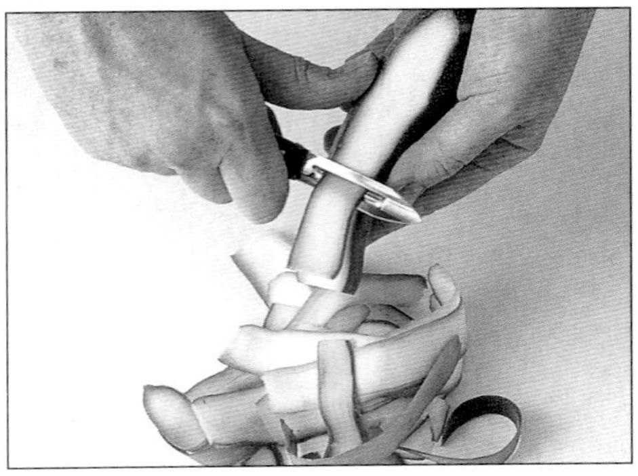

1 Preheat the oven to 200°C/400°F/Gas 6. Using a potato peeler, carefully slice the courgettes lengthways into thin strips.

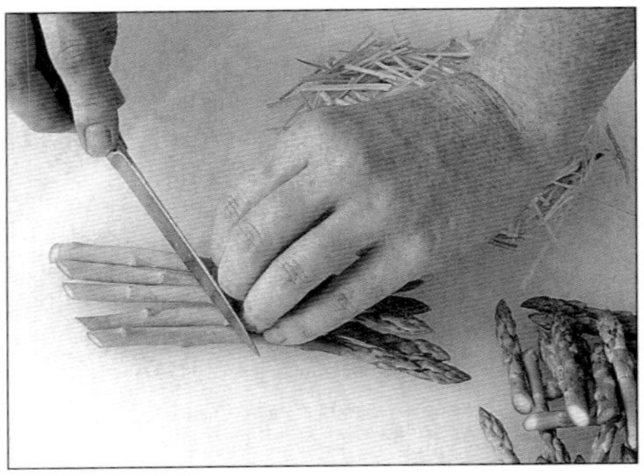

2 Cut the leek into very fine julienne strips and cut the asparagus evenly into 5cm/2in lengths.

3 Cut out four sheets of greaseproof paper measuring 30 × 38cm/12 × 15in and fold each one in half. Draw a large curve to make a heart shape when unfolded. Cut along the inside of the line and open out.

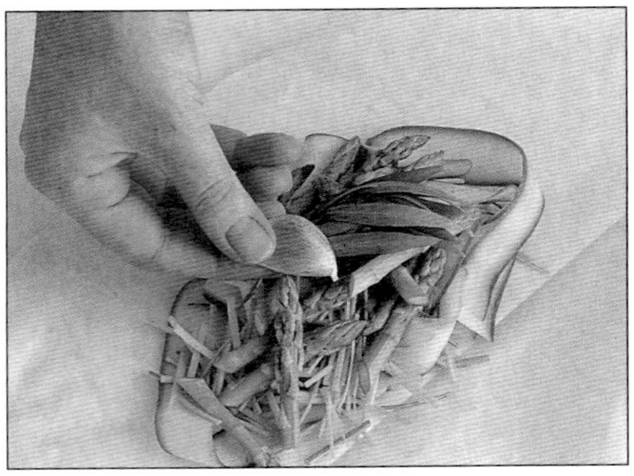

4 Divide the courgettes, leek and asparagus evenly between each paper heart, positioning the filling on one side of the fold line, then top each portion with a sprig of tarragon and an unpeeled garlic clove. Season to taste.

5 Brush the edges of the paper lightly with the beaten egg and fold over.

6 Twist the edges of the paper together so that each parcel is completely sealed. Lay the parcels on a baking sheet.

7 Bake in the preheated oven for 10 minutes. Serve the parcels immediately.

NUTRITIONAL NOTES

Per portion:

Energy	110Kcals/460kJ
Total fat	2.29g
Saturated fat	0.49g
Cholesterol	48mg
Fibre	6.73g

GREEN BEANS WITH TOMATOES

This is a real Italian summer favourite using the best ripe plum tomatoes and French beans. It is ideal served as an accompaniment or with fresh Italian bread for a tasty lunch or supper dish.

INGREDIENTS

15ml/1 tbsp olive oil
1 large onion, thinly sliced
2 garlic cloves, finely chopped
6 large ripe plum tomatoes, peeled, deseeded and coarsely chopped
150ml/¼ pint/⅔ cup dry white wine
450g/1lb French green beans, sliced in half lengthways
16 stoned black olives
10ml/2 tsp lemon juice
salt and freshly ground black pepper

SERVES 4

1 Heat the oil in a large frying pan. Add the onion and garlic and cook for about 5 minutes until the onion is softened but not brown, stirring occasionally.

2 Add the chopped tomatoes, white wine, beans, olives and lemon juice and cook over a gentle heat for a further 20 minutes, stirring occasionally, until the sauce is thickened and the beans are tender. Season with salt and pepper to taste and serve at once.

COOK'S TIP

French beans need little preparation – you simply top and tail them. When choosing, make sure that the beans snap easily – this is a sure sign of freshness.

NUTRITIONAL NOTES

Per portion:

Energy	69Kcals/278kJ
Total fat	2.7g
Saturated fat	0.4g
Cholesterol	0mg
Fibre	2.4g

VARIATION

Any leftovers of this dish are delicious eaten cold, as a salad, with plenty of crusty Italian bread to mop up the juices.

CAPONATA

This dish is a quintessential part of Sicilian antipasti and is a rich, spicy mixture of aubergine, tomatoes, capers and celery. Serve with warm crusty bread and olives.

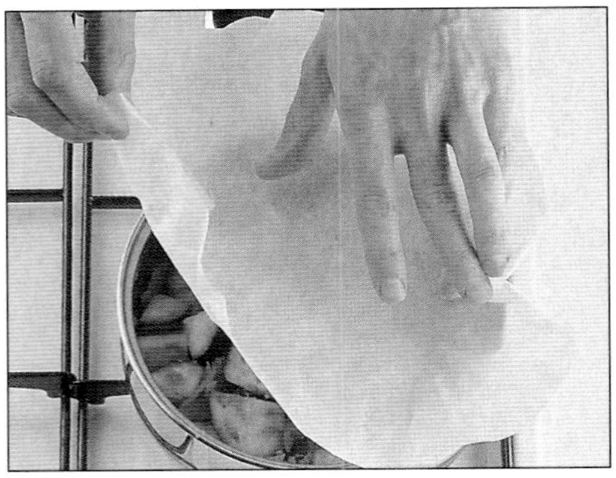

3 Cover the surface of the vegetables with a circle of greaseproof paper and simmer for 8–10 minutes. Remove and discard the paper.

4 Add the capers and olives to the pan, then season to taste with salt and mix together well.

5 Spoon the caponata into a bowl, garnish with chopped fresh parsley and serve at room temperature.

INGREDIENTS

20ml/4 tsp olive oil
1 large onion, sliced
2 celery sticks, sliced
450g/1lb aubergines, diced
5 ripe tomatoes, chopped
1 garlic clove, crushed
45ml/3 tbsp red wine vinegar
15ml/1 tbsp sugar
30ml/2 tbsp capers
12 olives
pinch of salt
60ml/4 tbsp chopped fresh parsley, to garnish

SERVES 4

1 Heat half the oil in a large heavy-based saucepan. Add the onion and celery and cook over a gentle heat for 3–4 minutes to soften, stirring occasionally.

2 Add the remainder of the oil with the aubergines and stir to mix. Cook until the aubergines begin to colour, stirring occasionally, then stir in the tomatoes, garlic, vinegar and sugar.

NUTRITIONAL NOTES
Per portion:

Energy	81Kcals/340kJ
Total fat	4.7g
Saturated fat	0.7g
Cholesterol	0mg
Fibre	2.9g

KOHLRABI STUFFED WITH PEPPERS

The slightly sharp flavour of the peppers is an excellent foil to the more earthy flavour of the kohlrabi in this delicious low-fat Italian-style vegetable dish.

INGREDIENTS

4 small kohlrabies, about 175–225g/6–8oz each
about 400ml/14fl oz/1⅔ cups hot vegetable stock
15ml/1 tbsp sunflower oil
1 onion, chopped
1 small red pepper, deseeded and sliced
1 small green pepper, deseeded and sliced
salt and freshly ground black pepper
fresh flat leaf parsley, to garnish (optional)

SERVES 4

1 Preheat the oven to 180ºC/350ºF/Gas 4. Trim, top and tail the kohlrabies and arrange in an ovenproof dish.

2 Pour over enough stock to come about halfway up the vegetables. Cover and braise in the oven for about 30 minutes, until tender. Transfer to a plate and allow to cool, reserving the stock.

3 Heat the oil in a frying pan and fry the onion over a gentle heat for 3–4 minutes, stirring occasionally. Add the peppers and cook for a further 2–3 minutes, until the onion is lightly browned, stirring the vegetables occasionally.

4 Add the reserved vegetable stock and a little seasoning and allow to simmer, uncovered, over a moderate heat, until the stock has almost all evaporated, stirring occasionally.

5 Scoop out the insides of the kohlrabies and chop roughly. Stir into the onion and pepper mixture and adjust the seasoning to taste. Arrange the kohlrabi shells in a shallow ovenproof dish.

6 Spoon the pepper filling into the kohlrabi shells. Place in the oven for 5–10 minutes to heat through and then serve, garnished with a sprig of flat leaf parsley, if you like.

NUTRITIONAL NOTES

Per portion:

Energy	112Kcals/470kJ
Total fat	4.63g
Saturated fat	0.55g
Cholesterol	0mg
Fibre	5.8g

COURGETTES WITH ONION AND GARLIC

Use good-quality olive oil and sunflower oil for this dish. The olive oil gives the dish a delicious fragrance without overpowering the courgettes, making this an ideal vegetable accompaniment.

INGREDIENTS

10ml/2 tsp olive oil
10ml/2 tsp sunflower oil
1 large onion, chopped
1 garlic clove, crushed
4–5 courgettes, cut into 1cm/½in slices
150ml/¼ pint/⅔ cup vegetable stock
2.5ml/½ tsp chopped fresh oregano
salt and freshly ground black pepper
chopped fresh parsley, to garnish

SERVES 4

1 Heat the olive and sunflower oils in a large frying pan and fry the onion with the garlic over a moderate heat for 5–6 minutes, stirring occasionally, until the onion has softened and is beginning to brown.

2 Add the sliced courgettes and fry for about 4 minutes until they begin to be flecked with brown, stirring frequently.

3 Stir in the stock, oregano and seasoning and simmer gently for 8–10 minutes or until the liquid has almost evaporated, stirring occasionally.

4 Spoon the courgettes into a warmed serving dish, sprinkle with chopped parsley and serve.

NUTRITIONAL NOTES

Per portion:

Energy	47Kcals/192kJ
Total fat	4.1g
Saturated fat	0.5g
Cholesterol	0mg
Fibre	0.5g

COURGETTES IN CITRUS SAUCE

These tender baby courgettes served in a virtually fat-free citrus sauce make this a tasty and low-fat accompaniment to grilled or barbecued fish fillets.

INGREDIENTS

350g/12oz baby courgettes
4 spring onions, thinly sliced
2.5cm/1in piece of fresh root ginger, peeled and grated
30ml/2 tbsp white wine vinegar
15ml/1 tbsp light soy sauce
5ml/1 tsp soft light brown sugar
45ml/3 tbsp vegetable stock
finely grated rind and juice of 1/2 lemon and 1/2 orange
5ml/1 tsp cornflour

SERVES 4

1 Place the courgettes in a saucepan of lightly salted boiling water and cook for 3–4 minutes, or until just tender. Drain well and return to the pan. Set aside.

2 Meanwhile, put all the remaining ingredients, except the cornflour, into a saucepan and bring to the boil, stirring occasionally. Simmer for 3 minutes.

3 Blend the cornflour with 10ml/2 tsp cold water in a small bowl and stir into the sauce. Bring the sauce to the boil, stirring continuously, until the sauce has thickened.

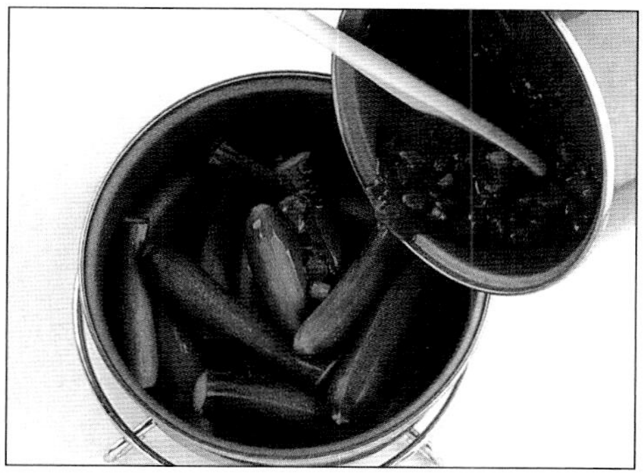

4 Pour the sauce over the courgettes in the pan and heat gently, shaking the pan to coat them evenly. Transfer to a warmed serving dish and serve.

COOK'S TIP

If baby courgettes are unavailable, you can use larger ones, but they should be cooked whole so that they don't absorb too much water. After cooking, halve them lengthways and cut them into 10cm/4in lengths.

NUTRITIONAL NOTES

Per portion:

Energy	33Kcals/138kJ
Total fat	2.18g
Saturated fat	0.42g
Cholesterol	0.09mg
Fibre	0.92g

POTATO GNOCCHI

Gnocchi are little Italian dumplings made either with mashed potato and flour, as here, or with semolina. They should be light in texture, and must not be overworked while being made.

Ingredients

1kg/2¼lb waxy potatoes, scrubbed
250–300g/9–11oz/2–2½ cups plain flour
1 egg
pinch of grated nutmeg
25g/1oz/2 tbsp butter
salt
a little grated fresh Parmesan cheese, to serve (optional)

Serves 6

1 Place the unpeeled potatoes in a large saucepan of salted water. Bring to the boil and cook until the potatoes are tender but not falling apart. Drain. Peel as soon as possible, while the potatoes are still hot.

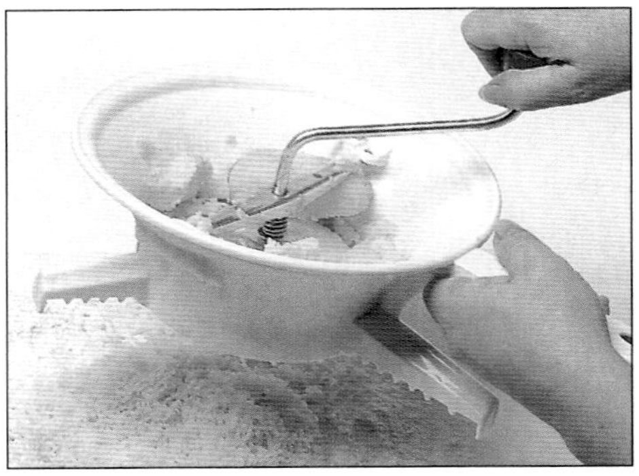

2 On a work surface, spread out a layer of flour. Mash the hot potatoes with a food mill, dropping them on to the flour. Sprinkle with about half of the remaining flour. Mix the flour very lightly into the potatoes.

Nutritional Notes

Per portion:

Energy	256Kcals/1083kJ
Total fat	4.6g
Saturated fat	2.4g
Cholesterol	37.8mg
Fibre	2.6g

3 Break the egg into the mixture, add the nutmeg and knead lightly, drawing in more flour as necessary. When the dough is light to the touch and no longer moist or sticky it is ready to be rolled. Do not overwork or the gnocchi will be heavy.

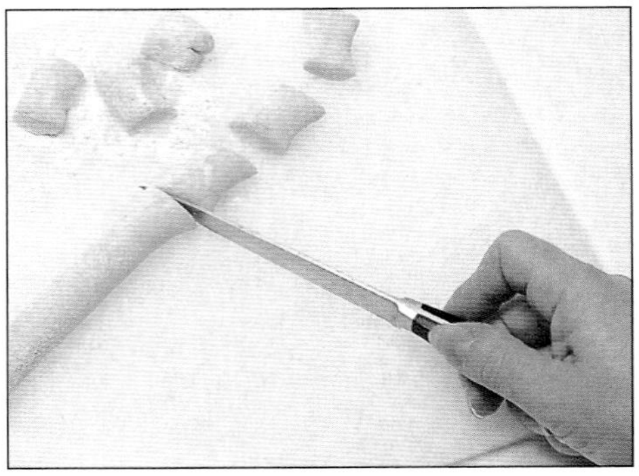

4 Divide the dough into four parts. On a lightly floured board, form each part into a roll about 2cm/¾in in diameter, taking care not to overhandle the dough. Cut the rolls crossways into pieces about 2cm/¾in long.

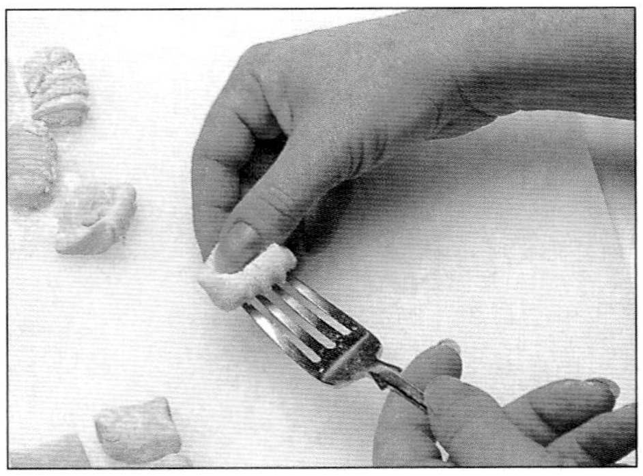

5 Hold an ordinary table fork with long tines sideways, leaning on the board. One by one, press and roll the gnocchi lightly along the tines of the fork towards the points, making ridges on one side and a depression from your thumb on the other.

6 Bring a large saucepan of water to a fast boil. Add salt and drop in about half the gnocchi.

7 When they rise to the surface, after 3–4 minutes, the gnocchi are done. Scoop them out, allow to drain and place in a warmed serving bowl. Dot with butter. Keep warm while the remaining gnocchi are boiling.

8 As soon as they are cooked, toss the drained gnocchi with the butter, sprinkle with a little grated Parmesan, if using, and serve.

Variation

Green gnocchi are made in exactly the same way as potato gnocchi, with the addition of fresh or frozen spinach. Use 675g/1½lb fresh spinach, or 400g/14oz frozen leaf spinach. Mix with the potato and the flour in Step 2. Almost any pasta sauce is suitable for serving with gnocchi; they are particularly good with Gorgonzola sauce, or simply drizzled with a little olive oil. Gnocchi can also be served in clear soup.

MEAT AND POULTRY PASTA DISHES

Freshly cooked PASTA *topped or tossed with a tasty* LOW-FAT *sauce made with* MEAT *or poultry and served with crusty Italian* BREAD *or a salad provides an appealing meal for all to* ENJOY. *Choose from a* VARIETY *of low-fat Italian recipes all packed full of* FLAVOUR, *including low-fat versions of classic dishes such as Spaghetti* BOLOGNESE, *Lasagne and Spaghetti alla* CARBONARA.

SPAGHETTI BOLOGNESE

A very popular Italian dish, this tasty spaghetti Bolognese is full of flavour and is low in fat too.

Ingredients

1 onion, chopped
2–3 garlic cloves, crushed
300ml/½ pint/1¼ cups beef or chicken stock
450g/1lb extra-lean minced turkey or beef
2 × 400g/14oz cans chopped tomatoes
5ml/1 tsp dried basil
5ml/1 tsp dried oregano
60ml/4 tbsp tomato purée
450g/1lb button mushrooms, quartered and sliced
150ml/¼ pint/⅔ cup red wine
450g/1lb dried spaghetti
salt and freshly ground black pepper

Serves 8

1 Put the chopped onion and garlic into a non-stick saucepan with half of the stock. Bring to the boil and cook for 5 minutes until the onion is tender and the stock has reduced completely, stirring occasionally.

2 Add the turkey or beef and cook for 5 minutes, breaking up the meat with a fork. Add the tomatoes, herbs and tomato purée, bring to the boil, then cover, reduce the heat and simmer for 1 hour, stirring occasionally.

3 Meanwhile, cook the mushrooms with the wine for 5 minutes in a non-stick saucepan or until the wine has evaporated, stirring occasionally. Add the mushrooms to the meat with salt and pepper to taste and stir to mix.

4 Meanwhile, cook the pasta in a large saucepan of boiling salted water for 8–12 minutes until tender or *al dente*. Drain thoroughly. Serve the cooked spaghetti topped with the meat sauce.

Cook's Tip

Sautéing vegetables in stock rather than oil is an easy way of cutting down calories and fat. Choose fat-free stock to reduce even more.

Nutritional Notes

Per portion:

Energy	321Kcals/1350kJ
Total fat	4.1g
Saturated fat	1.3g
Cholesterol	33mg
Fibre	2.7g

CHILLI MINCE AND PIPE RIGATE

Fresh chilli-flavoured cooked minced meat combines well with pasta to create a flavourful and filling low-fat Italian supper dish.

INGREDIENTS

450g/1lb extra-lean minced beef or turkey
1 onion, finely chopped
2–3 garlic cloves, crushed
1–2 fresh red chillies, deseeded and finely chopped
400g/14oz can chopped tomatoes
45ml/3 tbsp tomato purée
5ml/1 tsp dried mixed herbs
450g/1lb/4 cups dried pipe rigate
400g/14oz can red kidney beans, drained
salt and freshly ground black pepper

SERVES 6

1 Cook the minced beef or turkey in a non-stick saucepan, breaking up any large pieces with a wooden spoon, until browned all over.

2 Stir in the onion, garlic and chilli, cover the pan with a lid and cook gently for 5 minutes.

3 Stir in the tomatoes, tomato purée, herbs, 450ml/¾ pint/1¾ cups water and seasoning. Bring to the boil, then reduce the heat and simmer for 1½ hours, stirring occasionally. Remove the pan from the heat and leave to cool slightly.

4 Meanwhile, cook the pasta in a large saucepan of boiling, salted water until tender or *al dente*. Drain thoroughly. Meanwhile, skim off and discard any fat from the surface of the mince. Add the red kidney beans and cook for 5–10 minutes until piping hot, stirring occasionally. Pour the sauce over the cooked pasta, and serve.

NUTRITIONAL NOTES

Per portion:

Energy	246Kcals/1042kJ
Total fat	1.8g
Saturated fat	0.4g
Cholesterol	38.5mg
Fibre	6g

SPAGHETTI WITH MEATBALLS

Italian-style meatballs simmered in a sweet and spicy tomato sauce are truly delicious served with spaghetti, making an ideal low-fat dish for all the family to enjoy.

Ingredients

350g/12oz extra-lean minced beef
1 egg
60ml/4 tbsp roughly chopped fresh flat leaf parsley
2.5ml/½ tsp crushed dried red chillies
1 thick slice of white bread, crusts removed
30ml/2 tbsp semi-skimmed milk
15ml/1 tbsp olive oil
300ml/½ pint/1¼ cups passata
400ml/14fl oz/1⅔ cups vegetable stock
5ml/1 tsp sugar
450g/1lb dried spaghetti
salt and freshly ground black pepper
40g/1½oz grated fresh Parmesan cheese, to serve

Serves 8

1 Put the minced beef in a large bowl. Add the egg, half the parsley and half the crushed chillies. Season with plenty of salt and pepper. Mix well.

2 Tear the bread into small pieces and place in a small bowl. Moisten with the milk. Leave to soak for a few minutes, then squeeze out and discard the excess milk and crumble the bread over the meat mixture. Mix everything together with a wooden spoon, then use your hands to squeeze and knead the mixture so that it becomes smooth and quite sticky.

3 Wash your hands, rinse them under the cold tap, then pick up small pieces of the mixture and roll them between your palms to make about 40–60 small balls.

4 Place the meatballs on a tray and chill in the fridge for about 30 minutes.

5 Heat the oil in a large non-stick frying pan. Cook the meatballs in batches until browned all over. Set aside.

6 Pour the passata and stock into a large saucepan. Heat gently, then add the remaining chillies and the sugar, with salt and pepper to taste. Add the meatballs to the passata mixture, then bring to the boil. Reduce the heat, cover and simmer for 20 minutes, stirring occasionally.

7 Cook the pasta in a large saucepan of boiling salted water, according to the packet instructions until it is tender or *al dente*. Drain well and tip it into a warmed large bowl. Pour the sauce over the pasta and toss gently to mix. Sprinkle with the remaining parsley and serve with grated Parmesan handed separately.

Nutritional Notes

Per portion:

Energy	148Kcals/622kJ
Total fat	5g
Saturated fat	1.9g
Cholesterol	44.8mg
Fibre	0.9g

SPAGHETTI WITH SPICY MINCED BEEF SAUCE

This is a delicious spicy version of spaghetti Bolognese, which is not an authentic Italian dish. It was "invented" by Italian émigrés in America in the 1960s in response to popular demand.

Ingredients

10ml/2 tsp olive oil
1 onion, finely chopped
1 garlic clove, crushed
5ml/1 tsp dried mixed herbs
1.5ml/¼ tsp cayenne pepper
450g/1lb extra-lean minced beef
400g/14oz can chopped Italian plum tomatoes
45ml/3 tbsp tomato ketchup
15ml/1 tbsp sun-dried tomato purée
5ml/1 tsp Worcestershire sauce
5ml/1 tsp dried oregano
450ml/¾ pint/scant 2 cups beef or vegetable stock
45ml/3 tbsp red wine
450g/1lb dried spaghetti
salt and freshly ground black pepper
25g/1oz grated fresh Parmesan cheese, to serve (optional)

Serves 6

1 Heat the oil in a medium saucepan, add the onion and garlic and cook over a low heat, stirring frequently, for about 5 minutes until softened. Stir in the mixed herbs and cayenne and cook for a further 2–3 minutes. Add the minced beef and cook gently for about 5 minutes, stirring frequently and breaking up any lumps in the meat with a wooden spoon.

2 Stir in the tomatoes, tomato ketchup, sun-dried tomato purée, Worcestershire sauce, oregano and plenty of ground black pepper. Pour in the stock and red wine and bring to the boil, stirring. Cover the pan, reduce the heat and leave the sauce to simmer for 30 minutes, stirring occasionally.

3 Meanwhile, cook the pasta in a large saucepan of boiling salted water, according to the packet instructions, until tender or *al dente*. Drain, and divide among warmed bowls. Taste the meat sauce and add a little salt if necessary, then spoon it on top of the pasta and sprinkle with a little grated Parmesan, if using. Serve immediately.

Nutritional Notes

Per portion:

Energy	207Kcals/874kJ
Total fat	4.9g
Saturated fat	1.5g
Cholesterol	39.1mg
Fibre	1.8g

LASAGNE

This is a delicious low-fat version of the classic Italian lasagne, ideal served with a mixed salad and crusty bread for an appetizing supper with friends.

INGREDIENTS

1 large onion, chopped
2 garlic cloves, crushed
500g/1¼lb extra-lean minced beef or turkey
450g/1lb passata
5ml/1 tsp dried mixed herbs
225g/8oz frozen leaf spinach, defrosted
200g/7oz lasagne verdi
200g/7oz low-fat cottage cheese
mixed salad, to serve

FOR THE SAUCE

25g/1oz low-fat spread
25g/1oz plain flour
300ml/½ pint/1¼ cups skimmed milk
1.5ml/¼ tsp ground nutmeg
25g/1oz grated fresh Parmesan cheese
salt and freshly ground black pepper

SERVES 8

1 Put the onion, garlic and minced meat into a non-stick saucepan. Cook quickly for 5 minutes, stirring with a wooden spoon to separate the pieces, until the meat is lightly browned all over.

COOK'S TIP

Make sure you use the type of lasagne that does not require any pre-cooking for this recipe.

2 Add the passata, herbs and seasoning and stir to mix. Bring to the boil, cover, then reduce the heat and simmer for about 30 minutes, stirring occasionally.

3 Make the sauce: put all the sauce ingredients, except the Parmesan cheese, into a saucepan. Cook until the sauce thickens, whisking continuously until bubbling and smooth. Turn the heat off. Adjust the seasoning to taste, add the Parmesan cheese to the sauce and stir to mix.

NUTRITIONAL NOTES

Per portion:

Energy	244Kcals/1032kJ
Total fat	4.8g
Saturated fat	1.9g
Cholesterol	37.9mg
Fibre	2g

4 Preheat the oven to 190°C/375°F/Gas 5. Lay the spinach leaves out on sheets of absorbent kitchen paper and pat them until they are dry.

5 Layer the meat mixture, lasagne, cottage cheese and spinach leaves in a 2 litre/3½ pint/8 cup ovenproof dish, starting and ending with a layer of meat.

6 Spoon the sauce over the top to cover the meat completely and bake in the oven for 40–50 minutes or until bubbling. Serve with a mixed salad.

TAGLIATELLE WITH MEAT SAUCE

This recipe is an authentic meat sauce – ragù – from the city of Bologna in Emilia-Romagna. It is quite rich and very delicious, and is always served with tagliatelle, never with spaghetti.

INGREDIENTS

450g/1lb dried tagliatelle
salt and freshly ground black pepper
grated fresh Parmesan cheese, to serve (optional)

FOR THE BOLOGNESE MEAT SAUCE

1 onion
2 carrots
2 celery sticks
2 garlic cloves
15ml/1 tbsp olive oil
115g/4oz lean back bacon, diced
250g/9oz extra-lean minced beef
250g/9oz extra-lean minced pork
120ml/4fl oz/½ cup dry white wine
2 × 400g/14oz cans crushed Italian plum tomatoes
475–750ml/16fl oz–1¼ pints/2–3 cups beef stock

SERVES 8

1 Make the meat sauce. Chop all the fresh vegetables finely. Heat the oil in a large frying pan or saucepan. Add the chopped vegetables and the bacon and cook over a medium heat, stirring frequently, for 10 minutes or until the vegetables have softened.

2 Add the minced beef and pork, reduce the heat and cook gently for 10 minutes, stirring frequently and breaking up any lumps in the meat with a wooden spoon.

3 Stir in salt and pepper to taste, then add the wine and stir again. Simmer for about 5 minutes, or until reduced.

4 Add the tomatoes and 250ml/8fl oz/ 1 cup of the stock and bring to the boil. Stir the sauce well, then reduce the heat. Half cover the pan with a lid and leave to simmer very gently for 2 hours. Stir occasionally and add more stock as it becomes absorbed.

5 Simmer the sauce, without a lid, for a further 30 minutes, stirring frequently. Meanwhile, cook the pasta in a large saucepan of boiling salted water, according to the packet instructions, until tender or *al dente*. Taste the sauce and adjust the seasoning. Drain the cooked pasta and tip it into a warmed bowl. Pour the meat sauce over the pasta and toss well. Serve immediately, sprinkled with grated Parmesan, if using.

NUTRITIONAL NOTES

Per portion:

Energy	185Kcals/782kJ
Total fat	5g
Saturated fat	1.7g
Cholesterol	36.3mg
Fibre	1.8g

LAMB AND SWEET PEPPER SAUCE

This simple sauce is a speciality of the Abruzzo-Molise region of Italy, east of Rome, where it is traditionally served with *maccheroni alla chitarra* – square-shaped long macaroni.

Ingredients

15ml/1 tbsp olive oil
250g/9oz boneless lean lamb neck fillet, diced quite small
2 garlic cloves, finely chopped
2 bay leaves, torn
250ml/8fl oz/1 cup dry white wine
4 ripe Italian plum tomatoes, skinned and chopped
2 large red peppers, deseeded and diced
450g/1lb dried spaghetti
salt and freshly ground black pepper

Serves 6

Nutritional Notes

Per portion:

Energy	179Kcals/755kJ
Total fat	5g
Saturated fat	1.8g
Cholesterol	28mg
Fibre	1.4g

1 Heat the oil in a medium frying pan or saucepan, add the lamb and a little salt and pepper. Cook over a medium to high heat for about 10 minutes, stirring frequently, until browned all over.

Cook's Tip

You can make your own fresh *maccheroni alla chitarra* or buy the dried pasta from an Italian delicatessen. Alternatively, this sauce is just as good served with ordinary spaghetti or long or short macaroni.

2 Sprinkle in the garlic and add the bay leaves, then pour in the wine and let it bubble until reduced.

3 Add the tomatoes and peppers and stir to mix. Season again. Cover with the lid, bring to the boil, then reduce the heat and simmer gently for 45–55 minutes or until the lamb is very tender. Stir occasionally during cooking and add a little water if the sauce becomes too dry. Meanwhile, cook the pasta in a large saucepan of boiling salted water, according to the packet instructions, until tender or *al dente*. Drain well. Remove and discard the bay leaves from the lamb sauce before serving it with the cooked pasta.

Variation

The peppers don't have to be red. Use yellow, orange or green if you prefer; either one colour or a mixture.

TAGLIOLINI WITH MEATY TOMATO SAUCE

Serve cooked tagliolini or tagliarini with this delicious meat-flavoured tomato sauce for an appetizing main course or supper.

INGREDIENTS

1 small onion
1 small carrot
2 celery sticks
2 garlic cloves
1 small handful of fresh flat leaf parsley
50g/2oz lean ham or bacon, finely chopped
60–90ml/4–6 tbsp dry white wine, or more to taste
500g/1 1/4lb ripe Italian plum tomatoes, chopped
350g/12oz dried tagliolini or tagliarini
salt and freshly ground black pepper
fresh flat leaf parsley sprigs, to garnish

SERVES 4

1 Chop the onion, carrot and celery finely in a food processor. Add the garlic cloves and parsley and process until finely chopped. Alternatively, chop everything by hand.

2 Put the chopped vegetable mixture in a medium shallow saucepan or skillet with the ham or bacon and cook, stirring, over a low heat for about 5 minutes. Add the wine, with salt and pepper to taste, and simmer for 5 minutes, then stir in the tomatoes. Bring to the boil, reduce the heat and simmer for 40 minutes, stirring occasionally and adding a little hot water if the sauce seems too dry.

3 Have ready a large sieve placed over a large bowl. Carefully pour in the sauce and press it through the sieve with the back of a metal spoon, leaving behind the tomato skins and any tough pieces of vegetable that won't go through. Discard the contents of the sieve.

4 Return the sauce to the rinsed-out saucepan and heat it through, adding a little more wine or hot water if it is too thick. Taste the sauce and adjust the seasoning. Meanwhile, cook the pasta in a large saucepan of boiling salted water, according to the packet instructions, until tender or *al dente*. Drain thoroughly. Toss the cooked pasta with the tomato sauce and serve immediately, garnished with fresh parsley sprigs.

NUTRITIONAL NOTES

Per portion:

Energy	187Kcals/790kJ
Total fat	3.3g
Saturated fat	1g
Cholesterol	8.8mg
Fibre	2.7g

RIGATONI WITH PORK

This is an excellent and very tasty, low-fat meat sauce made using lean minced pork rather than the more usual minced beef. You could serve it with tagliatelle or spaghetti instead of rigatoni.

INGREDIENTS

1 small onion
1/2 carrot
1/2 celery stick
2 garlic cloves
15ml/1 tbsp olive oil
150g/5oz extra-lean minced pork
60ml/4 tbsp dry white wine
400g/14oz can chopped Italian plum tomatoes
a few fresh basil leaves, plus extra basil leaves, to garnish
400g/14oz/3 1/2 cups dried rigatoni
salt and freshly ground black pepper
freshly shaved Parmesan cheese, to serve (optional)

SERVES 4

1 Chop the fresh vegetables and garlic finely, in a food processor or by hand. Heat the oil in a large frying pan or saucepan until just sizzling, add the vegetables and cook over a medium heat, stirring frequently, for 3–4 minutes.

VARIATION

To give the sauce a more intense flavour, soak 15g/1/2oz dried porcini mushrooms in 175ml/6fl oz/3/4 cup warm water for 15–20 minutes, then drain, chop and add with the meat.

2 Add the minced pork and cook gently for 2–3 minutes, breaking up any lumps in the meat with a wooden spoon.

3 Reduce the heat and cook for a further 2–3 minutes, stirring frequently, then stir in the wine. Mix in the tomatoes, whole basil leaves, salt to taste and plenty of pepper. Bring to the boil, then reduce the heat, cover and simmer for 40 minutes, stirring occasionally.

4 Cook the pasta in a large saucepan of boiling salted water, according to the packet instructions, until tender or *al dente*. Just before draining it, add a ladleful or two of the cooking water to the sauce. Stir well, then taste the sauce and adjust the seasoning.

5 Drain the pasta, add it to the pan of sauce and toss well. Serve immediately, sprinkled with the basil leaves and shaved Parmesan, if using.

NUTRITIONAL NOTES

Per portion:

Energy	70Kcals/293kJ
Total fat	2.5g
Saturated fat	0.4g
Cholesterol	0mg
Fibre	2.4g

TAGLIATELLE WITH MILANESE SAUCE

Tagliatelle is served with a tasty, low-fat version of the classic Milanese sauce to create this flavourful dish, ideal for a family meal.

INGREDIENTS

1 onion, finely chopped
1 celery stick, finely chopped
1 red pepper, deseeded and diced
1–2 garlic cloves, crushed
150ml/¼ pint/⅔ cup vegetable or chicken stock
400g/14oz can tomatoes
15ml/1 tbsp tomato purée
10ml/2 tsp caster sugar
5ml/1 tsp dried mixed herbs
350g/12oz tagliatelle
115g/4oz button or small cap mushrooms, sliced
60ml/4 tbsp dry white wine
115g/4oz lean cooked ham, coarsely diced
salt and freshly ground black pepper
15ml/1 tbsp chopped fresh parsley, to garnish

SERVES 4

1 Put the onion, celery, red pepper and garlic into a saucepan.

2 Add the stock, bring to the boil and cook for 5 minutes or until tender, stirring occasionally.

3 Add the tomatoes, tomato purée, sugar and dried herbs. Season with salt and pepper.

4 Bring to the boil then reduce the heat and simmer for 30 minutes, stirring occasionally, until the sauce is thick.

5 Cook the pasta in a large saucepan of boiling salted water, according to the packet instructions, until tender or *al dente*. Drain thoroughly.

6 Meanwhile, put the mushrooms into a small saucepan with the white wine, cover and cook for 3–4 minutes until the mushrooms are tender and all the wine has been absorbed, stirring occasionally.

7 Stir the mushrooms and ham into the tomato sauce and reheat gently over a low heat until piping hot.

8 Transfer the pasta to a warmed serving dish and spoon the sauce on top. Garnish with chopped parsley and serve.

NUTRITIONAL NOTES

Per portion:

Energy	405Kcals/1700kJ
Total fat	3.5g
Saturated fat	0.8g
Cholesterol	17mg
Fibre	4.5g

COOK'S TIP

To reduce the calorie and fat content even more, omit the ham and use sweetcorn kernels or cooked broccoli florets instead.

SPAGHETTI ALLA CARBONARA

This is a low-fat variation of the classic Italian charcoal burner's spaghetti, using lean smoked back bacon rashers and low-fat cream cheese. Serve with a few Parmesan cheese shavings.

INGREDIENTS

150g/5oz lean smoked back bacon rashers
1 onion, chopped
1–2 garlic cloves, crushed
150ml/¼ pint/⅔ cup chicken stock
150ml/¼ pint/⅔ cup dry white wine
200g/7oz low-fat soft cheese
450g/1lb chilli and garlic-flavoured dried spaghetti
30ml/2 tbsp chopped fresh parsley
salt and freshly ground black pepper
15g/½oz shaved fresh Parmesan cheese, to serve

SERVES 4

1 Cut the bacon rashers into 1cm/½in strips. Fry quickly in a non-stick frying pan for 2–3 minutes, stirring. Add the onion, garlic and stock to the pan. Bring to the boil, cover, then reduce the heat and simmer for about 5 minutes until tender.

2 Add the wine and boil rapidly until reduced by half. Whisk in the cheese and season to taste with salt and pepper.

3 Meanwhile, cook the spaghetti in a large saucepan of boiling, salted water for 10–12 minutes, until tender or *al dente*. Drain thoroughly.

4 Return the cooked spaghetti to the pan with the sauce and parsley, toss well and serve immediately topped with a few thin shavings of Parmesan cheese.

NUTRITIONAL NOTES

Per portion:

Energy	428Kcals/1815kJ
Total fat	4.6g
Saturated fat	1.6g
Cholesterol	9.96mg
Fibre	3g

PAPPARDELLE WITH RABBIT SAUCE

This delicious low-fat pasta dish comes from the north of Italy, where rabbit sauces for pasta are very popular. Serve with crusty fresh bread and a mixed leaf salad for a filling meal.

INGREDIENTS

15g/1/2oz/1/4 cup dried porcini mushrooms
175ml/6fl oz/3/4 cup warm water
1 small onion
1/2 carrot
1/2 celery stick
2 bay leaves
15ml/1 tbsp olive oil
40g/1 1/2oz lean back bacon, chopped
15ml/1 tbsp roughly chopped fresh flat leaf parsley, plus extra to garnish
350g/12oz boneless lean rabbit meat
90ml/6 tbsp dry white wine
200g/7oz can chopped Italian plum tomatoes or 200ml/7fl oz/scant 1 cup passata
450g/1lb dried pappardelle
salt and freshly ground black pepper

SERVES 6

1 Put the dried mushrooms in a bowl, pour over the warm water and leave to soak for 15–20 minutes. Finely chop the fresh vegetables. Make a tear in each bay leaf, so they release their flavour.

2 Heat the oil in a frying pan or medium saucepan. Add the vegetables, bacon and parsley and cook for about 5 minutes, stirring occasionally.

3 Add the pieces of rabbit and fry on both sides for 3–4 minutes, stirring frequently. Pour the wine over and let it bubble and reduce for a few minutes, then add the tomatoes or passata. Drain the mushrooms and pour the soaking liquid into the pan. Chop the mushrooms and add them to the pan with the bay leaves and salt and pepper to taste. Stir well, cover, bring to the boil, then reduce the heat and simmer for 35–40 minutes until the rabbit is tender, stirring occasionally.

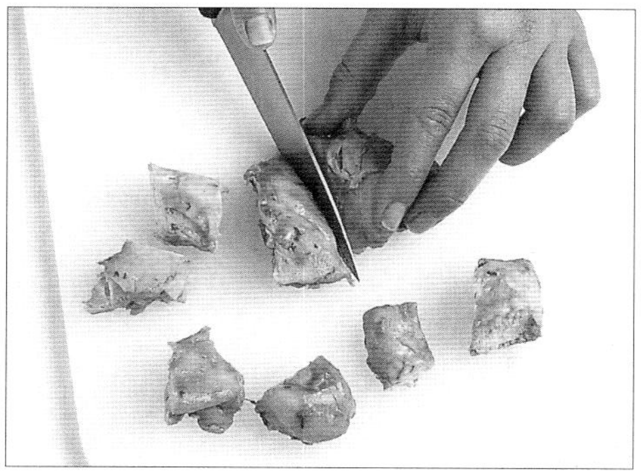

4 Remove from the heat and lift out the rabbit with a slotted spoon. Cut into bite-size chunks and stir into the sauce. Remove the bay leaves. Add more salt and pepper, if needed. Cook the pasta in a large saucepan of boiling salted water, according to the packet instructions, until tender or *al dente*. Meanwhile, reheat the sauce until piping hot. Drain the pasta and toss with the sauce in a warmed bowl. Serve immediately, sprinkled with parsley.

NUTRITIONAL NOTES

Per portion:

Energy	166Kcals/699kJ
Total fat	4.7g
Saturated fat	1.4g
Cholesterol	33.9mg
Fibre	1.4g

FISH AND SHELLFISH PASTA DISHES

The wide variety of different SHAPES, *sizes and* FLAVOURS *of fresh and dried pasta creates a wonderful basis for many delicious and* NUTRITIOUS *low-fat Italian fish and shellfish* PASTA *dishes. We include a tempting selection of no-fuss recipes, using a variety of* FISH *and* SHELLFISH, *to please every palate. Choose from Farfalle with* TUNA, *Smoked Trout Cannelloni, Tagliatelle with Scallops or Vermicelli with* CLAM *Sauce.*

FUSILLI WITH SMOKED TROUT

Fusilli pasta is served with a delicious smoked trout and vegetable sauce to create a flavourful lunch or supper dish. Smoked salmon may be used in place of the trout, for a tasty change.

INGREDIENTS

2 carrots, cut into julienne sticks
1 leek, cut into julienne sticks
2 celery sticks, cut into julienne sticks
150ml/1/4 pint/2/3 cup vegetable or fish stock
225g/8oz smoked trout fillets, skinned and cut into strips
200g/7oz low-fat soft cheese
150ml/1/4 pint/2/3 cup medium sweet white wine or fish stock
15ml/1 tbsp chopped fresh dill or fennel
225g/8oz dried fusilli lunghi
salt and freshly ground black pepper
fresh dill sprigs, to garnish

SERVES 6

1 Put the carrots, leek and celery into a saucepan with the vegetable or fish stock. Bring to the boil and cook quickly for 4–5 minutes until the vegetables are tender and most of the stock has evaporated, stirring occasionally. Turn the heat off and stir in the smoked trout. Set aside.

2 To make the sauce, put the soft cheese and wine or fish stock into a saucepan and cook, whisking until smooth. Season. Stir in the dill or fennel.

3 Meanwhile, cook the pasta in a large saucepan of boiling salted water according to the instructions, until tender or *al dente*. Drain thoroughly. Return to the pan, add the sauce, toss and transfer to a serving bowl. Top with the vegetables and trout. Serve garnished with dill sprigs.

NUTRITIONAL NOTES

Per portion:

Energy	234Kcals/989kJ
Total fat	3.7g
Saturated fat	1.3g
Cholesterol	40mg
Fibre	1.7g

PASTA WITH TOMATO AND TUNA

Pasta shells are topped with a tasty tuna and tomato sauce to create this delicious, low-fat Italian-style pasta dish.

INGREDIENTS

1 onion, finely chopped
1 celery stick, finely chopped
1 red pepper, deseeded and diced
1 garlic clove, crushed
150ml/¼ pint/⅔ cup chicken stock
400g/14oz can chopped tomatoes
15ml/1 tbsp tomato purée
10ml/2 tsp caster sugar
15ml/1 tbsp chopped fresh basil
15ml/1 tbsp chopped fresh parsley
450g/1lb/4 cups dried conchiglie
400g/14oz can tuna in brine, drained
30ml/2 tbsp capers in vinegar, drained
salt and freshly ground black pepper

SERVES 6

1 Put the onion, celery, red pepper and garlic into a saucepan. Add the stock, bring to the boil and cook for 5 minutes until the stock has reduced significantly.

2 Add the tomatoes, tomato purée, sugar and herbs. Season to taste with salt and pepper and bring to the boil. Reduce the heat and simmer for about 30 minutes until thick, stirring occasionally.

VARIATION

If fresh herbs are not available, use a 400g/14oz can of chopped tomatoes with herbs and add 5–10ml/1–2 tsp dried mixed herbs, in place of the fresh herbs.

3 Meanwhile, cook the pasta in a large saucepan of boiling, salted water according to the packet instructions, until tender or *al dente*. Drain thoroughly and transfer to a warm serving dish.

4 Flake the tuna into large chunks and add to the sauce with the capers. Cook gently for 1–2 minutes, stirring, then pour over the pasta, toss gently and serve immediately.

NUTRITIONAL NOTES

Per portion:

Energy	369Kcals/1549kJ
Total fat	2.1g
Saturated fat	0.4g
Cholesterol	34mg
Fibre	4g

SAFFRON PAPPARDELLE

Serve this flavourful and low-fat Italian pasta dish with a mixed green salad and fresh Italian bread for a wholesome and nutritious meal.

Ingredients

large pinch of saffron strands
4 sun-dried tomatoes, chopped
5ml/1 tsp chopped fresh thyme
12 large fresh whole prawns in their shells
225g/8oz baby squid
225g/8oz skinless monkfish fillet
2–3 garlic cloves, crushed
2 small onions, quartered
1 small bulb fennel, trimmed and sliced
150ml/¼ pint/⅔ cup white wine
225g/8oz dried pappardelle
salt and freshly ground black pepper
30ml/2 tbsp chopped fresh parsley, to garnish

Serves 4

1 Put the saffron, sun-dried tomatoes and thyme into a bowl with 60ml/4 tbsp hot water. Leave to soak for 30 minutes.

Cook's Tip

Make sure you use the sun-dried tomatoes for soaking in Step 1, rather than the ones preserved in oil. Do not try to substitute turmeric for the saffron in this recipe; although the colour will be similar, the flavour will be quite different.

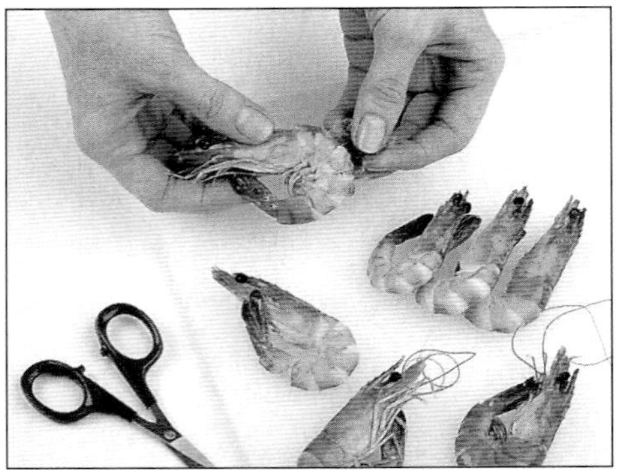

2 Wash the prawns and carefully remove and discard the shells, but leave the heads and tails intact. Pull the head from the body of each squid and remove and discard the quill. Cut the tentacles from the head and rinse under cold water. Pull off and discard the outer skin and cut the flesh into 5mm/¼in rings. Cut the monkfish into 2.5cm/1in cubes. Set aside.

3 Put the garlic, onions and fennel into a pan with the wine. Cover and simmer for 5 minutes until tender. Stir occasionally.

Nutritional Notes

Per portion:

Energy	381Kcals/1602kJ
Total fat	3.5g
Saturated fat	0.6g
Cholesterol	34mg
Fibre	3.2g

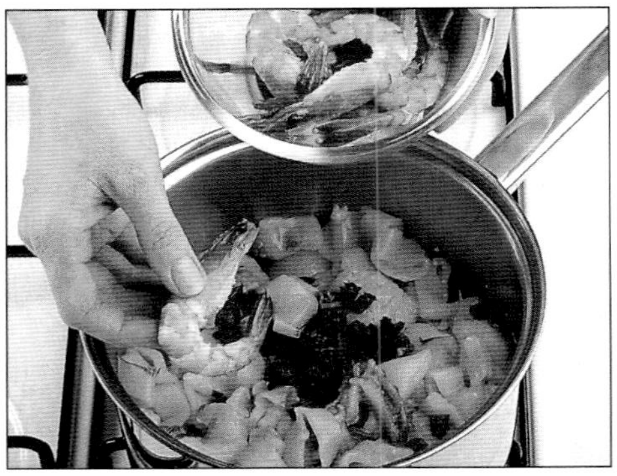

4 Stir in the monkfish and the saffron mixture. Cover and cook for 3 minutes, then stir in the prawns and squid. Cover and cook gently for 1–2 minutes (do not overcook). Season to taste.

5 Meanwhile, cook the pasta in a large saucepan of boiling, salted water according to the packet instructions, until tender or *al dente*. Drain thoroughly.

6 Divide the pasta among four serving dishes and top with the sauce. Sprinkle with parsley and serve at once.

FARFALLE WITH TUNA

This is a quick and simple dish that makes a good low-fat weekday supper if you have canned tomatoes and tuna in the store cupboard. Serve with crusty fresh Italian bread.

INGREDIENTS

15ml/1 tbsp olive oil
1 small onion, finely chopped
1 garlic clove, finely chopped
400g/14oz can chopped Italian plum tomatoes
45ml/3 tbsp dry white wine
8–10 stoned black olives, sliced into rings
10ml/2 tsp chopped fresh oregano or 5ml/1 tsp dried oregano, plus extra fresh oregano, to garnish
350g/12oz/3 cups dried farfalle
175g/6oz can tuna in brine
salt and freshly ground black pepper

SERVES 4

1 Heat the olive oil in a medium frying pan or saucepan, and add the chopped onion and garlic.

2 Cook gently for 2–3 minutes until the onion is soft and golden, stirring occasionally.

3 Add the tomatoes and bring to the boil, then add the white wine and simmer for a minute or so. Stir in the olives and oregano, with salt and pepper to taste, then cover and cook for 20–25 minutes, stirring occasionally.

4 Meanwhile, cook the pasta in a large saucepan of boiling salted water according to the packet instructions, until tender or *al dente*.

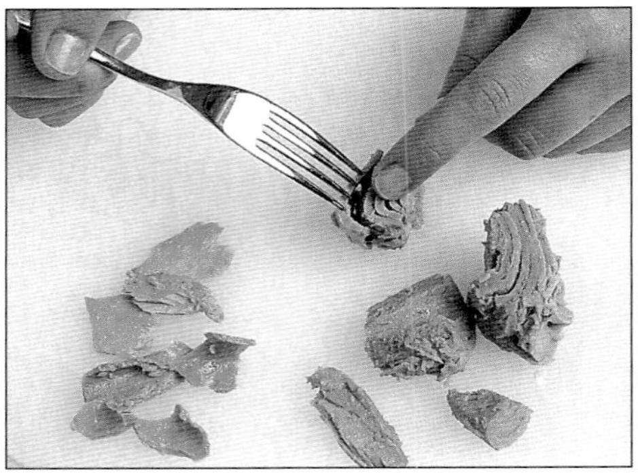

5 Drain the tuna and flake it with a fork. Add to the sauce with about 60ml/4 tbsp of the pasta water and stir to mix. Adjust the seasoning to taste.

6 Drain the pasta well and tip it into a warmed serving bowl. Pour the sauce over the top and toss to mix. Serve immediately, garnished with oregano.

NUTRITIONAL NOTES

Per portion:

Energy	387Kcals/1643kJ
Total fat	4.9g
Saturated fat	0.8g
Cholesterol	21.3mg
Fibre	3.5g

MACARONI WITH BROCCOLI AND CAULIFLOWER

This is a typical southern Italian dish, full of flavour and low in fat too. Without the anchovies, it can be served to vegetarians.

INGREDIENTS

175g/6oz cauliflower florets, cut into small sprigs
175g/6oz broccoli florets, cut into small sprigs
350g/12oz/3 cups dried short-cut macaroni
15ml/1 tbsp extra virgin olive oil
1 onion, finely chopped
30ml/2 tbsp pine nuts (optional)
1 sachet of saffron powder, dissolved in 15ml/1 tbsp warm water
15ml/1 tbsp raisins
30ml/2 tbsp sun-dried tomato purée
4 bottled or canned anchovies in olive oil, drained and chopped
salt and freshly ground black pepper
grated fresh Pecorino cheese, to serve (optional)

SERVES 4

1 Cook the cauliflower in a large saucepan of boiling salted water for 3 minutes. Add the broccoli and boil for a further 2 minutes. Remove the vegetables from the pan with a large slotted spoon, place on a plate and set aside.

2 Add the pasta to the vegetable cooking water and bring back to the boil. Cook the pasta according to the packet instructions, until it is tender or *al dente*.

3 Meanwhile, heat the olive oil in a large frying pan or saucepan, add the onion and cook over a low to medium heat, stirring frequently, for 2–3 minutes or until golden. Add the pine nuts, if using, the broccoli and cauliflower, and the saffron water. Add the raisins, sun-dried tomato purée and a couple of ladlefuls of the pasta cooking water until the mixture has the consistency of a sauce. Finally, add plenty of pepper.

4 Stir well, cook for 1–2 minutes, then add the chopped anchovies. Drain the pasta and tip it into the vegetable mixture. Toss well, then taste for seasoning and add salt if necessary. Serve the pasta immediately in four warmed bowls, sprinkled with freshly grated Pecorino, if using.

NUTRITIONAL NOTES

Per portion:

Energy	339Kcals/1438kJ
Total fat	5g
Saturated fat	0.7g
Cholesterol	0mg
Fibre	4.5g

SMOKED TROUT CANNELLONI

Cannelloni are stuffed with a tasty smoked trout filling, topped with a low-fat cheese sauce and oven-baked to create this appetizing Italian lunch or supper dish.

INGREDIENTS

1 large onion, finely chopped
1 garlic clove, crushed
60ml/4 tbsp vegetable stock
2 × 400g/14oz cans chopped tomatoes
2.5ml/½ tsp dried mixed herbs
1 smoked trout, weighing about 400g/14oz
75g/3oz/¾ cup frozen peas, thawed
75g/3oz/1½ cups fresh breadcrumbs
16 cannelloni tubes
salt and freshly ground black pepper
mixed salad, to serve

FOR THE CHEESE SAUCE

25g/1oz/2 tbsp low-fat spread
25g/1oz/¼ cup plain flour
350ml/12fl oz/1½ cups skimmed milk
freshly grated nutmeg
15g/½oz/1½ tbsp finely grated fresh Parmesan cheese

SERVES 6

1 Simmer the onion, garlic and stock in a large covered saucepan for 3 minutes. Uncover and continue to cook, stirring occasionally, until reduced entirely.

COOK'S TIP

Smoked trout can be bought already filleted or whole. If you buy fillets, you'll need 225g/8oz fish.

2 Stir in the tomatoes and herbs. Simmer uncovered for a further 10 minutes, or until very thick, stirring occasionally.

3 Meanwhile, skin the smoked trout with a sharp knife. Carefully flake the flesh and discard all the bones. Mix with the tomato mixture, peas, breadcrumbs, salt and pepper in a large bowl.

4 Preheat the oven to 190°C/375°F/Gas 5. Spoon the filling into the cannelloni tubes and arrange in an ovenproof dish. Set aside.

5 Make the sauce. Put the low-fat spread, flour and milk into a saucepan and cook over a medium heat, whisking until the sauce thickens. Simmer for 2–3 minutes, stirring continuously. Season to taste with salt, pepper and nutmeg.

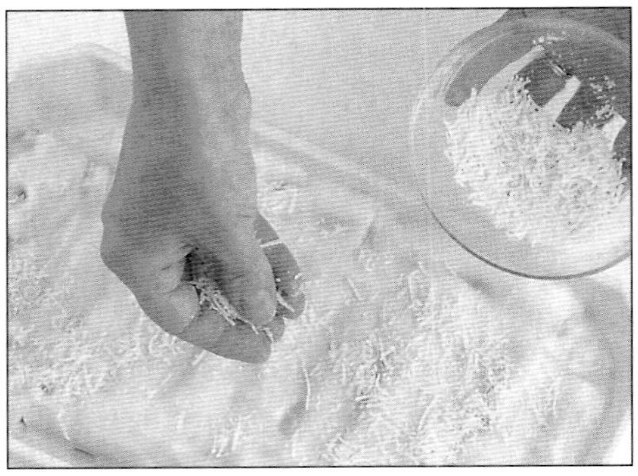

6 Pour the sauce over the cannelloni and sprinkle with the Parmesan cheese. Bake in the oven for 35–40 minutes, or until the top is golden brown. Serve with a mixed salad.

NUTRITIONAL NOTES

Per portion:

Energy	306Kcals/1298kJ
Total fat	5g
Saturated fat	1.3g
Cholesterol	45.8mg
Fibre	3g

SPAGHETTI WITH TUNA SAUCE

A speedy low-fat midweek meal, which can also be made with other pasta shapes, this tasty Italian pasta dish is ideal for all the family.

INGREDIENTS

225g/8oz dried spaghetti, or 450g/1lb fresh
1 garlic clove, crushed
400g/14oz can chopped tomatoes
425g/15oz can tuna fish in brine, drained and flaked
2.5ml/½ tsp chilli sauce (optional)
4 stoned black olives, chopped
salt and freshly ground black pepper

SERVES 4

1 Cook the spaghetti in a large saucepan of boiling salted water for 12 minutes or until just tender or *al dente*. Drain well and keep hot.

2 Add the garlic and tomatoes to the saucepan and bring to the boil. Simmer, uncovered, for 2–3 minutes, stirring the mixture occasionally.

3 Add the tuna fish, chilli sauce, if using, the olives and spaghetti. Heat gently until hot, stirring. Add seasoning to taste and serve hot.

COOK'S TIP

If fresh tuna is available, use 450g/1lb, cut into small chunks, and add after Step 2. Simmer for 6–8 minutes, then add the chilli, olives and pasta.

NUTRITIONAL NOTES

Per portion:

Energy	306Kcals/1288kJ
Total fat	2.02g
Saturated fat	0.37g
Cholesterol	48.45mg
Fibre	2.46g

PASTA WITH HERBY SCALLOPS

Low-fat fromage frais, cooked with mustard, garlic, herbs and scallops, makes this deceptively creamy and delicious sauce ideal for serving with cooked pasta for a flavourful meal.

INGREDIENTS

120ml/4fl oz/½ cup low-fat fromage frais
10ml/2 tsp wholegrain mustard
2 garlic cloves, crushed
30–45ml/2–3 tbsp fresh lime juice
60ml/4 tbsp chopped fresh parsley
30ml/2 tbsp snipped fresh chives
350g/12oz dried black tagliatelle
12 large fresh scallops
60ml/4 tbsp white wine
150ml/¼ pint/⅔ cup fish stock
salt and freshly ground black pepper
lime wedges and fresh parsley sprigs, to garnish

SERVES 4

1 To make the sauce, mix the fromage frais, mustard, garlic, lime juice, chopped parsley, chives and seasoning together in a mixing bowl. Set aside.

2 Cook the pasta in a large saucepan of boiling salted water according to the packet instructions, until tender or *al dente*. Drain thoroughly and keep hot.

3 Slice the scallops in half, horizontally. Keep any coral whole. Put the wine and fish stock into a saucepan and heat to simmering point. Add the scallops and cook very gently for 3–4 minutes (but not for any longer or they will toughen).

4 Remove the scallops, place on a plate and keep warm. Boil the wine and stock to reduce by half and then add the green sauce to the pan. Heat gently to warm through, stirring, then return the scallops to the pan and cook for 1 minute. Spoon the sauce over the cooked pasta and garnish with lime wedges and fresh parsley sprigs. Serve.

NUTRITIONAL NOTES

Per portion:

Energy	368Kcals/1561kJ
Total fat	4.01g
Saturated fat	0.98g
Cholesterol	99mg
Fibre	1.91g

TAGLIATELLE WITH SCALLOPS

Scallops and brandy add a taste of luxury to this appetizing pasta sauce, ideal as a supper dish.

INGREDIENTS

200g/7oz scallops, sliced
30ml/2 tbsp plain flour
15ml/1 tbsp olive oil
2 spring onions, cut into thin rings
1/2–1 small fresh red chilli, deseeded and very finely chopped
30ml/2 tbsp finely chopped fresh flat leaf parsley
60ml/4 tbsp brandy
105ml/7 tbsp fish stock
275g/10oz fresh spinach-flavoured tagliatelle
salt and freshly ground black pepper

SERVES 4

1 Toss the scallops in the flour, shaking the excess. Bring a large saucepan of salted water to the boil for the pasta. Meanwhile, heat the oil in a frying pan. Add the spring onions, chilli and half the parsley and cook, stirring frequently, for 1–2 minutes over a medium heat. Add the scallops and toss for 1–2 minutes.

2 Pour the brandy over the scallops, then set it alight. When the flames have died down, pour in the stock, season and stir. Simmer for 2–3 minutes, then cover and remove from the heat. Cook the pasta according to the packet instructions. Drain, add to the sauce and toss over a medium heat until mixed. Serve at once.

NUTRITIONAL NOTES

Per portion:

Energy	372Kcals/1576kJ
Total fat	4.8g
Saturated fat	0.7g
Cholesterol	0.0mg
Fibre	2.2g

SPAGHETTI WITH SQUID AND PEAS

In Tuscany, squid is often cooked with peas in a tomato sauce. This low-fat recipe is a tasty variation on the theme, and it works very well.

INGREDIENTS

450g/1lb prepared squid
10ml/2 tsp olive oil
1 small onion, finely chopped
400g/14oz can chopped Italian plum tomatoes
1 garlic clove, finely chopped
15ml/1 tbsp red wine vinegar
5ml/1 tsp sugar
10ml/2 tsp finely chopped fresh rosemary
115g/4oz/1 cup frozen peas
275g/10oz dried spaghetti
15ml/1 tbsp chopped fresh flat leaf parsley
salt and freshly ground black pepper

SERVES 4

1 Cut the prepared squid into strips about 5mm/1/4in wide. Finely chop any tentacles. Set aside. Heat the oil in a frying pan, add the onion and cook gently, stirring, for about 5 minutes until softened. Add the squid, tomatoes, garlic, vinegar and sugar and stir to mix.

NUTRITIONAL NOTES

Per portion:

Energy	285Kcals/1206kJ
Total fat	4g
Saturated fat	0.4g
Cholesterol	0.0mg
Fibre	3g

2 Add the rosemary and seasoning. Bring to the boil, stirring, then cover, reduce the heat, and simmer for 20 minutes, stirring occasionally. Stir in the peas and cook for a further 10 minutes. Cook the pasta according to the packet instructions. Serve with the sauce and the parsley.

HOT SPICY PRAWNS WITH CAMPANELLE

This low-fat prawn sauce tossed with hot pasta creates an ideal Italian-style suppertime dish. Add less or more chilli depending on how hot you like your food.

INGREDIENTS

225g/8oz cooked, peeled tiger prawns
1–2 garlic cloves, crushed
finely grated rind of 1 lemon
15ml/1 tbsp fresh lemon juice
1.5ml/¼ tsp red chilli paste or 1 large pinch of chilli powder
15ml/1 tbsp light soy sauce
150g/5oz lean smoked back bacon rashers
1 shallot or small onion, finely chopped
60ml/4 tbsp dry white wine
225g/8oz/2 cups dried campanelle or other dried pasta shapes
60ml/4 tbsp fish stock
4 firm ripe tomatoes, peeled, deseeded and chopped
30ml/2 tbsp chopped fresh parsley
salt and freshly ground black pepper

SERVES 4

1 In a glass bowl, mix the prawns with the garlic, lemon rind and juice, then stir in the chilli paste or powder and soy sauce.

2 Season with salt and pepper, then cover and leave to marinate in a cool place for at least 1 hour.

3 Grill the bacon rashers under a hot grill until cooked, then cut them into 5mm/¼in dice. Set aside.

4 Put the shallot or onion and white wine into a saucepan, bring to the boil, cover and cook for 2–3 minutes or until it is tender and the wine has reduced by half. Set aside.

5 Meanwhile, cook the pasta in a large saucepan of boiling salted water according to the packet instructions, until tender or *al dente*. Drain thoroughly and keep hot.

6 Just before serving, put the prawns with their marinade into a large frying pan, bring to the boil quickly and add the cooked bacon and fish stock. Heat through for 1 minute, stirring.

7 Add to the hot pasta with the shallot or onion mixture, chopped tomatoes and parsley. Toss quickly to mix and serve at once.

COOK'S TIP

To save time later, the prawns and marinade ingredients can be mixed together, covered and chilled in the fridge overnight, until ready to use.

NUTRITIONAL NOTES

Per portion:

Energy	214Kcals/908kJ
Total fat	3g
Saturated fat	0.9g
Cholesterol	37.5mg
Fibre	1.4g

TRENETTE WITH SHELLFISH

Colourful and delicious, this typical pasta dish from the Genoese region of Italy is ideal for a low-fat lunch or supper. The sauce is quite runny, so serve it with spoons and crusty Italian bread.

INGREDIENTS

20ml/4 tsp olive oil
1 small onion, finely chopped
1 garlic clove, crushed
1/2 fresh red chilli, deseeded and finely chopped
200g/7oz can chopped Italian plum tomatoes
30ml/2 tbsp chopped fresh flat leaf parsley
450g/1lb fresh clams in their shells
450g/1lb fresh mussels in their shells
60ml/4 tbsp dry white wine
450g/1lb/4 cups dried trenette
a few fresh basil leaves
90g/3 1/2oz/2/3 cup cooked, peeled prawns, thawed and thoroughly dried if frozen
salt and freshly ground black pepper
chopped fresh herbs, to garnish

SERVES 6

1 Heat half the oil in a frying pan. Add the onion, garlic and chilli and cook over a medium heat for 1–2 minutes, stirring continuously. Stir in the tomatoes, half the parsley and pepper to taste. Bring to the boil, cover, reduce the heat and simmer for 15 minutes, stirring occasionally.

2 Scrub the clams and mussels under cold running water. Discard any that are open or that do not close when sharply tapped against the work surface.

3 In a large saucepan, heat the remaining oil. Add the clams and mussels, with the rest of the parsley and toss over a high heat for a few seconds. Pour in the white wine, then cover tightly. Cook for about 5 minutes, shaking the pan frequently, until the clams and mussels have opened.

4 Remove the pan from the heat and transfer the clams and mussels to a bowl with a slotted spoon, discarding any shellfish that have failed to open.

NUTRITIONAL NOTES

Per portion:

Energy	414Kcals/1755kJ
Total fat	5g
Saturated fat	0.7g
Cholesterol	21mg
Fibre	2.7g

5 Strain the cooking liquid into a measuring jug and set aside. Reserve a few clams and mussels in their shells for the garnish, then remove the rest from their shells.

6 Cook the pasta in a large saucepan of boiling salted water, according to the packet instructions, until tender or *al dente*. Meanwhile, add 120ml/4fl oz/1/2 cup of the seafood liquid to the tomato sauce. Bring to the boil over a high heat, stirring. Reduce the heat, tear in the basil and add the prawns with the shelled clams and mussels. Stir well, then adjust the seasoning to taste.

7 Drain the pasta and tip it into a warmed bowl. Add the seafood sauce and toss well to combine. Serve sprinkled with chopped herbs and garnish each portion with the reserved clams and mussels.

LINGUINE WITH CRAB

This pasta recipe comes from Rome. It makes a tasty low-fat first course served on its own, or it can be served for lunch or supper with crusty Italian bread.

INGREDIENTS

about 250g/9oz shelled white crab meat
15ml/1 tbsp olive oil
1 small handful of fresh flat leaf parsley, roughly chopped, plus extra to garnish
1 garlic clove, crushed
350g/12oz ripe Italian plum tomatoes, skinned and chopped
60–90ml/4–6 tbsp dry white wine
350g/12oz dried linguine
salt and freshly ground black pepper

SERVES 4

1 Put the crab meat in a mortar and pound to a rough pulp with a pestle, or use a sturdy bowl and the end of a rolling pin. Set aside.

2 Heat the oil in a large saucepan. Add the parsley and garlic, season to taste, and cook until the garlic begins to brown, stirring occasionally.

3 Stir in the tomatoes, pounded crab meat and wine, cover the pan, bring to the boil, then reduce the heat and simmer for 15 minutes, stirring occasionally.

4 Meanwhile, cook the pasta in a large saucepan of boiling salted water, according to the packet instructions, draining it the moment it is tender or *al dente*, and reserving a little of the cooking water. Return the pasta to the clean pan.

5 Add the tomato and crab mixture to the pasta and toss to mix, adding a little cooking water if necessary. Adjust the seasoning to taste. Serve hot, in warmed bowls, sprinkled with chopped parsley.

NUTRITIONAL NOTES

Per portion:

Energy	308Kcals/1307kJ
Total fat	5g
Saturated fat	0.7g
Cholesterol	32.1mg
Fibre	2.3g

COOK'S TIP

Ask a fishmonger to remove crab meat from the shell, or buy dressed crab at the supermarket. Alternatively, use drained canned crab meat.

SPAGHETTI WITH CLAM SAUCE

This is one of Italy's most famous pasta dishes, sometimes translated as "white clam sauce" to distinguish it from that other classic, clams in tomato sauce.

INGREDIENTS

1kg/2¼lb fresh clams
15ml/1 tbsp olive oil
45ml/3 tbsp chopped fresh flat leaf parsley
120ml/4fl oz/½ cup dry white wine
275g/10oz dried spaghetti
2 garlic cloves
salt and freshly ground black pepper

SERVES 4

1 Scrub the clams under cold running water, discarding any that are open or that do not close when sharply tapped against the work surface.

2 Heat half the oil in a large saucepan, add the clams and 15ml/1 tbsp of the parsley and cook over a high heat for a few seconds. Pour in the wine, then cover tightly. Cook for about 5 minutes, shaking the pan frequently, until the clams have opened. Meanwhile, cook the pasta in a large saucepan of boiling salted water, according to the packet instructions, until tender or *al dente*.

3 Using a slotted spoon, transfer the clams to a bowl, discarding any that have failed to open. Strain the liquid and set it aside. Put eight clams to one side, then remove the rest from their shells.

4 Heat the remaining oil in a clean saucepan. Cook the whole garlic cloves over a medium heat until golden, crushing them with the back of a spoon. Remove the garlic with a slotted spoon and discard.

5 Add the shelled clams to the pan, gradually add some of the strained liquid from the clams, then add plenty of pepper. Cook for 1–2 minutes, gradually adding more liquid as the sauce reduces. Add the remaining parsley and cook for 1–2 minutes, stirring occasionally.

6 Drain the pasta, add it to the pan and toss well. Serve in individual dishes, scooping the shelled clams from the bottom of the pan and placing some of them on top of each serving. Garnish with the reserved clams in their shells and serve immediately.

NUTRITIONAL NOTES

Per portion:

Energy	425Kcals/1789kJ
Total fat	4.5g
Saturated fat	0.4g
Cholesterol	0mg
Fibre	1.5g

VERMICELLI WITH CLAM SAUCE

This recipe originates from the city of Naples, where both fresh tomato sauce and seafood are traditionally served with vermicelli. The two are combined for a tasty, low-fat dish.

INGREDIENTS

1kg/2¼lb fresh clams
250ml/8fl oz/1 cup dry white wine
2 garlic cloves, bruised
1 large handful of fresh flat leaf parsley
10ml/2 tsp olive oil
1 small onion, finely chopped
8 ripe Italian plum tomatoes, peeled, deseeded and finely chopped
½–1 fresh red chilli, deseeded and finely chopped
350g/12oz dried vermicelli
salt and freshly ground black pepper

SERVES 4

1 Scrub the clams thoroughly under cold running water and discard any that are open or that do not close when sharply tapped against the work surface.

2 Pour the white wine into a large saucepan, add the bruised garlic cloves and half the parsley, then add the clams. Cover tightly with the lid and bring to the boil over a high heat. Cook for about 5 minutes, shaking the pan frequently, until the clams have opened.

3 Tip the clams into a large colander set over a bowl and let the liquid drain through. Leave the clams until cool enough to handle, then remove about two-thirds of them from their shells, tipping the clam liquor into the bowl of cooking liquid.

4 Discard any clams that have failed to open. Set both shelled and unshelled clams aside, keeping the unshelled clams warm in a bowl covered with a lid. Reserve the cooking liquid and set aside.

5 Heat the oil in a saucepan, add the onion and cook gently, stirring frequently, for about 5 minutes until softened. Add the tomatoes, then the clam liquid. Add the chilli, season to taste, and stir.

6 Bring to the boil, half cover, then simmer gently for 15–20 minutes, stirring occasionally. Meanwhile, cook the pasta in a large saucepan of boiling salted water, according to the packet instructions. Chop the remaining parsley finely.

NUTRITIONAL NOTES

Per portion:

Energy	536Kcals/2262kJ
Total fat	4.7g
Saturated fat	0.4g
Cholesterol	0mg
Fibre	2.4g

7 Add the shelled clams to the sauce, stir well and heat through very gently for 2–3 minutes, stirring occasionally.

8 Drain the cooked pasta well and tip it into a warmed bowl. Taste the clam and tomato sauce and adjust the seasoning, then pour the sauce over the pasta and toss everything together well. Garnish with the reserved clams in their shells, sprinkle the chopped parsley over the pasta and serve immediately.

VEGETARIAN PASTA DISHES

This appetizing MEDLEY *of vegetarian pasta dishes brings together a wealth of* DELICIOUS *ingredients to create a collection of low-fat recipes* PACKED *with goodness and the flavours of Italy for family and friends to* RELISH. *Select from recipes such as Tagliatelle with Sun-Dried* TOMATOES, *Mushroom Bolognese, Penne with Artichokes or* TAGLIATELLE *with Hazelnut Pesto.*

CONCHIGLIE WITH TOMATOES AND ROCKET

Cooked pasta shells, tossed together with lightly cooked tomatoes and fresh rocket, makes a tasty low-fat dish that is ideal for a summer lunch or supper.

Ingredients

450g/1lb/4 cups dried conchiglie
450g/1lb ripe cherry tomatoes
75g/3oz fresh rocket
15ml/1 tbsp extra virgin olive oil
15g/½oz fresh Parmesan cheese
salt and freshly ground black pepper

Serves 4

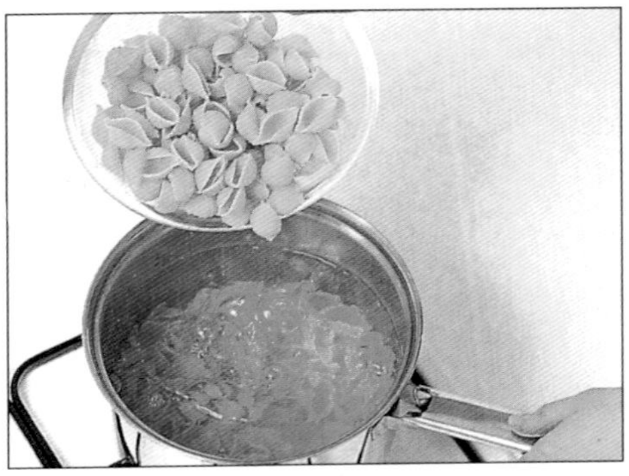

1 Cook the pasta in a large saucepan of boiling salted water, according to the packet instructions, until tender or *al dente*. Stir occasionally.

2 While the pasta is cooking, halve the cherry tomatoes. Trim, wash and dry the rocket.

3 Heat the oil in a large saucepan, add the halved tomatoes and cook for barely 1 minute. The tomatoes should only just heat through and not disintegrate.

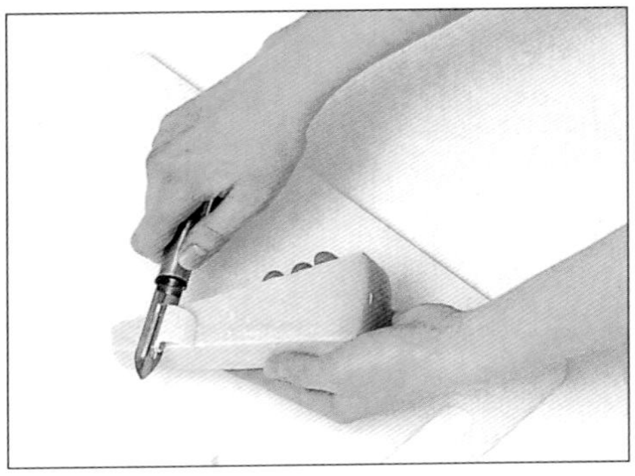

4 Meanwhile, cut the Parmesan cheese into fine shavings, using a swivel vegetable peeler.

Cook's Tip

This pasta dish relies for its success on a salad green called rocket. Available in most large supermarkets, it is a leaf that is easily grown in the garden or a window-box and tastes slightly peppery. When you buy rocket, make sure the leaves are very fresh with no sign of wilting. Rocket does not keep well unless it has been pre-packaged. To keep it for a day or two, wrap it in damp kitchen paper and store in the fridge.

5 Drain the pasta and tip it into the pan with the tomatoes.

6 Add the rocket and then carefully stir to mix and heat through. Season well with salt and pepper and serve immediately, topped with a little shaved Parmesan cheese.

Variations

- You might like to try adding 1.5ml/¼ tsp dried chilli flakes and 2 finely chopped garlic cloves to this dish. Simply add them to the oil and fry gently for a minute or so before adding the tomatoes.
- Use a different type of pasta such as fusilli in place of the conchiglie.
- In place of the rocket, try fresh watercress.

Nutritional Notes

Per portion:

Energy	329Kcals/1396kJ
Total fat	5g
Saturated fat	1.2g
Cholesterol	2.3mg
Fibre	3.5g

TAGLIATELLE WITH SUN-DRIED TOMATOES

Tagliatelle tossed in a delicious fresh and sun-dried tomato sauce is an ideal main-course meal for all the family to enjoy.

INGREDIENTS

1 garlic clove, crushed
1 celery stick, thinly sliced
115g/4oz/1 cup sun-dried tomatoes, finely chopped
90ml/6 tbsp red wine
8 plum tomatoes
350g/12oz dried tagliatelle
salt and freshly ground black pepper

SERVES 4

1 Put the garlic, celery, sun-dried tomatoes and wine into a saucepan. Cook gently for 15 minutes, stirring occasionally.

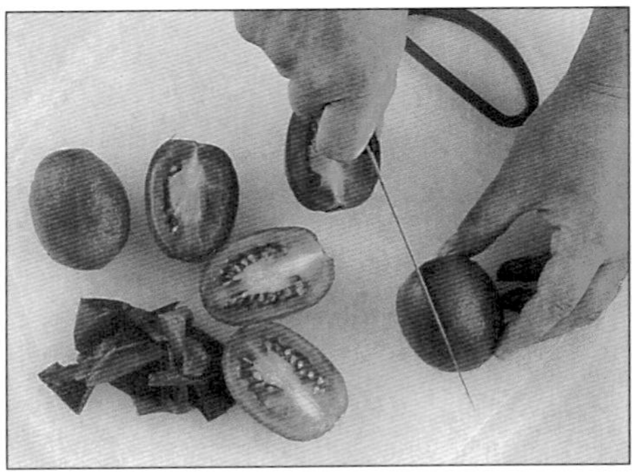

2 Meanwhile, plunge the plum tomatoes into a saucepan of boiling water for 1 minute, then into a saucepan of cold water. Drain, then slip off and discard their skins. Halve the tomatoes, remove and discard the seeds and cores and roughly chop the flesh.

3 Add the plum tomatoes to the saucepan, stir to mix and simmer for a further 5 minutes. Season to taste with salt and pepper.

4 Meanwhile, cook the tagliatelle in a large saucepan of boiling salted water for 8–10 minutes, or until tender or *al dente*. Drain well. Toss the cooked pasta with half the tomato sauce and serve on warmed plates, topped with the remaining tomato sauce.

NUTRITIONAL NOTES

Per portion:

Energy	357Kcals/1499kJ
Total fat	2.32g
Saturated fat	0.32g
Cholesterol	0mg
Fibre	5.09g

COOK'S TIP

Choose plain sun-dried tomatoes for this sauce, instead of those preserved in oil, which will increase the fat content of the dish.

SPAGHETTI WITH MIXED BEAN SAUCE

Mixed beans are flavoured with fresh chilli and garlic and cooked in a tomato sauce in this quick and easy pasta dish.

INGREDIENTS

1 onion, finely chopped
1–2 garlic cloves, crushed
1 large green chilli, deseeded and finely chopped
150ml/¼ pint/⅔ cup vegetable stock
400g/14oz can chopped tomatoes
30ml/2 tbsp tomato purée
120ml/4fl oz/½ cup red wine
5ml/1 tsp dried oregano
200g/7oz French beans, sliced
400g/14oz can red kidney beans, drained
400g/14oz can cannellini beans, drained
400g/14oz can chick-peas, drained
450g/1lb dried spaghetti
salt and freshly ground black pepper

SERVES 6

1 Put the onion, garlic and chilli into a non-stick saucepan with the stock. Bring to the boil and cook for 5 minutes until tender, stirring occasionally.

NUTRITIONAL NOTES

Per portion:

Energy	431Kcals/1811kJ
Total fat	3.6g
Saturated fat	0.2g
Cholesterol	0mg
Fibre	9.9g

2 Stir in the tomatoes, tomato purée, wine, oregano and seasoning. Bring to the boil, cover, then reduce the heat and simmer for 20 minutes, stirring the mixture occasionally.

3 Meanwhile, cook the French beans in a saucepan of boiling, salted water for about 5–6 minutes until tender. Drain the beans thoroughly.

4 Add all the beans and the chick-peas to the sauce, stir to mix and simmer for a further 10 minutes. Meanwhile, cook the spaghetti in a large saucepan of boiling salted water, according to the packet instructions, until tender or *al dente*. Drain thoroughly. Transfer the pasta to a serving dish and top with the bean sauce. Serve immediately.

TAGLIATELLE WITH BROCCOLI AND SPINACH

This is an excellent Italian vegetarian supper dish. It is nutritious, filling and low-fat and needs no accompaniment. If you like, you can use tagliatelle flecked with herbs.

2 Add salt to the water in the steamer and fill the steamer saucepan with boiling water, then add the pasta and cook, according to the packet instructions, until tender or *al dente*. Meanwhile, chop the broccoli and spinach in the colander.

INGREDIENTS

2 heads of broccoli
450g/1lb fresh spinach, stalks removed
freshly grated nutmeg
350g/12oz dried egg tagliatelle
15ml/1 tbsp extra virgin olive oil
juice of 1/2 lemon, or to taste
salt and freshly ground black pepper
15g/1/2oz grated fresh Parmesan cheese, to serve

SERVES 4

NUTRITIONAL NOTES

Per portion:

Energy	288Kcals/1218kJ
Total fat	4.9g
Saturated fat	1g
Cholesterol	1.9mg
Fibre	4.5g

1 Put the broccoli in the basket of a steamer, cover and steam over a saucepan of boiling water for 10 minutes. Add the spinach to the broccoli, cover and steam for 4–5 minutes or until both are tender. Towards the end of the cooking time, sprinkle the vegetables with freshly grated nutmeg and salt and pepper to taste. Transfer the vegetables to a colander and set aside.

3 Drain the pasta. Heat the oil in the pasta pan, add the pasta and chopped vegetables and toss over a medium heat until evenly mixed. Sprinkle in the lemon juice and plenty of black pepper, then taste and add more lemon juice, salt and nutmeg if you like. Serve immediately, sprinkled with freshly grated Parmesan and black pepper.

VARIATION

If you like, add a sprinkling of crushed dried chillies with the black pepper in Step 3.

PENNE WITH GREEN VEGETABLE SAUCE

Lightly cooked fresh green vegetables are tossed with pasta to create this low-fat Italian dish, ideal for a light lunch or supper.

INGREDIENTS

2 carrots
1 courgette
75g/3oz French beans
1 small leek, washed
2 ripe Italian plum tomatoes
1 handful of fresh flat leaf parsley
15ml/1 tbsp extra virgin olive oil
2.5ml/½ tsp sugar
115g/4oz/1 cup frozen peas
350g/12oz/3 cups dried penne
salt and freshly ground black pepper

SERVES 4

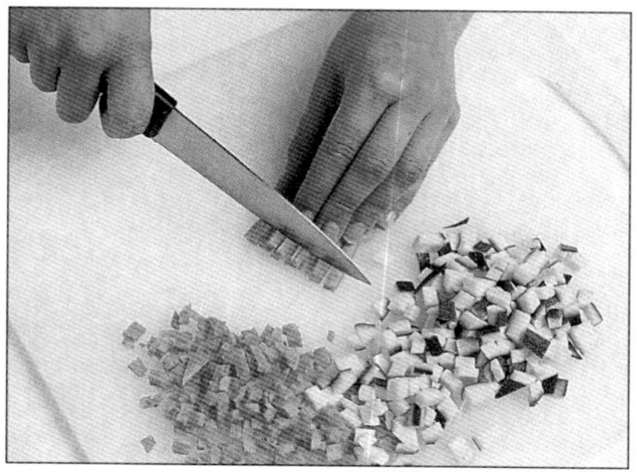

1 Dice the carrots and the courgette finely. Top and tail the French beans, then cut them into 2cm/¾in lengths. Slice the leek thinly. Skin and dice the tomatoes. Finely chop the parsley and set aside.

2 Heat the oil in a medium frying pan or saucepan. Add the carrots and leek. Sprinkle the sugar over and cook, stirring frequently, for about 5 minutes.

3 Stir in the courgette, French beans, peas and plenty of salt and pepper. Cover and cook over a low to medium heat for 5–8 minutes until the vegetables are tender, stirring occasionally.

4 Meanwhile, cook the pasta in a large saucepan of boiling salted water, according to the packet instructions, until it is tender or *al dente*. Drain the pasta well and keep it hot until it is ready to serve.

5 Stir the parsley and chopped plum tomatoes into the vegetable mixture and adjust the seasoning to taste. Toss with the cooked pasta and serve at once.

NUTRITIONAL NOTES

Per portion:

Energy	328Kcals/1392kJ
Total fat	4.5g
Saturated fat	0.7g
Cholesterol	0mg
Fibre	5g

PAPPARDELLE AND SUMMER VEGETABLE SAUCE

A delicious low-fat sauce of tomatoes and fresh vegetables adds colour and robust flavour to pasta in this tasty Italian-style dish.

INGREDIENTS

2 small red onions, peeled, root left intact
150ml/1/4 pint/2/3 cup vegetable stock
1–2 garlic cloves, crushed
60ml/4 tbsp red wine
2 courgettes, cut into fingers
1 yellow pepper, deseeded and sliced
400g/14oz can tomatoes
10ml/2 tsp chopped fresh thyme
5ml/1 tsp caster sugar
350g/12oz dried pappardelle
salt and freshly ground black pepper
fresh thyme and 6 black olives, stoned and roughly chopped, to garnish

SERVES 4

1 Cut each onion into eight wedges through the root end, to hold them together during cooking. Put into a saucepan with the stock and garlic. Bring to the boil, cover then reduce the heat and simmer for 5 minutes, until tender.

2 Add the wine, courgettes, yellow pepper, tomatoes, chopped thyme and sugar. Season with salt and pepper and stir to mix. Bring to the boil and cook gently for 5–7 minutes, shaking the pan occasionally to coat the vegetables with the sauce. (Do not overcook the vegetables as they are much nicer if they are slightly crunchy.)

3 Meanwhile, cook the pasta in a large saucepan of boiling salted water, according to the packet instructions, until tender or *al dente*. Drain thoroughly.

NUTRITIONAL NOTES

Per portion:

Energy	334Kcals/1426kJ
Total fat	2.1g
Saturated fat	0.3g
Cholesterol	0mg
Fibre	4g

4 Transfer the pasta to a warmed serving dish and top with the vegetables. Garnish with fresh thyme and chopped black olives and serve immediately.

PASTA PRIMAVERA

You can use any mixture of fresh, young spring vegetables to make this delicately flavoured low-fat pasta dish, ideal for a quick and tasty supper.

INGREDIENTS

225g/8oz thin asparagus spears, chopped in half
115g/4oz mangetouts, topped and tailed
115g/4oz baby sweetcorn
225g/8oz whole baby carrots, trimmed
1 small red pepper, deseeded and chopped
8 spring onions, sliced
225g/8oz dried torchietti or other pasta shapes
150ml/1/4 pint/2/3 cup low-fat cottage cheese
150ml/1/4 pint/2/3 cup low-fat yogurt
15ml/1 tbsp lemon juice
15ml/1 tbsp chopped fresh parsley
15ml/1 tbsp snipped fresh chives
skimmed milk (optional)
salt and freshly ground black pepper
sun-dried tomato bread, to serve

SERVES 4

1 Cook the asparagus spears in a saucepan of boiling, salted water for 3–4 minutes. Add the mangetouts halfway through the cooking time. Drain and rinse both under cold water to stop further cooking. Set aside.

2 Cook the baby corn, carrots, red pepper and spring onions in the same way in a saucepan of boiling salted water until tender. Drain, rinse and set aside.

3 Meanwhile, cook the pasta in a large saucepan of boiling salted water, according to the packet instructions, until tender or *al dente*. Drain thoroughly and keep hot.

4 Put the cottage cheese, yogurt, lemon juice, parsley, chives and seasoning into a blender or food processor and blend until smooth. Thin the sauce with a little skimmed milk, if necessary. Put the sauce into a large saucepan with the cooked pasta and vegetables, heat gently and toss carefully to mix. Serve at once with sun-dried tomato breadsticks.

NUTRITIONAL NOTES

Per portion:

Energy	320Kcals/1344kJ
Total fat	3.1g
Saturated fat	0.4g
Cholesterol	3mg
Fibre	6.2g

LENTIL BOLOGNESE

Served with cooked spaghetti, this delicious lentil Bolognese sauce provides an excellent low-fat pasta dish for all vegetarians.

INGREDIENTS

15ml/1 tbsp olive oil
1 onion, chopped
2 garlic cloves, crushed
2 carrots, coarsely grated
2 celery sticks, chopped
115g/4oz/2/3 cup red lentils
400g/14oz can chopped tomatoes
30ml/2 tbsp tomato purée
450ml/3/4 pint/scant 2 cups stock
15ml/1 tbsp chopped fresh marjoram, or 5ml/1 tsp dried marjoram
450g/1lb dried spaghetti
salt and freshly ground black pepper

SERVES 6

1 Heat the oil in a large saucepan, add the onion, garlic, carrots and celery and cook gently for about 5 minutes, until the vegetables are soft, stirring occasionally.

2 Add the lentils, tomatoes, tomato purée, stock, marjoram and seasoning and stir to mix.

3 Bring the mixture to the boil, then partially cover with a lid, reduce the heat and simmer for about 20 minutes until thick and soft, stirring occasionally.

4 Meanwhile, cook the pasta in a large saucepan of boiling salted water, according to the packet instructions, until tender or *al dente*. Drain well.

5 Serve the cooked pasta on warmed serving plates, with the lentil sauce spooned on top.

NUTRITIONAL NOTES

Per portion:

Energy	335Kcals/1423kJ
Total fat	3.4g
Saturated fat	0.4g
Cholesterol	3.9mg
Fibre	0g

TAGLIATELLE WITH HAZELNUT PESTO

Hazelnuts add a delicious flavour to this reduced-fat alternative to the classic Italian pesto sauce. Serve with cooked pasta such as tagliatelle or fettucine.

2 Cook the tagliatelle in a large saucepan of boiling salted water, according to the packet instructions, until tender or *al dente*, then drain well.

3 Add the pesto sauce to the hot pasta, tossing together until well mixed. Sprinkle with pepper and serve hot.

INGREDIENTS

2 garlic cloves, crushed
25g/1oz/1 cup fresh basil leaves
25g/1oz/¼ cup hazelnuts
200g/7oz/⅞ cup skimmed milk soft cheese
225g/8oz dried tagliatelle, or 450g/1lb fresh
salt and freshly ground black pepper

SERVES 4

1 Place the garlic, basil, hazelnuts and soft cheese in a blender or food processor and blend to a thick paste. Set aside.

NUTRITIONAL NOTES

Per portion:

Energy	227Kcals/960kJ
Total fat	4.7g
Saturated fat	0.7g
Cholesterol	2.1mg
Fibre	1.7g

PASTA WITH TOMATO AND CHILLI SAUCE

This is a speciality of Lazio. In Italian it is called *pasta all'arrabbiata* – the word *arrabbiata* means rabid or angry, and describes the heat that comes from the chilli.

INGREDIENTS

500g/1¼lb sugocasa
2 garlic cloves, crushed
150ml/¼ pint/⅔ cup dry white wine
15ml/1 tbsp sun-dried tomato purée
1 fresh red chilli
300g/11oz dried penne or tortiglioni
60ml/4 tbsp finely chopped fresh flat leaf parsley
salt and freshly ground black pepper
15g/½oz grated fresh Pecorino cheese, to serve

SERVES 4

1 Put the sugocasa, garlic, wine, tomato purée and whole chilli in a saucepan and bring to the boil. Cover, reduce the heat and simmer gently, stirring occasionally.

2 Drop the pasta into a large saucepan of rapidly boiling salted water and simmer for 10–12 minutes or until tender or *al dente*.

3 Remove the chilli from the sauce and add half the parsley. Add seasoning to taste. If you prefer a hotter taste, finely chop some or all of the chilli and return it to the sauce.

4 Drain the pasta and tip it into a warmed serving bowl. Pour the sauce over the pasta and toss to mix. Serve at once, sprinkled with a little grated Pecorino cheese and the remaining parsley.

NUTRITIONAL NOTES

Per portion:

Energy	287Kcals/1220kJ
Total fat	2.1g
Saturated fat	0.7g
Cholesterol	2.2mg
Fibre	3g

PENNE WITH ARTICHOKES

Artichokes are a very popular vegetable in Italy, and are often used in sauces for pasta. This sauce is garlicky and richly flavoured, perfect for a delicious light lunch or supper.

INGREDIENTS

juice of 1/2–1 lemon
2 globe artichokes
15ml/1 tbsp olive oil
1 small fennel bulb, thinly sliced, with feathery tops reserved
1 onion, finely chopped
4 garlic cloves, finely chopped
1 handful of fresh flat leaf parsley, roughly chopped
400g/14oz can chopped Italian plum tomatoes
150ml/1/4 pint/2/3 cup dry white wine
350g/12oz/3 cups dried penne
10ml/2 tsp capers, chopped
salt and freshly ground black pepper

SERVES 6

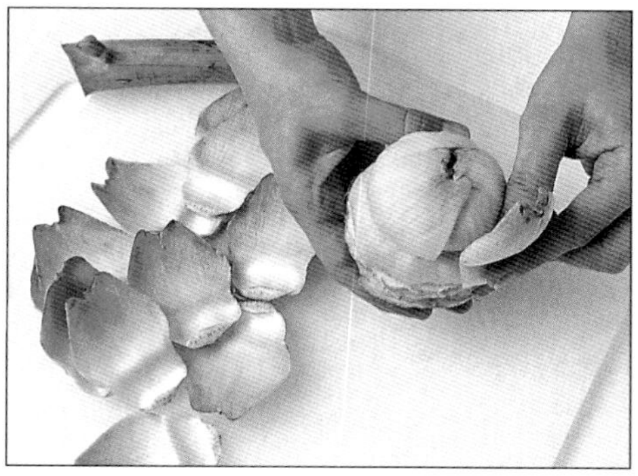

1 Have ready a bowl of cold water to which you have added the juice of half a lemon. Cut off the artichoke stalks, then discard the outer leaves until the pale inner leaves that are almost white at the base remain.

2 Cut off the tops of these leaves so that the base remains. Cut the base in half lengthways, then prise the hairy choke out of the centre with the tip of the knife and discard. Cut the artichokes lengthways into 5mm/1/4in slices, adding them immediately to the bowl of water.

3 Bring a large saucepan of water to the boil. Add a good pinch of salt, then drain the artichokes and add them immediately to the water. Boil for 5 minutes, drain and set aside.

4 Heat the oil in a large frying pan or saucepan and add the fennel, onion, garlic and parsley. Cook over a low to medium heat, stirring frequently, for about 10 minutes until the fennel has softened and is lightly coloured.

5 Add the tomatoes and wine, with salt and pepper to taste. Bring to the boil, stirring, then cover, reduce the heat and simmer for 10–15 minutes, stirring occasionally. Stir in the artichokes, replace the lid and simmer for a further 10 minutes.

6 Meanwhile, cook the pasta in a large saucepan of water, according to the packet instructions. Drain, reserving a little cooking water. Stir the capers into the sauce, then adjust the seasoning and add the remaining lemon juice if you like.

7 Tip the pasta into a warmed serving bowl, pour the sauce over and mix, adding a little cooking water if necessary. Serve, garnished with fennel fronds.

NUTRITIONAL NOTES

Per portion:

Energy	269Kcals/1140kJ
Total fat	3g
Saturated fat	0.4g
Cholesterol	0mg
Fibre	2.7g

CHIFFERI RIGATI WITH AUBERGINE SAUCE

Full of flavour, this excellent Italian vegetarian sauce goes well with any short pasta shape, such as chifferi rigati or penne, to create an appetizing lunch or supper dish.

INGREDIENTS

30ml/2 tbsp olive oil
1 small fresh red chilli
2 garlic cloves
2 handfuls of fresh flat leaf parsley
450g/1lb aubergines, roughly chopped
1 handful of fresh basil leaves
200ml/7fl oz/scant 1 cup water
1 vegetable stock cube
8 ripe Italian plum tomatoes, skinned and finely chopped
60ml/4 tbsp red wine
5ml/1 tsp sugar
1 sachet saffron powder
2.5ml/½ tsp ground paprika
450g/1lb dried short pasta such as chifferi rigati or penne
salt and freshly ground black pepper

SERVES 6

1 Heat the oil in a large frying pan or saucepan and add the whole chilli and whole garlic cloves. Roughly chop the parsley and add half to the pan. Smash the garlic cloves with a wooden spoon to release their juice, then cover the pan and cook the mixture over a low to medium heat for about 10 minutes, stirring occasionally.

2 Remove and discard the chilli. Add the aubergines to the pan with the remaining parsley and all the basil. Pour in half the water. Crumble in the stock cube and stir until it is dissolved, then cover and cook, stirring frequently, for about 10 minutes.

3 Add the tomatoes, wine, sugar, saffron and paprika, with salt and pepper to taste, then pour in the remaining water. Stir well, replace the lid and cook for a further 30–40 minutes, stirring occasionally. Adjust the seasoning to taste.

4 Meanwhile, cook the pasta in a large saucepan of boiling salted water, according to the packet instructions, until tender or *al dente*. Drain well.

5 Add the aubergine sauce to the cooked pasta, toss together to ensure it is thoroughly mixed and serve immediately.

NUTRITIONAL NOTES

Per portion:

Energy	300Kcals/1274kJ
Total fat	3.6g
Saturated fat	0.6g
Cholesterol	0mg
Fibre	4.1g

RIGATONI WITH WINTER TOMATO SAUCE

In winter, when fresh tomatoes are not at their best, this is the sauce the Italians make. Try to use good-quality canned plum tomatoes from Italy.

INGREDIENTS

1 onion
1 carrot
1 celery stick
15ml/1 tbsp olive oil
1 garlic clove, thinly sliced
a few leaves each of fresh basil, thyme and oregano or marjoram, plus extra to garnish (optional)
2 × 400g/14oz cans chopped Italian plum tomatoes
15ml/1 tbsp sun-dried tomato purée
5ml/1 tsp sugar
about 90ml/6 tbsp dry red or white wine (optional)
350g/12oz/3 cups dried rigatoni
salt and freshly ground black pepper
15g/½oz coarsely shaved fresh Parmesan cheese, to serve (optional)

SERVES 4

1 Chop the onion, carrot and celery finely, either in a food processor or by hand.

2 Heat the oil in a medium saucepan, add the garlic slices and stir over a very low heat for 1–2 minutes.

3 Add the chopped vegetables and the fresh herbs. Cook over a low heat, stirring frequently, for 5–7 minutes until the vegetables have softened and have become lightly coloured.

4 Add the canned tomatoes, tomato purée and sugar, then stir in the wine, if using. Add salt and pepper to taste. Bring to the boil, stirring, then reduce the heat to a gentle simmer. Cook, uncovered, for about 45 minutes, stirring occasionally.

5 Meanwhile, cook the pasta in a large saucepan of boiling salted water, according to the packet instructions, until tender or *al dente*. Drain the pasta and tip it into a warmed bowl. Taste the sauce and adjust the seasoning. Pour the sauce over the pasta and toss well to mix. Serve immediately, with shavings of Parmesan handed separately, if using. If you like, garnish with extra chopped fresh herbs.

NUTRITIONAL NOTES

Per portion:

Energy	351Kcals/1491kJ
Total fat	4.4g
Saturated fat	0.6g
Cholesterol	0mg
Fibre	4g

FUSILLI WITH TOMATO AND BALSAMIC VINEGAR

The intense, sweet-and-sour flavour of balsamic vinegar gives a pleasant kick to this sauce made with canned tomatoes. It makes an appetizing low-fat pasta meal.

INGREDIENTS

2 × 400g/14oz cans chopped Italian plum tomatoes
2 pieces of drained sun-dried tomatoes in olive oil, thinly sliced
2 garlic cloves, crushed
15ml/1 tbsp olive oil
5ml/1 tsp sugar
350g/12oz/3 cups dried fusilli
45ml/3 tbsp balsamic vinegar
salt and freshly ground black pepper
15g/½oz coarsely shaved fresh Pecorino cheese and rocket salad, to serve (optional)

SERVES 4

1 Put the canned and sun-dried tomatoes in a medium saucepan with the garlic, olive oil and sugar. Add salt and pepper to taste. Bring to the boil, stirring. Reduce the heat and simmer for about 30 minutes until reduced, stirring the mixture occasionally.

2 Meanwhile, cook the pasta in a large saucepan of boiling salted water, according to the packet instructions, until tender or *al dente*.

3 Add the balsamic vinegar to the tomato sauce and stir to mix evenly. Cook for 1–2 minutes then remove from the heat and adjust the seasoning to taste.

4 Drain the pasta and turn it into a warmed bowl. Pour the sauce over the cooked pasta and toss well to mix. Serve immediately, with the rocket salad and shaved Pecorino handed round separately, if using.

VARIATION

The flavour of carrots goes well with balsamic vinegar. Try adding some fine batons to the saucepan with the tomatoes and garlic in Step 1.

NUTRITIONAL NOTES

Per portion:

Energy	360Kcals/1531kJ
Total fat	4.5g
Saturated fat	0.6g
Cholesterol	0mg
Fibre	4.1g

SPAGHETTI WITH FRESH TOMATO SAUCE

This is the famous Neapolitan sauce from Italy that is made in summer when tomatoes are very ripe and sweet. Spaghetti is the traditional choice of pasta for a low-fat, flavourful Italian meal.

INGREDIENTS

675g/1½lb ripe Italian plum tomatoes
15ml/1 tbsp olive oil
1 onion, finely chopped
350g/12oz dried spaghetti
1 small handful of fresh basil leaves
salt and freshly ground black pepper
15g/½oz coarsely shaved fresh Parmesan cheese, to serve

SERVES 4

1 With a sharp knife, cut a cross in the bottom (flower) end of each tomato. Bring a medium saucepan of water to the boil and remove from the heat. Plunge a few of the tomatoes into the water, leave for 30 seconds or so, then lift them out with a slotted spoon. Repeat the process with the remaining tomatoes, then peel off and discard the skins and roughly chop the flesh. Set aside.

2 Heat the oil in a large saucepan, add the onion and cook over a low heat, stirring frequently, for about 5 minutes until softened and lightly coloured. Add the tomatoes, with salt and pepper to taste. Bring to a gentle boil then cover the pan, reduce the heat and simmer for 30–40 minutes, stirring occasionally, until thick.

3 Meanwhile, cook the pasta in a large saucepan of boiling salted water, according to the packet instructions, until tender or *al dente*. Shred the fresh basil leaves finely.

4 Remove the sauce from the heat, stir in the basil and adjust the seasoning to taste. Drain the pasta, tip it into a warmed bowl, pour the sauce over and toss well to mix. Serve immediately, with a little shaved Parmesan handed separately.

NUTRITIONAL NOTES

Per portion:

Energy	330Kcals/1399kJ
Total fat	5g
Saturated fat	1.1g
Cholesterol	2.2mg
Fibre	4.05g

PASTA WITH CHICK-PEA SAUCE

This is a delicious, and very speedy, low-fat Italian-style dish, ideal for an appetizing lunch or supper.

Ingredients

450g/1lb dried penne or other dried pasta shapes
10ml/2 tsp olive oil
1 onion, thinly sliced
1 red pepper, deseeded and sliced
400g/14oz can chopped tomatoes
425g/15oz can chick-peas
30ml/2 tbsp dry vermouth (optional)
5ml/1 tsp dried oregano
1 large bay leaf
30ml/2 tbsp capers
salt and freshly ground black pepper
fresh oregano sprigs, to garnish

Serves 6

1 Cook the pasta in a large saucepan of boiling salted water, according to the packet instructions, until tender or *al dente*. Drain and keep hot. Meanwhile, heat the olive oil in a large saucepan and gently fry the sliced onion and pepper for about 5 minutes, stirring occasionally, until softened.

2 Add the tomatoes, chick-peas with their liquid, vermouth, if using, herbs and capers and stir well to mix.

3 Season to taste with salt and pepper and bring to the boil, then reduce the heat and simmer for about 10 minutes, stirring occasionally. Remove and discard the bay leaf. Add the hot pasta to the sauce, toss to mix and serve hot, garnished with fresh oregano sprigs.

Cook's Tip

Choose whatever pasta shapes you like, although hollow shapes, such as penne (quills) or shells are particularly good with this sauce.

Nutritional Notes

Per portion:

Energy	372Kcals/1579kJ
Total fat	4.9g
Saturated fat	0.6g
Cholesterol	0mg
Fibre	6g

TAGLIATELLE WITH MUSHROOMS

Freshly cooked tagliatelle is tossed with a flavourful mixed mushroom sauce, to create this very tasty, low-fat pasta dish.

Ingredients

1 small onion, finely chopped
2 garlic cloves, crushed
150ml/¼ pint/⅔ cup vegetable stock
225g/8oz mixed fresh mushrooms, such as field, chestnut, oyster or chanterelle
60ml/4 tbsp white or red wine
10ml/2 tsp tomato purée
15ml/1 tbsp soy sauce
5ml/1 tsp chopped fresh thyme
30ml/2 tbsp chopped fresh parsley, plus extra to garnish
225g/8oz fresh sun-dried tomato and herb tagliatelle
salt and freshly ground black pepper
15g/½oz shaved fresh Parmesan cheese, to serve (optional)

Serves 4

1 Put the onion and garlic into a saucepan with the vegetable stock, then cover and cook for 5 minutes or until tender, stirring occasionally.

2 Add the mushrooms (quartered or sliced if large; left whole if small), wine, tomato purée and soy sauce. Cover and cook for 5 minutes, stirring occasionally.

3 Remove the lid from the pan and boil until the liquid has reduced by half, stirring occasionally. Stir in the chopped fresh herbs and season to taste with salt and pepper.

4 Meanwhile, cook the fresh pasta in a large saucepan of boiling, salted water for 2–5 minutes, until tender or *al dente*. Drain thoroughly, then toss the pasta lightly with the mushroom sauce. Serve, garnished with parsley and shavings of Parmesan cheese, if you like.

Nutritional Notes

Per portion:

Energy	241Kcals/1010kJ
Total fat	2.4g
Saturated fat	0.7g
Cholesterol	45mg
Fibre	3g

MUSHROOM BOLOGNESE

A quick – and exceedingly tasty – vegetarian version of the classic Italian dish. This dish is easy to prepare and makes a very satisfying low-fat meal.

INGREDIENTS

450g/1lb mushrooms
15ml/1 tbsp olive oil
1 onion, chopped
1 garlic clove, crushed
15ml/1 tbsp tomato purée
400g/14oz can chopped tomatoes
45ml/3 tbsp chopped fresh oregano
450g/1lb fresh pasta, such as spaghetti or tagliatelle
salt and freshly ground black pepper
15g/½oz shaved fresh Parmesan cheese, to serve (optional)

SERVES 4

1 Trim the mushroom stems neatly, then cut each mushroom into quarters. Set them aside.

2 Heat the olive oil in a large pan. Add the onion and garlic and cook them for 2–3 minutes, stirring occasionally.

3 Add the prepared mushrooms to the pan and mix them gently with the olive oil and crushed garlic. Cook over a high heat for about 3–4 minutes, stirring the mixture occasionally.

4 Stir in the tomato purée, chopped tomatoes and 15ml/1 tbsp of the oregano. Cover, reduce the heat, then cook for about 5 minutes, stirring occasionally.

5 Meanwhile, bring a large saucepan of salted water to the boil. Cook the pasta in the boiling water for 2–3 minutes, or according to the packet instructions, until tender or *al dente*.

6 Season the mushroom Bolognese sauce with salt and pepper. Drain the pasta, turn it into a bowl and add the mushroom mixture. Toss to mix well. Serve in individual bowls, topped with shavings of fresh Parmesan, if using, and the remaining chopped fresh oregano.

COOK'S TIP

If you prefer to use dried pasta, make this the first thing that you cook. It will take 10–12 minutes to cook, during which time you can make the mushroom mixture. Use 350g/12oz dried pasta.

NUTRITIONAL NOTES

Per portion:

Energy	404Kcals/1717kJ
Total fat	4.9g
Saturated fat	0.6g
Cholesterol	0mg
Fibre	5g

TAGLIATELLE WITH SPINACH GNOCCHI

Italian-style gnocchi are extremely smooth and light and make a delicious accompaniment to this flavourful low-fat pasta dish.

INGREDIENTS

450g/1lb mixed flavoured fresh tagliatelle
15g/½oz shaved fresh Parmesan cheese, to garnish (optional)

FOR THE SPINACH GNOCCHI

450g/1lb frozen chopped spinach
1 small onion, finely chopped
1 garlic clove, crushed
1.5ml/¼ tsp ground nutmeg
400g/14oz low-fat cottage cheese
115g/4oz dried white breadcrumbs
75g/3oz semolina or plain flour
50g/2oz grated fresh Parmesan cheese
3 egg whites

FOR THE TOMATO SAUCE

1 onion, finely chopped
1 celery stick, finely chopped
1 red pepper, deseeded and diced
1 garlic clove, crushed
150ml/¼ pint/⅔ cup vegetable stock
400g/14oz can tomatoes
15ml/1 tbsp tomato purée
10ml/2 tsp caster sugar
5ml/1 tsp dried oregano
salt and freshly ground black pepper

SERVES 6

1 To make the tomato sauce, put the onion, celery, pepper and garlic into a non-stick saucepan. Add the stock, bring to the boil and cook for 5 minutes or until tender, stirring occasionally.

2 Stir in the tomatoes, tomato purée, sugar and oregano. Season to taste, bring to the boil, then reduce the heat and simmer for 30 minutes until thick, stirring occasionally. Keep hot.

3 Meanwhile, make the gnocchi. Put the spinach, onion and garlic into a saucepan, cover and cook until the spinach is defrosted. Remove the lid for a minute or so, and increase the heat. Cook until the liquid has evaporated. Season with salt, pepper and nutmeg. Turn into a bowl and leave to cool. Mix in the remaining gnocchi ingredients. Shape into about 30 ovals and refrigerate for 30 minutes.

4 Cook the spinach gnocchi in a large saucepan of boiling salted water for about 5 minutes. Remove with a slotted spoon and drain. Keep hot. Meanwhile, cook the tagliatelle in a large saucepan of boiling salted water, according to the packet instructions, until tender or *al dente*. Drain well. Transfer the pasta to serving plates, top with the gnocchi, the tomato sauce and shavings of Parmesan cheese, if using. Serve immediately.

NUTRITIONAL NOTES

Per portion:

Energy	189Kcals/803kJ
Total fat	2g
Saturated fat	0.8g
Cholesterol	3.3mg
Fibre	2.9g

RATATOUILLE PENNE BAKE

Mixed Mediterranean vegetables and penne are tossed together and grilled until lightly toasted to create this delicious and low-fat pasta meal.

INGREDIENTS

1 small aubergine
2 courgettes, thickly sliced
200g/7oz firm tofu, cubed
45ml/3 tbsp dark soy sauce
2–3 garlic cloves, crushed
10ml/2 tsp sesame seeds
1 small red pepper, deseeded and sliced
1 onion, finely chopped
150ml/¼ pint/⅔ cup vegetable stock
3 firm ripe tomatoes, skinned, deseeded and quartered
15ml/1 tbsp chopped fresh mixed herbs
225g/8oz dried penne
salt and freshly ground black pepper
crusty bread, to serve

SERVES 6

1 Wash and cut the aubergine into 2.5cm/1in cubes. Put into a colander with the courgettes, sprinkle with salt and leave to drain for 30 minutes. Rinse thoroughly, drain and set aside.

2 Mix the tofu with the soy sauce, 1 crushed garlic clove and the sesame seeds. Cover and leave to marinate for 30 minutes.

NUTRITIONAL NOTES

Per portion:

Energy	208Kcals/873kJ
Total fat	3.7g
Saturated fat	0.5g
Cholesterol	0mg
Fibre	3.9g

3 Put the aubergine, courgettes, pepper, onion and remaining garlic into a saucepan, with the stock. Bring to the boil, cover and cook for about 10 minutes until tender, stirring occasionally. Remove the lid and boil until all the stock has evaporated. Add the prepared tomatoes and herbs and cook for a further 3 minutes, stirring occasionally. Season to taste with salt and pepper.

4 Meanwhile cook the pasta in a large saucepan of boiling salted water, according to the packet instructions, until tender or *al dente*. Drain thoroughly. Toss the pasta with the vegetable mixture, the tofu and the marinade. Transfer to a shallow 25cm/10in square ovenproof dish and cook under a hot grill until lightly toasted. Transfer the bake to a serving dish and serve immediately with fresh crusty bread.

BREADS

It's hard to beat the AROMA *of freshly baked bread and once you've mastered the basic techniques it's* EASY *to make your own* BREAD. *We bring you a selection of Italian breads ideal for breakfast, brunch or a picnic* al fresco. *Choose from traditional* CIABATTA *and Focaccia breads, Olive and Oregano Bread, Sun-dried* TOMATO *Breadsticks or, for a slightly sweet bread, try the tempting Italian* CHOCOLATE *Bread.*

CIABATTA

This irregular-shaped Italian bread is so called because it looks like an old shoe or slipper. It is made with a wet dough flavoured with olive oil, and is a great accompaniment to low-fat dishes.

Ingredients

For the biga starter

10g/¼oz fresh yeast
175–200ml/6–7fl oz/scant 1 cup lukewarm water
350g/12oz/3 cups unbleached plain flour, plus extra for dusting

For the dough

15g/½oz fresh yeast
400ml/14fl oz/1⅔ cups lukewarm water
60ml/4 tbsp lukewarm semi-skimmed milk
500g/1¼lb/5 cups unbleached strong white bread flour
10ml/2 tsp salt
45ml/3 tbsp extra virgin olive oil

Makes 3 loaves, Serves 12

1 In a small bowl, cream the yeast for the biga starter with a little of the water. Sift the flour into a bowl. Gradually mix in the yeast mixture and enough of the remaining water to form a firm dough.

2 Turn out the biga starter dough on to a lightly floured surface and knead for about 5 minutes until smooth. Return the dough to the bowl, cover with lightly oiled clear film and leave in a warm place for 12–15 hours, or until the dough has risen and is starting to collapse.

3 Sprinkle three baking sheets with flour and set aside. Mix the yeast for the dough with a little of the water until creamy, then mix in the remaining water. Add the yeast mixture to the biga and mix well. Mix in the milk, beating thoroughly with a wooden spoon. Mix in the flour by hand for 15 minutes, lifting the dough, to form a very wet mixture.

4 Beat in the salt and olive oil. Cover with lightly oiled clear film and leave to rise, in a warm place, for 1½–2 hours, or until doubled in bulk.

5 Using a spoon, tip one-third of the dough at a time on to each prepared baking sheet, trying to avoid knocking back the dough in the process.

6 Using floured hands, shape into oblong loaves, about 2.5cm/1in thick. Flatten slightly. Sprinkle with flour and leave to rise in a warm place for 30 minutes. Meanwhile, preheat the oven to 220°C/425°F/Gas 7. Bake the loaves for 25–30 minutes or until golden brown. Transfer to a wire rack to cool.

Nutritional Notes

Per portion:

Energy	268Kcals/1137kJ
Total fat	3.7g
Saturated fat	0.6g
Cholesterol	0.4mg
Fibre	2.2g

OLIVE OIL BREAD ROLLS

The Italians adore interesting and elaborately shaped rolls. This distinctively flavoured bread dough, enriched with olive oil, can be used for making rolls or shaped as one large loaf.

INGREDIENTS

450g/1lb/4 cups unbleached strong white bread flour
10ml/2 tsp salt
15g/½oz fresh yeast
250ml/8fl oz/1 cup lukewarm water
60ml/4 tbsp extra virgin olive oil, plus 15ml/1 tbsp extra for brushing

MAKES 16 ROLLS

1 Lightly oil three baking sheets and set aside. Sift the flour and salt together in a large bowl and make a well in the centre. In a jug, cream the yeast with half the water, then stir in the rest. Add to the well with the oil and mix to form a dough. Turn on to a lightly floured surface. Knead for 8–10 minutes until smooth and elastic. Place in an oiled bowl, cover with oiled clear film and let rise, in a warm place, for 1 hour, or until nearly doubled in bulk.

2 Turn out on to a lightly floured surface and knock back. Divide into 12 equal pieces of dough and shape into rolls as described in Steps 3, 4 and 5.

3 For *tavalli* (spiral rolls): roll each piece into a strip about 30cm/12in long and 4cm/1½in wide. Twist into a loose spiral and join the ends to make a circle. Place on the baking sheets, well spaced. Lightly brush with oil, cover with oiled clear film and leave to rise, in a warm place, for 20–30 minutes.

NUTRITIONAL NOTES

Per portion:

Energy	119Kcals/503kJ
Total fat	3.1g
Saturated fat	0.4g
Cholesterol	0mg
Fibre	0.9g

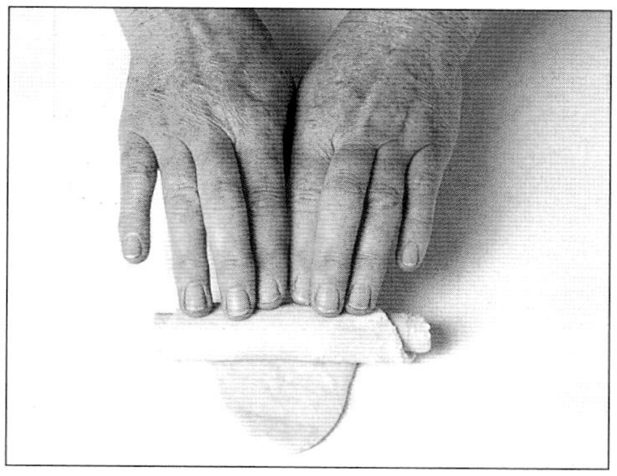

4 For *filoncini* (finger rolls): flatten each piece into an oval and roll to 23cm/9in without changing the shape. Make it 5cm/2in wide at one end and 10cm/4in at the other. Roll up from the wider end. Stretch to 20–23cm/8–9in long. Cut in half. Place on the baking sheets, well spaced. Lightly brush with oil, cover with oiled clear film and leave to rise, in a warm place, for 20–30 minutes.

5 For *carciofi* (artichoke-shaped rolls): shape each piece into a ball and space well apart on the baking sheets. Brush with oil, cover with oiled clear film and let rise, in a warm place, for 20–30 minutes. Preheat the oven to 200°C/400°F/Gas 6. Using scissors, snip 5mm/¼in deep cuts in a circle on the top of each roll, then five larger horizontal cuts around the sides. Bake all the rolls for 15 minutes. Transfer to a wire rack to cool. Serve warm or cold.

TUSCANY BREAD

This bread from Tuscany is made without salt and probably originates from the days when salt was heavily taxed. To compensate for the lack of salt, serve with salty foods such as olives.

INGREDIENTS

500g/1¼lb/5 cups unbleached strong white flour
350ml/12fl oz/1½ cups boiling water
15g/½oz fresh yeast
60ml/4 tbsp lukewarm water

MAKES 1 LOAF, SERVES 8

1 First make the starter. Sift 175g/6oz/1½ cups of the flour into a large bowl. Pour over the boiling water, leave for a couple of minutes, then mix well. Cover the bowl with a damp dish towel and leave for 10 hours.

2 Lightly flour a baking sheet and set aside. In a bowl, cream the yeast with the lukewarm water. Mix well into the starter.

3 Gradually add the remaining flour and mix to form a dough. Turn out on to a lightly floured surface and knead for 5–8 minutes until smooth and elastic.

4 Place in a lightly oiled bowl, cover with lightly oiled clear film and leave to rise, in a warm place, for 1–1½ hours, or until doubled in bulk.

NUTRITIONAL NOTES

Per portion:

Energy	213Kcals/906kJ
Total fat	0.8g
Saturated fat	0.1g
Cholesterol	0mg
Fibre	1.9g

5 Turn the dough out on to a lightly floured surface, knock back, and shape into a round.

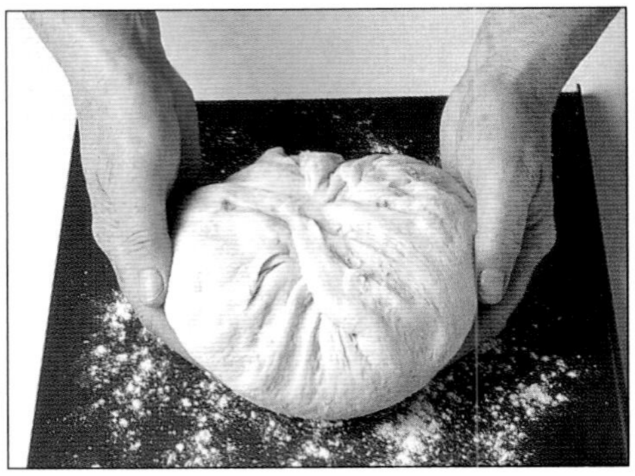

6 Fold the sides of the round into the centre and seal. Place seam side up on the prepared baking sheet. Cover with oiled clear film and leave to rise, in a warm place, for 30–45 minutes, or until doubled in bulk.

7 Flatten the loaf to about half its risen height and flip over. Cover with a large upturned bowl and leave to rise again, in a warm place, for 30 minutes.

8 Meanwhile, preheat the oven to 220°C/425°F/Gas 7. Slash the top of the loaf, using a sharp knife, if wished. Bake for 30–35 minutes, or until golden. Transfer to a wire rack to cool. Serve in slices or wedges.

POLENTA BREAD

Polenta is widely used in Italian cooking. Here it is combined with pine nuts to make a truly Italian bread with a fantastic flavour. Serve in slices topped with mixed salad and low-fat cheese.

INGREDIENTS

50g/2oz/1/3 cup polenta
300ml/1/2 pint/1 1/4 cups luke-warm water
15g/1/2oz fresh yeast
2.5ml/1/2 tsp clear honey
225g/8oz/2 cups unbleached strong white bread flour
25g/1oz/2 tbsp butter
30ml/2 tbsp pine nuts
7.5ml/1 1/2 tsp salt

FOR THE TOPPING

1 egg yolk
15ml/1 tbsp water
15ml/1 tbsp pine nuts (optional)

MAKES 1 LOAF, SERVES 8

1 Lightly grease a baking sheet and set aside. Mix the polenta and 250ml/8fl oz/1 cup of the water together in a saucepan and slowly bring to the boil, stirring continuously with a large wooden spoon. Reduce the heat and let simmer for 2–3 minutes, stirring occasionally. Remove from the heat and set aside to cool for 10 minutes, or until just warm.

2 In a small bowl, mix the yeast with the remaining water and honey until creamy. Sift 115g/4oz/1 cup of the flour into a large bowl. Gradually beat in the yeast mixture, then stir in the polenta mixture gradually to combine. Turn out on to a lightly floured surface and knead for 5 minutes until smooth and elastic. Cover the bowl with lightly oiled clear film. Leave the dough to rise, in a warm place, for about 2 hours, or until it has doubled in bulk.

3 Meanwhile, melt the butter in a small saucepan, add the pine nuts and cook over a medium heat, stirring, until pale golden. Remove the pan from the heat and set aside to cool.

4 Add the remaining flour and the salt to the polenta dough and mix to form a soft dough. Knead in the pine nuts. Turn out on to a lightly floured surface and knead for 5 minutes until smooth and elastic.

5 Place in an oiled bowl, cover with clear film and leave to rise, in a warm place, for 1 hour, until doubled in bulk.

NUTRITIONAL NOTES

Per portion:

Energy	139Kcals/585kJ
Total fat	4.9g
Saturated fat	1.7g
Cholesterol	27.5mg
Fibre	0.8g

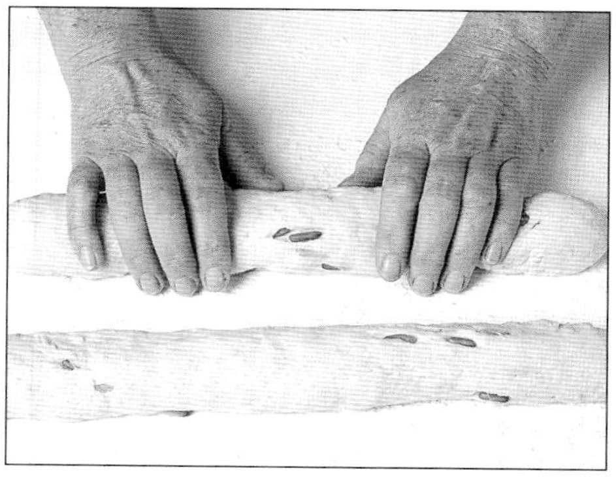

6 Knock back the dough and turn it out on to a lightly floured surface. Cut the dough into two equal pieces and roll each piece into a fat sausage about 38cm/15in long. Plait together and place on the prepared baking sheet. Cover with lightly oiled clear film and leave to rise, in a warm place, for 45 minutes. Preheat the oven to 200°C/400°F/Gas 6.

7 Mix the egg yolk and water and brush over the loaf. Sprinkle with pine nuts, if using, and bake for 30 minutes, or until golden and sounding hollow. Transfer to a wire rack to cool.

SICILIAN SCROLL

A wonderful pale yellow, crusty-topped loaf, enhanced with a nutty flavour from the sesame seeds. It's perfect for serving with low-fat cheese or cooked lean meats.

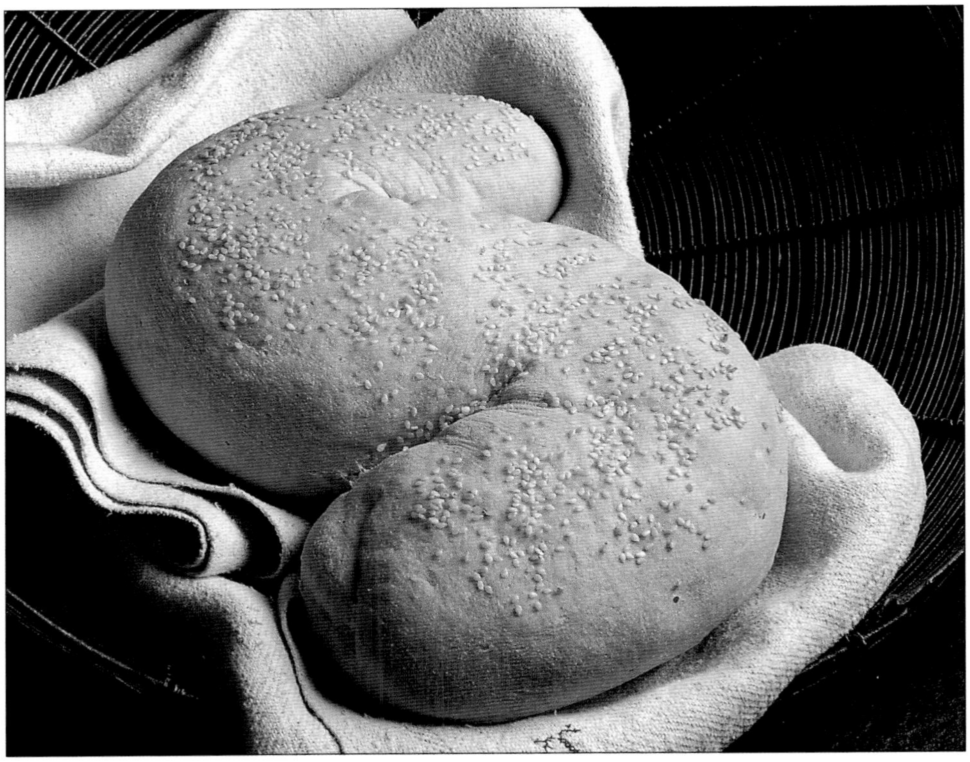

Ingredients

450g/1lb finely ground semolina
115g/4oz/1 cup unbleached strong white bread flour
10ml/2 tsp salt
20g/¾oz fresh yeast
360ml/12½fl oz/generous 1½ cups lukewarm water
30ml/2 tbsp extra virgin olive oil
30ml/2 tbsp sesame seeds, for sprinkling

Makes 1 loaf, Serves 8

Nutritional Notes

Per portion:

Energy	197Kcals/833kJ
Total fat	4.1g
Saturated fat	0.6g
Cholesterol	0mg
Fibre	0.5g

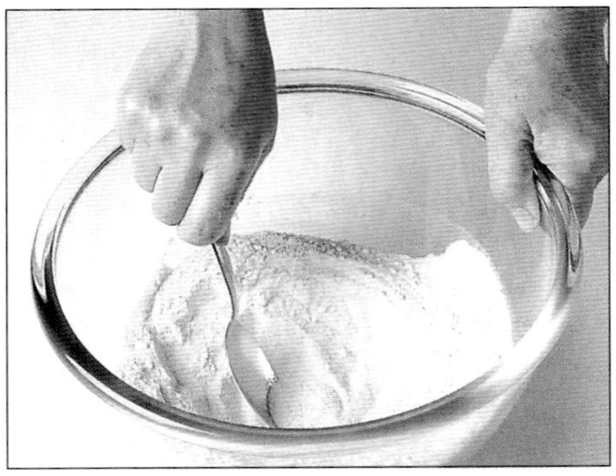

1 Lightly grease a baking sheet and set aside. Mix the semolina, white bread flour and salt together in a large bowl and make a well in the centre.

2 In a jug, cream the yeast with half the water, then stir in the remaining water. Add the creamed yeast to the centre of the semolina mixture with the olive oil. Gradually incorporate the semolina and flour to form a firm dough.

3 Turn the dough out on to a lightly floured surface. Knead for 8–10 minutes until smooth and elastic. Place in a lightly oiled bowl, cover with lightly oiled clear film and leave to rise, in a warm place, for 1–1½ hours, or until the dough has doubled in bulk.

4 Turn out on to a lightly floured surface and knock back. Knead, then shape the dough into a fat roll about 50cm/20in long. Form into an "S" shape.

5 Transfer to the prepared baking sheet, cover with oiled clear film and leave to rise, in a warm place, for 30–45 minutes, or until doubled in size.

6 Meanwhile, preheat the oven to 220°C/425°F/Gas 7. Brush the top of the scroll with water and sprinkle with the sesame seeds. Bake for 10 minutes. Spray the inside of the oven with water twice during this time.

7 Reduce the oven temperature to 200°C/400°F/Gas 6 and bake for a further 25–30 minutes, or until golden. Transfer to a wire rack to cool. Serve in slices.

PROSCIUTTO LOAF

This savoury Italian bread from Parma is spiked with the local dried ham. Just a small amount fills the loaf with marvellous flavour and creates a delicious low-fat accompaniment or snack.

INGREDIENTS

350g/12oz/3 cups unbleached strong white bread flour
7.5ml/1 1/2 tsp salt
15g/1/2 oz fresh yeast
250ml/8fl oz/1 cup lukewarm water
40g/1 1/2 oz prosciutto, torn into small pieces
5ml/1 tsp ground black pepper

MAKES 1 LOAF, SERVES 6

1 Lightly grease a baking sheet and set aside. Sift the flour and salt into a bowl and make a well in the centre. In a small bowl, cream the yeast with 30ml/2 tbsp of the water, then gradually mix in the rest. Pour into the centre of the flour.

2 Gradually beat in most of the flour with a wooden spoon to make a batter. Beat gently at first and then more vigorously as the batter thickens. When most of the flour is incorporated, mix in the rest with your hand to form a moist dough.

3 Turn out on to a lightly floured surface and knead for 5 minutes until smooth and elastic. Place in an oiled bowl, cover with lightly oiled clear film and leave to rise, in a warm place, for 1 1/2 hours, or until doubled in bulk.

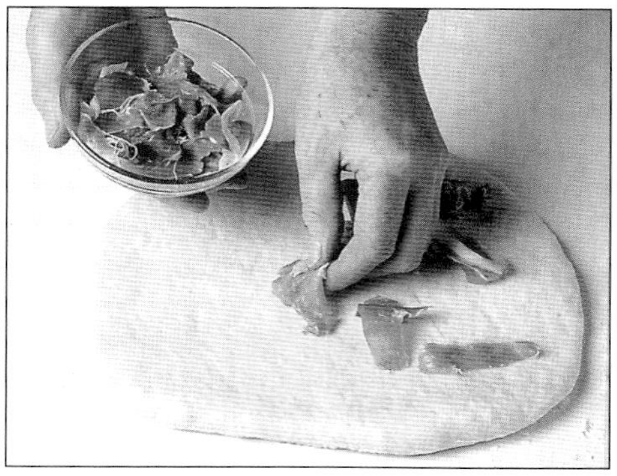

4 Turn the dough out on to a lightly floured surface, knock back and knead for 1 minute. Flatten to a round, then sprinkle with half the prosciutto and pepper. Fold in half and repeat with the remaining ham and pepper. Roll up, tucking in the sides.

5 Place on the prepared baking sheet, cover with oiled clear film and leave to rise, in a warm place, for 30 minutes. Turn out on to a lightly floured surface, roll into an oval, fold in half and seal the edges. Flatten and fold again. Seal and fold again to make a long loaf.

6 Roll into a stubby long loaf. Draw out the edges by rolling the dough under the palms of your hands. Place back on the prepared baking sheet, cover with oiled clear film and leave to rise, in a warm place, for 45 minutes, or until the loaf has doubled in bulk. Preheat the oven to 200°C/400°F/Gas 6.

7 Slash the top of the loaf diagonally three or four times, using a sharp knife, and bake in the oven for 30 minutes, or until golden. Transfer to a wire rack to cool. Serve in slices.

NUTRITIONAL NOTES

Per portion:

Energy	200Kcals/849kJ
Total fat	1.6g
Saturated fat	0.5g
Cholesterol	3.3mg
Fibre	1.7g

PARMA HAM AND PARMESAN BREAD

This nourishing Italian bread is ideal served in slices and topped with grilled vegetables for a tasty, low-fat lunch or supper.

Ingredients

225g/8oz/2 cups self-raising wholemeal flour
225g/8oz/2 cups self-raising white flour
5ml/1 tsp baking powder
5ml/1 tsp salt
5ml/1 tsp ground black pepper
75g/3oz Parma ham, chopped
25g/1oz/2 tbsp grated fresh Parmesan cheese
30ml/2 tbsp chopped fresh parsley
45ml/3 tbsp Meaux mustard
350ml/12fl oz/1 1/2 cups buttermilk
skimmed milk, to glaze

Makes 1 loaf, Serves 8

1 Preheat the oven to 200°C/400°F/Gas 6. Flour a baking sheet and set aside. Place the wholemeal flour in a bowl and sift in the white flour, baking powder and salt. Add the pepper and ham. Set aside about 15ml/1 tbsp of the grated Parmesan and stir the rest into the flour mixture. Stir in the parsley. Make a well in the centre of the mixture.

2 Mix the mustard and buttermilk together in a jug, pour into the flour mixture and quickly mix to a soft dough. Turn the dough out on to a lightly floured surface and knead briefly.

3 Shape the dough into an oval loaf, brush with milk and sprinkle with the remaining cheese. Place the loaf on the prepared baking sheet.

Nutritional Notes

Per portion:

Energy	250Kcals/1053kJ
Total fat	3.65g
Saturated fat	1.30g
Cholesterol	7.09mg
Fibre	3.81g

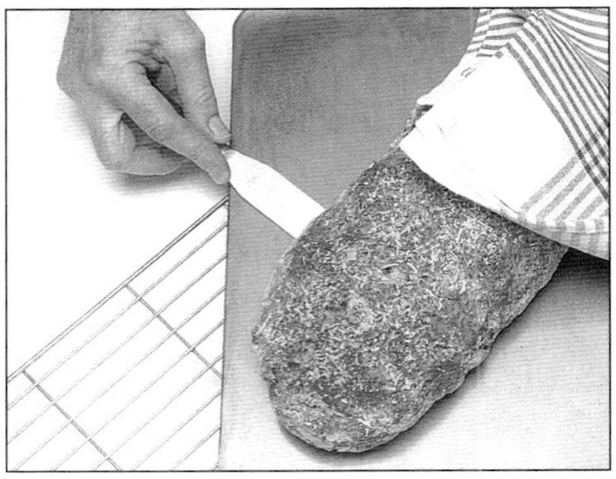

4 Bake in the oven for 25–30 minutes, or until golden brown. Transfer to a wire rack to cool. Serve in slices.

OLIVE AND HERB BREAD

Olive breads are popular all over the Mediterranean, especially in Italy. This delicious olive bread is an ideal low-fat accompaniment to pasta dishes or salads.

INGREDIENTS

2 red onions, thinly sliced
30ml/2 tbsp olive oil
225g/8oz/1½ cups stoned black or green olives
800g/1¾lb/7 cups strong white bread flour
7.5ml/1½ tsp salt
20ml/4 tsp easy-blend dried yeast
45ml/3 tbsp roughly chopped fresh parsley, coriander or mint
475ml/16fl oz/2 cups hand-hot water

MAKES 2 LOAVES
(EACH LOAF SERVES 10)

1 Fry the onions in the oil in a saucepan until soft. Remove the pan from the heat and set aside. Roughly chop the black or green olives and set aside.

2 Put the flour, salt, yeast and parsley, coriander or mint in a large bowl with the olives and fried onions and pour in the water. Mix to a dough using a round-bladed knife, adding a little more water if the mixture feels dry.

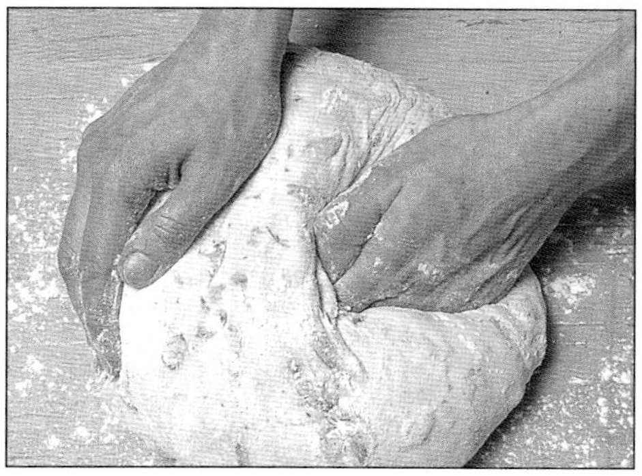

3 Turn out on to a lightly floured surface and knead for about 10 minutes, until smooth and elastic. Put in a clean bowl, cover with clear film and leave in a warm place until doubled in bulk.

4 Preheat the oven to 220°C/425°F/Gas 7. Lightly grease two baking sheets. Turn the dough out on to a lightly floured surface and cut in half. Shape into two rounds. Place on the prepared baking sheets, cover loosely with lightly oiled clear film and leave until doubled in bulk.

5 Slash the tops of the loaves with a sharp knife, then bake in the oven for about 40 minutes or until they sound hollow when tapped underneath. Transfer to a wire rack to cool. Serve in slices.

VARIATION

Shape the dough into 16 small rolls. Slash the tops as above and reduce the cooking time to 25 minutes.

NUTRITIONAL NOTES

Per portion:

Energy	157Kcals/664kJ
Total fat	2.9g
Saturated fat	0.41g
Cholesterol	0mg
Fibre	1.8g

OLIVE AND OREGANO BREAD

This tasty Italian bread is an excellent low-fat accompaniment to all salads and is particularly good served warm.

Ingredients

300ml/½ pint/1¼ cups warm water
5ml/1 tsp dried yeast
pinch of sugar
15ml/1 tbsp olive oil
1 onion, chopped
450g/1lb/4 cups strong white bread flour, plus extra for dusting
5ml/1 tsp salt
1.5ml/¼ tsp ground black pepper
50g/2oz/½ cup stoned black olives, roughly chopped
15ml/1 tbsp black olive paste
15ml/1 tbsp chopped fresh oregano
15ml/1 tbsp chopped fresh parsley

Makes 1 loaf, Serves 8

1 Put half the warm water in a jug. Sprinkle the yeast on top. Add the sugar, mix well and leave for 10 minutes.

Nutritional Notes

Per portion:

Energy	211Kcals/896kJ
Total fat	2.8g
Saturated fat	0.4g
Cholesterol	0mg
Fibre	2g

2 Heat the oil in a frying pan and fry the onion until golden brown, stirring occasionally. Remove the pan from the heat and set aside.

3 Sift the flour into a mixing bowl with the salt and pepper. Make a well in the centre. Add the yeast mixture, the fried onions (with the oil), the olives, olive paste, oregano, parsley and remaining water. Gradually incorporate the flour and mix to a soft dough, adding a little extra water if necessary.

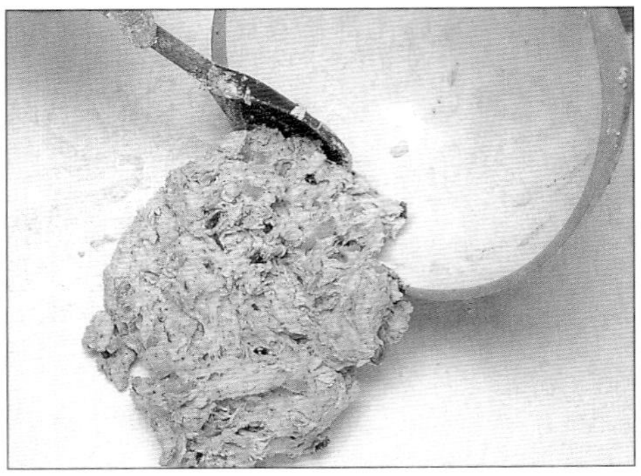

4 Turn the dough out on to a lightly floured surface and knead for 5 minutes until smooth and elastic. Place in a mixing bowl, cover with a damp dish towel and leave to rise in a warm place for about 2 hours until the dough has doubled in bulk. Lightly grease a baking sheet and set aside.

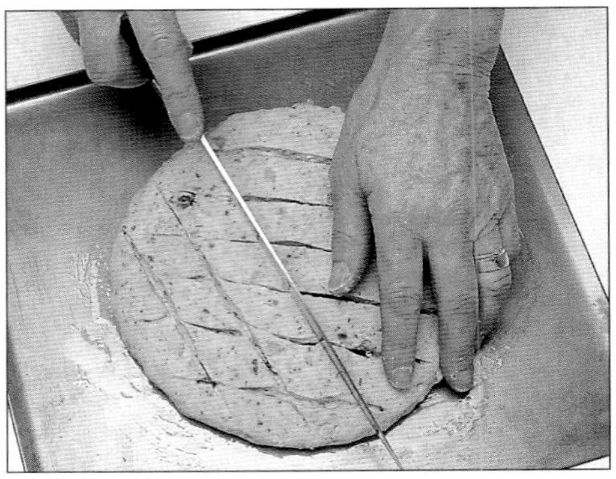

5 Turn the dough out on to a lightly floured surface and knead again for a few minutes. Shape into a 20cm/8in round and place on the prepared baking sheet. Using a sharp knife, make criss-cross cuts over the top of the dough. Cover and leave in a warm place for 30 minutes until well risen. Preheat the oven to 220°C/425°F/Gas 7.

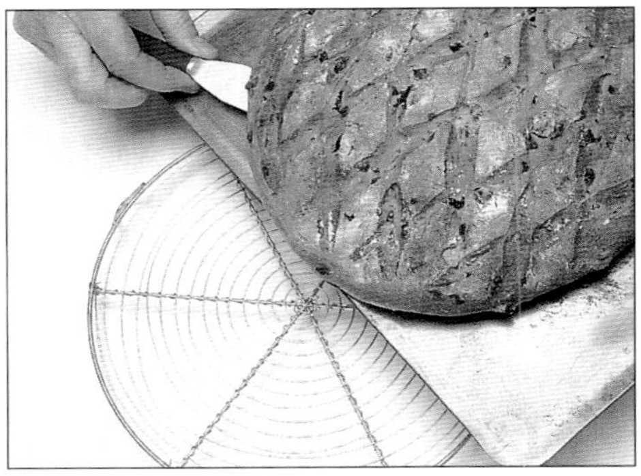

6 Dust the loaf with a little flour. Bake in the oven for 10 minutes then lower the oven temperature to 200°C/400°F/Gas 6. Bake for a further 20 minutes, or until the loaf sounds hollow when it is tapped underneath. Transfer to a wire rack to cool. Serve the bread warm or cold in slices or wedges.

MIXED OLIVE BREAD

Mixed black and green olives and good-quality fruity olive oil combine to make this strongly flavoured and irresistible Italian bread, ideal for a tasty low-fat snack.

Ingredients

275g/10oz/2½ cups unbleached strong white bread flour
50g/2oz/½ cup strong wholemeal bread flour
10g/¼ oz sachet easy-blend dried yeast
2.5ml/½ tsp salt
210ml/7½fl oz/scant 1 cup lukewarm water
15ml/1 tbsp extra virgin olive oil, plus 15ml/1 tbsp olive oil for brushing
115g/4oz/⅔ cup mixed stoned black and green olives, coarsely chopped

Makes 1 loaf, Serves 8

1 Lightly grease a baking sheet and set aside. Mix the flours, yeast and salt in a bowl and make a well in the centre.

2 Add the water and 15ml/1 tbsp oil to the centre of the flour and mix to form a soft dough. Knead the dough on a lightly floured surface for 8–10 minutes until smooth and elastic. Place in a lightly oiled bowl, cover with oiled clear film and leave to rise, in a warm place, for 1 hour, or until doubled in bulk.

3 Turn the dough out on to a lightly floured surface and knock back. Flatten out and sprinkle over the olives. Knead to distribute the olives evenly throughout the dough. Leave to rest for 5 minutes, then shape into an oval loaf. Place on the prepared baking sheet.

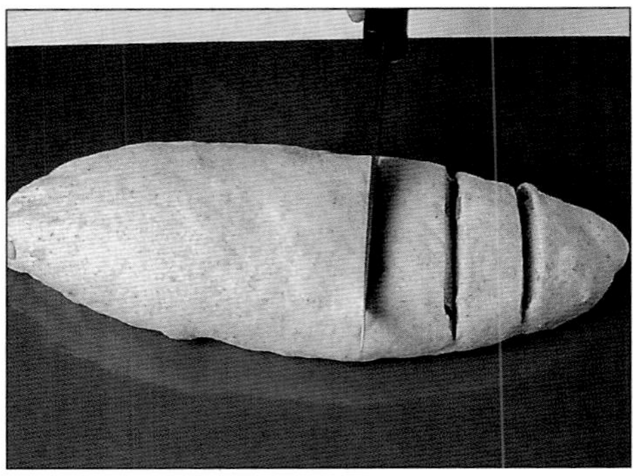

4 Make six deep cuts in the top of the dough and gently push the sections over. Cover with oiled clear film and leave to rise, in a warm place, for 30–45 minutes, or until doubled in bulk.

5 Meanwhile, preheat the oven to 200°C/400°F/Gas 6. Brush the bread with olive oil and bake in the oven for 35 minutes. Transfer to a wire rack to cool. Serve warm or cold in slices.

Nutritional Notes

Per portion:

Energy	165Kcals/697kJ
Total fat	3.5g
Saturated fat	0.5g
Cholesterol	0mg
Fibre	2g

HAM AND TOMATO SCONES

These delicious home-baked scones make an ideal accompaniment for low-fat soup. They are best eaten fresh on the day they are made, served either warm or cold.

INGREDIENTS

225g/8oz/2 cups self-raising flour
5ml/1 tsp dry mustard
5ml/1 tsp paprika, plus extra for sprinkling
2.5ml/½ tsp salt
25g/1oz/2 tbsp low-fat margarine
15ml/1 tbsp chopped fresh basil
50g/2oz/1 cup dry-packed sun-dried tomatoes, soaked in warm water, drained and chopped
50g/2oz cooked lean ham, chopped
90–120ml/3–4fl oz/6 tbsp–½ cup skimmed milk, plus extra for brushing

MAKES 12

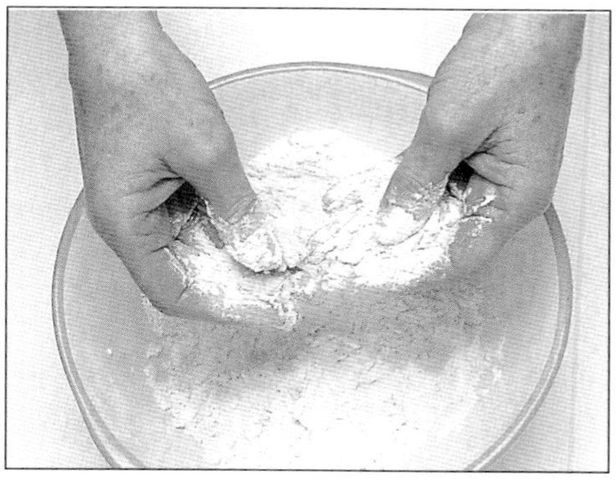

1 Preheat the oven to 200°C/400°F/Gas 6. Flour a large baking sheet and set aside. Sift the flour, mustard, paprika and salt into a bowl. Rub in the margarine until the mixture resembles breadcrumbs.

2 Stir in the basil, sun-dried tomatoes and ham, and mix lightly. Pour in enough milk to mix to a soft dough.

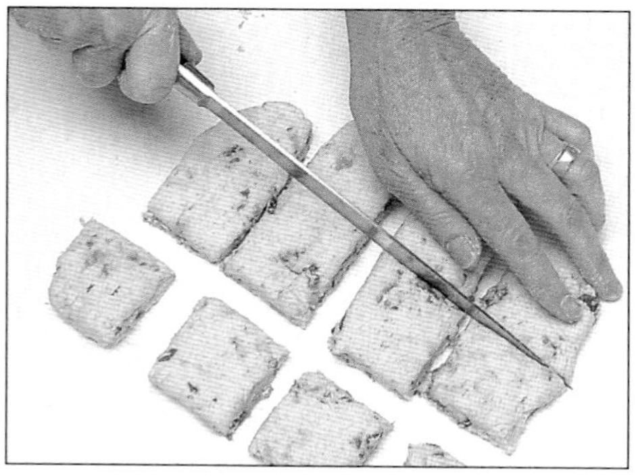

3 Turn out on to a lightly floured surface, knead briefly and roll out to a 20 × 15cm/8 × 6in rectangle. Cut into 5cm/2in squares and arrange on the baking sheet.

4 Brush the tops lightly with milk, sprinkle with paprika and bake in the oven for about 12–15 minutes. Transfer to a wire rack to cool. Serve warm or cold.

NUTRITIONAL NOTES

Per portion:

Energy	115Kcals/656kJ
Total fat	4.4g
Saturated fat	1g
Cholesterol	3.6mg
Fibre	1g

ROSEMARY AND SEA SALT FOCACCIA

Focaccia is an appetizing Italian flat bread made with olive oil. Here it is given added flavour with rosemary and coarse sea salt.

Ingredients

350g/12oz/3 cups plain flour
2.5ml/½ tsp salt
10ml/2 tsp easy-blend dried yeast
about 250ml/8fl oz/1 cup lukewarm water
45ml/3 tbsp olive oil
1 small red onion
leaves from 1 large fresh rosemary sprig
5ml/1 tsp coarse sea salt
oil, for greasing

Makes 1 loaf, Serves 8

1 Sift the flour and salt into a mixing bowl. Stir in the yeast, then make a well in the middle of the dry ingredients.

2 Pour in the water and 30ml/2 tbsp of the oil. Mix well to make a dough, adding a little more water if the mixture seems too dry.

Cook's Tip

Use flavoured olive oil, such as chilli or herb oil, for extra flavour. Wholemeal flour or a mixture of wholemeal and white flour works well with this recipe.

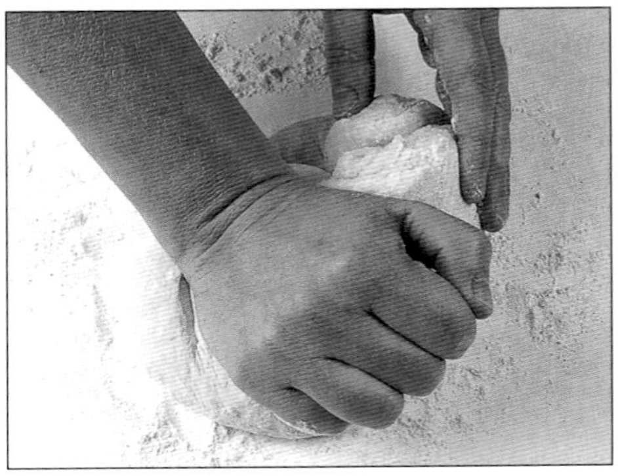

3 Turn the dough out on to a lightly floured surface and knead it for about 10 minutes until smooth and elastic.

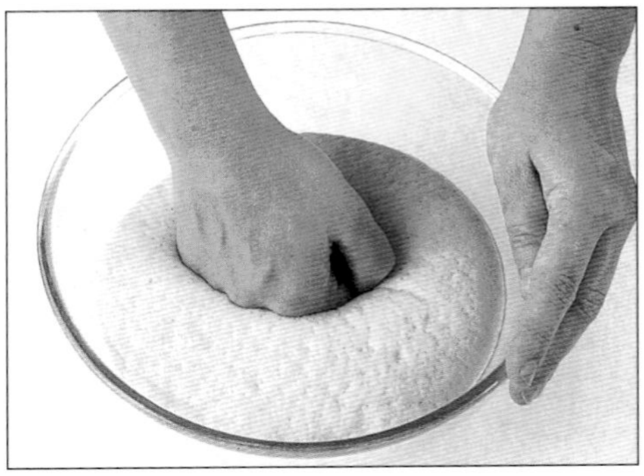

4 Place the dough in a greased bowl, cover and leave to rise in a warm place for about 1 hour until doubled in bulk. Knock back and knead the dough on a lightly floured surface for 2–3 minutes.

5 Preheat the oven to 220°C/425°F/Gas 7 and grease a baking sheet. Roll the dough to a circle 1cm/½in thick, transfer to the baking sheet and brush with remaining oil.

6 Halve the onion and chop it into thin slices. Press the slices lightly over the dough, with the rosemary and sea salt.

7 Using a finger, make deep indentations in the dough. Cover the surface with oiled clear film, then leave to rise in a warm place for 30 minutes. Remove and discard the clear film and bake the loaf in the oven for 25–30 minutes until golden. Transfer to a wire rack to cool. Serve in slices or wedges.

Nutritional Notes

Per portion:

Energy	191Kcals/807kJ
Total fat	4.72g
Saturated fat	0.68g
Cholesterol	0mg
Fibre	1.46g

SAFFRON FOCACCIA

A dazzling yellow bread with a distinctive flavour, this saffron focaccia makes a tasty snack or accompaniment.

Ingredients

For the dough

pinch of saffron threads
150ml/1/4 pint/2/3 cup boiling water
225g/8oz/2 cups plain flour
2.5ml/1/2 tsp salt
5ml/1 tsp easy-blend dried yeast
15ml/1 tbsp olive oil

For the topping

2 garlic cloves, sliced
1 red onion, cut into thin wedges
fresh rosemary sprigs
12 black olives, stoned and coarsely chopped
15ml/1 tbsp olive oil

Makes 1 loaf, Serves 10

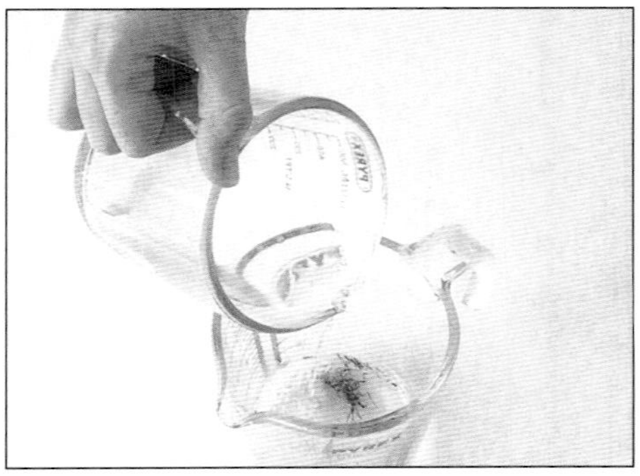

1 Make the dough. In a jug, infuse the saffron in the boiling water. Leave until cooled to lukewarm.

Variation

You might like to experiment with different topping ingredients for this bread. Green olives and sun-dried tomatoes are two others you could try.

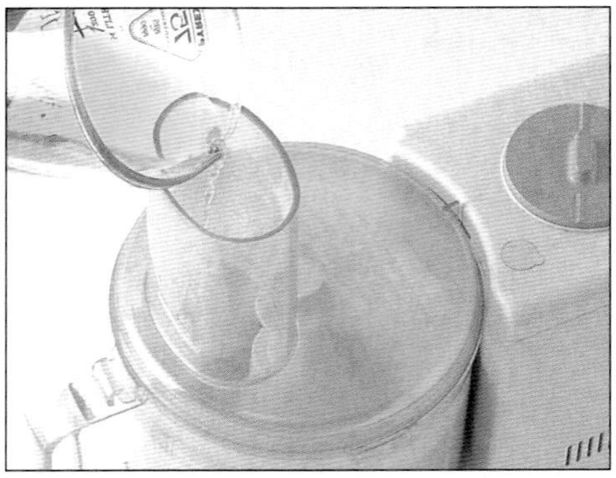

2 Place the flour, salt, yeast and olive oil in a food processor. Turn the processor on and gradually add the saffron and its liquid until the dough forms a ball.

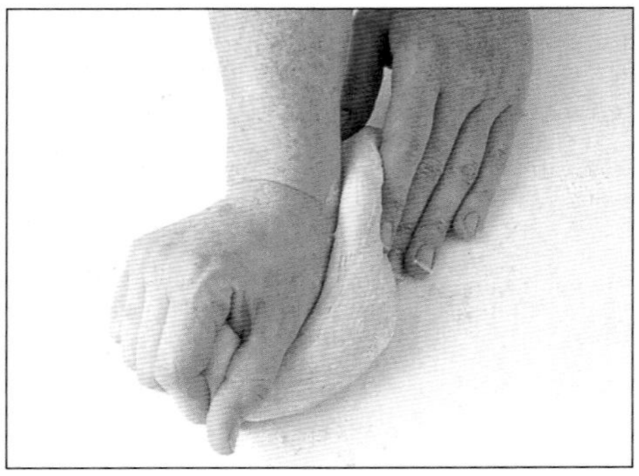

3 Transfer the dough on to a lightly floured work surface and knead for 10–15 minutes until smooth and elastic. Place in a bowl, cover and leave to rise in a warm place for about 30–40 minutes, until doubled in bulk. Lightly grease a baking sheet and set aside.

Nutritional Notes

Per portion:

Energy	177Kcals/754kJ
Total fat	4.7g
Saturated fat	0.7g
Cholesterol	0mg
Fibre	1.5g

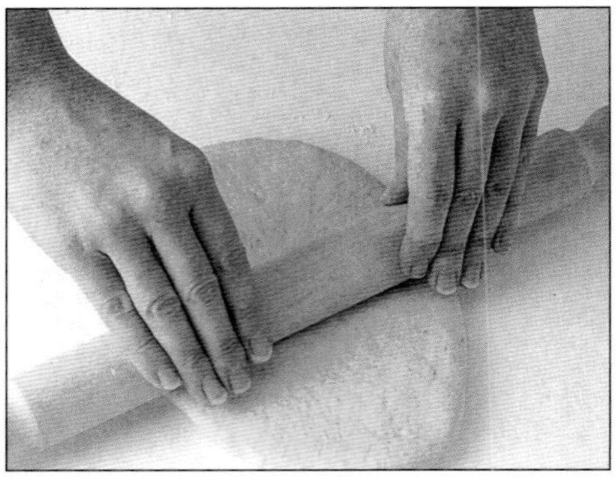

4 Knock back the risen dough on a lightly floured surface and roll out into an oval shape about 1cm/1/2in thick. Place on the prepared baking sheet and leave to rise in a warm place for 20–30 minutes.

5 Preheat the oven to 200°C/400°F/Gas 6. Use your fingers to press small indentations in the dough.

6 Cover the dough with the topping ingredients, brush lightly with the olive oil, and bake the loaf in the oven for about 25 minutes or until it sounds hollow when tapped underneath. Transfer to a wire rack to cool. Serve the focaccia in slices or wedges.

ONION FOCACCIA

This typical Italian pizza-like flat bread is characterized by its soft dimpled surface. This focaccia is flavoured with red onions and makes a tasty low-fat supper or snack.

INGREDIENTS

675g/1½lb/6 cups strong white bread flour
2.5ml/½ tsp salt
2.5ml/½ tsp caster sugar
15ml/1 tbsp easy-blend dried yeast
45ml/3 tbsp extra virgin olive oil
450ml/¾ pint/scant 2 cups hand-hot water

TO FINISH

2 red onions, thinly sliced
15ml/1 tbsp extra virgin olive oil
15ml/1 tbsp coarse salt

MAKES 2 LOAVES, SERVES 12

1 Sift the flour, salt and sugar into a large bowl. Stir in the yeast, oil and water and mix to a dough using a round-bladed knife, adding a little extra water if the dough is dry.

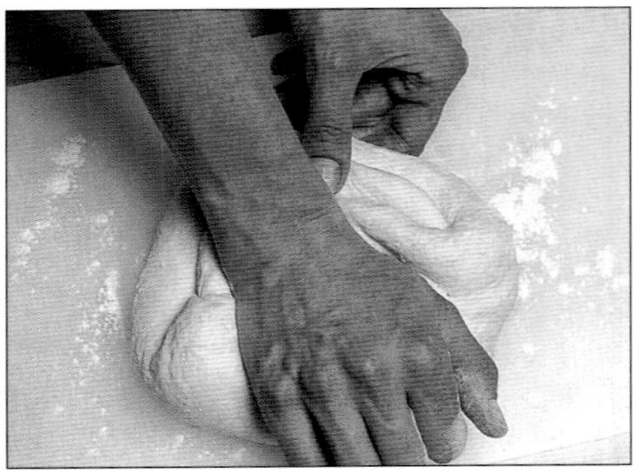

2 Turn the dough out on to a lightly floured surface and knead for about 10 minutes until smooth and elastic. Put the dough in a clean, lightly oiled bowl and cover with clear film. Leave to rise in a warm place until doubled in bulk.

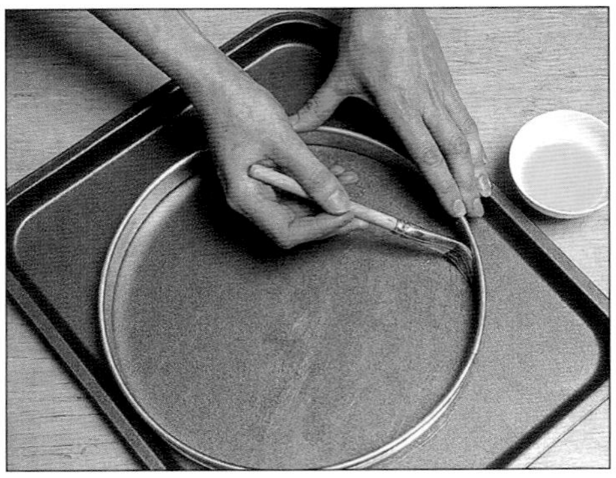

3 Place two 25cm/10in plain metal flan rings on baking sheets. Oil the sides of the rings and the baking sheets.

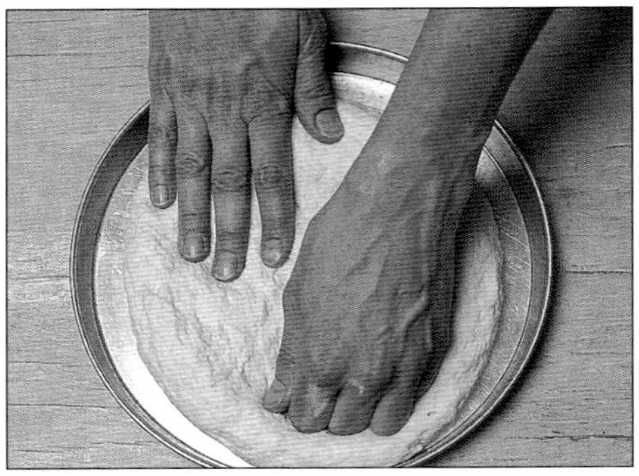

4 Preheat the oven to 200°C/400°F/Gas 6. Halve the dough and roll each piece of dough into a 25cm/10in round. Press into the prepared flan rings, cover with a damp dish towel and leave to rise in a warm place for 30 minutes.

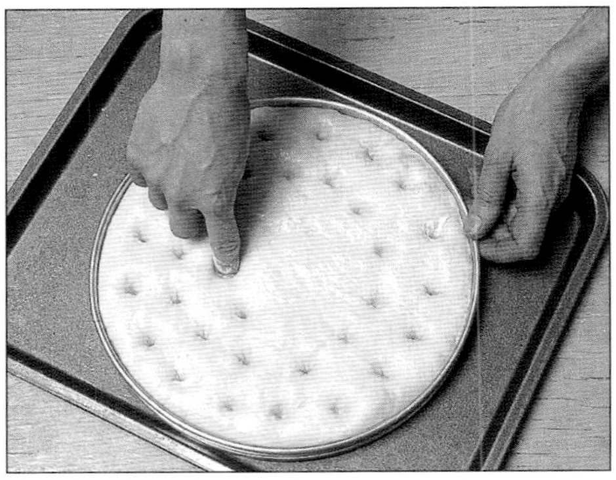

5 Using a finger, make deep holes, about 2.5cm/1in apart, in the dough. Cover and leave for a further 20 minutes.

6 To finish, scatter the dough with the onions and drizzle over the oil. Sprinkle with the salt, then a little cold water, to stop a crust from forming.

7 Bake in the oven for about 25 minutes until golden, sprinkling with water again during cooking. Transfer to a wire rack to cool. Serve in slices or wedges.

NUTRITIONAL NOTES

Per portion:

Energy	231Kcals/975kJ
Total fat	4.4g
Saturated fat	0.6g
Cholesterol	0mg
Fibre	1.9g

COOK'S TIP

When buying onions, look for ones with dry, papery skins. To slice them, cut a slice from the top and remove the skin. Halve lengthways and slice each half separately.

SAFFRON AND BASIL BREADSTICKS

Saffron lends its delicate aroma and flavour, as well as rich yellow colour, to these tasty breadsticks, ideal as a low-fat accompaniment, snack or nibble.

INGREDIENTS

generous pinch of saffron strands
30ml/2 tbsp hot water
450g/1lb/4 cups strong white bread flour
5ml/1 tsp salt
10ml/2 tsp easy-blend dried yeast
300ml/½ pint/1¼ cups lukewarm water
45ml/3 tbsp olive oil
45ml/3 tbsp chopped fresh basil

MAKES 32

1 In a small bowl, infuse the saffron strands in the hot water for 10 minutes.

2 Sift the flour and salt into a large mixing bowl. Stir in the yeast, then make a well in the centre of the dry ingredients. Pour in the lukewarm water and saffron liquid and start to mix a little.

3 Add the oil and basil and continue to mix to form a soft dough.

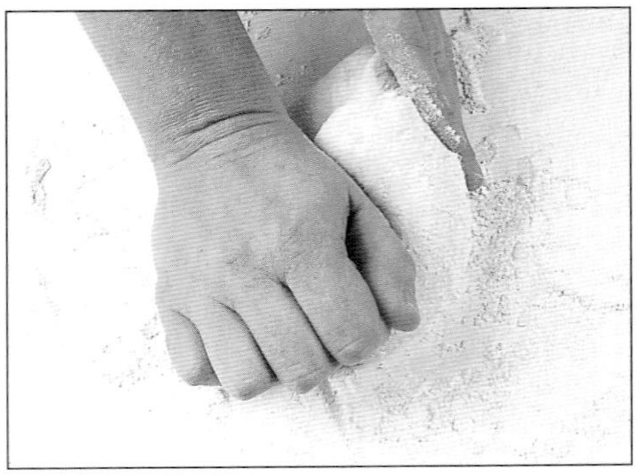

4 Knead the dough on a lightly floured surface for about 10 minutes until smooth and elastic.

5 Place in a greased bowl, cover with clear film and leave to rise in a warm place for about 1 hour until the dough has doubled in bulk.

COOK'S TIP

Use powdered saffron if saffron strands are not available. Turmeric is an inexpensive alternative: it imparts a lovely gold colour, but its flavour is not as delicate.

6 Knock back and knead the dough on a lightly floured surface for 2–3 minutes.

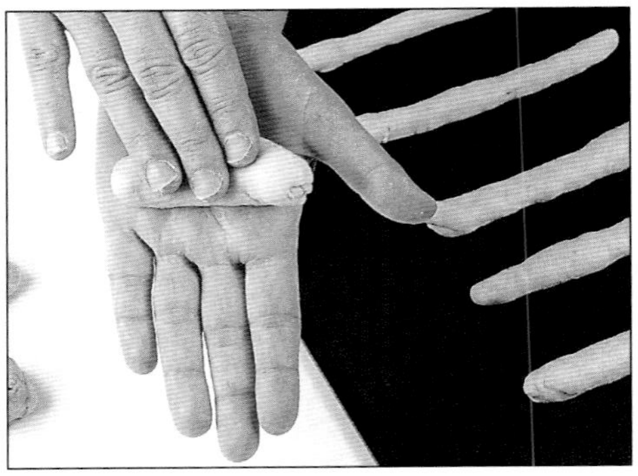

7 Preheat the oven to 220°C/425°F/Gas 7. Lightly grease two baking sheets and set aside. Divide the dough into 32 even pieces and shape into long sticks. Place them well apart on the prepared baking sheets, then leave them for a further 15–20 minutes until they become puffy. Bake in the oven for about 15 minutes until crisp and golden. Transfer to a wire rack to cool. Serve warm or cold.

NUTRITIONAL NOTES

Per portion:

Energy	59Kcals/249kJ
Total fat	1.3g
Saturated fat	1.17g
Cholesterol	0mg
Fibre	0.4g

SUN-DRIED TOMATO BREADSTICKS

Once you've tried this delicious and simple recipe you'll never buy manufactured breadsticks again. Serve with a low-fat dip or with low-fat cheese to end a meal.

INGREDIENTS

225g/8oz/2 cups plain flour
2.5ml/½ tsp salt
7.5ml/1½ tsp easy-blend dried yeast
5ml/1 tsp honey
5ml/1 tsp olive oil
150ml/¼ pint/⅔ cup warm water
6 halves sun-dried tomatoes in olive oil, drained and chopped
15ml/1 tbsp skimmed milk
10ml/2 tsp poppy seeds

MAKES 16

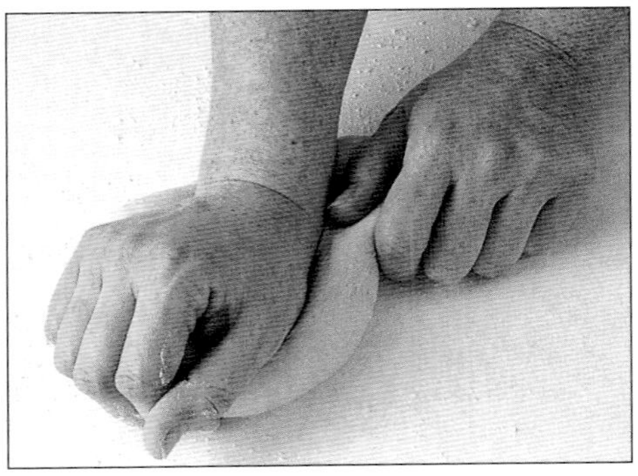

1 Place the flour, salt and yeast in a food processor. Add the honey and olive oil and, with the processor running, gradually pour in the water (you may not need to add it all as flours vary). Stop adding water as soon as the dough starts to cling together. Process for a further 1 minute. Turn the dough out on to a lightly floured surface. Knead for 3–4 minutes until smooth and elastic.

NUTRITIONAL NOTES

Per portion:

Energy	54Kcals/228kJ
Total fat	0.8g
Saturated fat	0.1g
Cholesterol	0.02mg
Fibre	0.5g

2 Once the dough is very smooth, knead in the chopped sun-dried tomatoes. Form the dough into a large ball and place in a lightly oiled bowl. Leave to rest for 5 minutes. Lightly oil a baking sheet and set aside. Preheat the oven to 150°C/300°F/Gas 2.

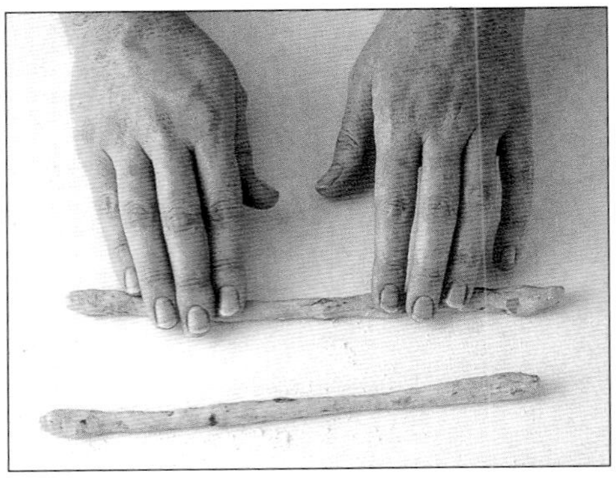

3 Divide the dough into 16 equal pieces and roll each piece into a 28cm × 1cm/11in × ½in long stick. Place on the prepared baking sheet and leave to rise in a warm place for 15 minutes.

4 Brush the sticks with milk and sprinkle with poppy seeds. Bake in the oven for 30 minutes. Place on a wire rack to cool.

CHOCOLATE BREAD

This slightly sweet chocolate bread from Italy is often served with a little creamy mascarpone as a special dessert. The dark chocolate pieces add texture to this light loaf.

INGREDIENTS

350g/12oz/3 cups unbleached strong white bread flour
25ml/1½ tbsp cocoa powder
2.5ml/½ tsp salt
25g/1oz/2 tbsp caster sugar
15g/½oz fresh yeast
250ml/8fl oz/1 cup lukewarm water
25g/1oz/2 tbsp butter, softened
75g/3oz plain continental chocolate, coarsely chopped
15ml/1 tbsp melted butter, for brushing

MAKES 1 LOAF, SERVES 12

NUTRITIONAL NOTES

Per portion:

Energy	154Kcals/651kJ
Total fat	4.8g
Saturated fat	2.8g
Cholesterol	7.4mg
Fibre	1.0g

1 Lightly grease a 15cm/6in deep round cake tin. Set aside. Sift the flour, cocoa and salt together in a large bowl. Stir in the sugar. Make a well in the centre.

2 Cream the yeast with 60ml/4 tbsp of the water, then stir in the remaining water. Add to the centre of the flour mixture and mix to a dough. Knead in the butter, then turn out and knead on a lightly floured surface until smooth and elastic. Place in an oiled bowl, cover with clear film and leave to rise, in a warm place, for 1 hour, or until doubled in bulk.

3 Turn the dough out on to a lightly floured surface and knock back. Knead in the chocolate, then cover with oiled clear film. Leave to rest for 5 minutes.

4 Shape the dough into a round and place in the prepared tin. Cover with lightly oiled clear film and leave to rise, in a warm place, for 45 minutes, or until doubled in bulk.

5 Preheat the oven to 220°C/425°F/Gas 7. Bake in the oven for 10 minutes, then reduce the oven temperature to 190°C/375°F/Gas 5 and bake for a further 25–30 minutes. Brush the hot bread with melted butter and transfer to a wire rack to cool. Serve in slices.

VARIATION

You can also bake this in one large or two small rounds on a baking sheet.

DESSERTS AND BAKES

Desserts provide the flavourful FINALE *to a meal, and we include a collection of delectable* HOT *and cold Italian desserts, all of which are* LOW *in fat too! Select from delights such as classic* ZABAGLIONE, *Grilled Nectarines with Ricotta and Spice,* SORBETS *such as* MANGO *and Lime Sorbet or Watermelon Sorbet, and bakes such as Chocolate* AMARETTI *or Biscotti.*

ZABAGLIONE

A much-loved, simple and very delicious Italian dessert traditionally made with Marsala, an Italian fortified wine, although Madeira is a good alternative.

Ingredients

4 egg yolks
50g/2oz/1/4 cup caster sugar
60ml/4 tbsp Marsala or Madeira
amaretti biscuits, to serve (optional)

Serves 6

1 Place the egg yolks and caster sugar in a large, clean, heatproof bowl and whisk with an electric beater until the mixture is pale and thick and forms fluffy peaks when the whisk is lifted out.

2 Gradually add the Marsala or Madeira, whisking well after each addition (at this stage the mixture will be quite runny).

Variation

If you don't have any Marsala or Madeira, you could use a medium-sweet sherry or a dessert wine.

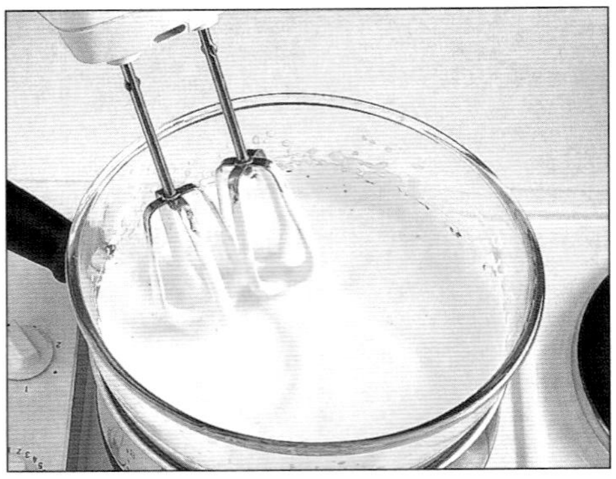

3 Now place the bowl over a pan of gently simmering water and continue to whisk for at least 5–7 minutes until the mixture becomes thick and mousse-like; when the beaters are lifted, they should leave a thick trail on the surface of the mixture.

4 Pour into six warmed, stemmed small glasses and serve immediately with the amaretti biscuits for dipping, if you like.

Nutritional Notes

Per portion:

Energy	93Kcals/388kJ
Total fat	4.1g
Saturated fat	1.2g
Cholesterol	150.9mg
Fibre	0g

STUFFED PEACHES WITH ALMOND LIQUEUR

Together amaretti biscuits and Amaretto liqueur have an intense almond flavour, and make a natural partner for peaches in this exquisite Italian low-fat dessert.

INGREDIENTS

4 ripe but firm peaches
50g/2oz/½ cup amaretti biscuits
30ml/2 tbsp low-fat spread
30ml/2 tbsp caster sugar
1 egg yolk
60ml/4 tbsp Amaretto liqueur
a little low-fat spread, for greasing
250ml/8fl oz/1 cup dry white wine
8 tiny sprigs of fresh basil, to decorate

SERVES 4

NUTRITIONAL NOTES

Per portion:

Energy	232Kcals/971kJ
Total fat	5g
Saturated fat	1.37g
Cholesterol	54.7mg
Fibre	1.9g

1 Preheat the oven to 180°C/350°F/Gas 4. Cut the peaches in half and remove and discard the stones. With a spoon, scrape out some of the flesh from each peach half, slightly enlarging the hollow left by the stone. Chop this flesh and set it aside. Set the peach halves aside.

2 Put the amaretti biscuits in a bowl and crush them finely with the end of a rolling pin. Set aside.

3 Cream the low-fat spread and sugar together in a separate bowl until smooth. Stir in the reserved chopped peach flesh, the egg yolk and half the liqueur with the amaretti crumbs. Mix well. Lightly grease an ovenproof dish that is just large enough to hold the peach halves in a single layer.

4 Stand the peach halves in the dish and spoon the amaretti stuffing into them. Mix the remaining liqueur with the wine, pour over the peaches and bake in the oven for 25 minutes or until the peaches feel tender. Decorate with basil sprigs and serve at once, with a little low-fat ice cream, if you like.

GRILLED NECTARINES WITH RICOTTA AND SPICE

This tasty Italian dessert is quick and easy to make at any time of year – use canned peach halves if fresh nectarines or peaches are not available.

INGREDIENTS

4 ripe nectarines or peaches
15ml/1 tbsp light muscovado sugar
115g/4oz/½ cup ricotta cheese or fromage frais
2.5ml/½ tsp ground star anise

SERVES 4

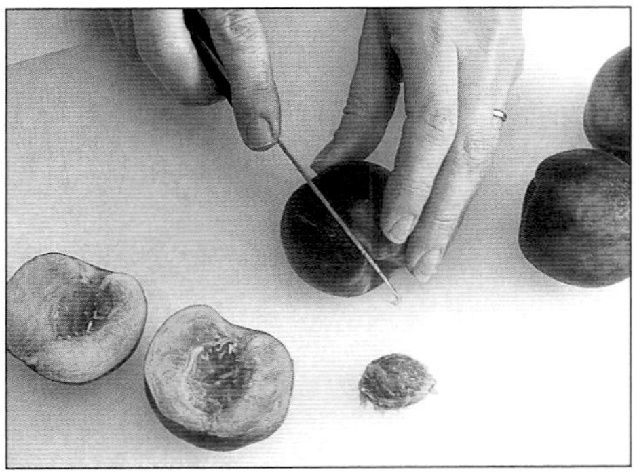

1 Cut the nectarines or peaches in half and remove and discard the stones.

2 Arrange the halved nectarines or peaches, cut side up, in a wide flameproof dish or on a baking sheet.

3 Stir the sugar into the ricotta or fromage frais. Using a teaspoon, spoon the mixture into the hollow of each nectarine or peach half.

4 Sprinkle with the star anise. Place the nectarines or peaches under a moderately hot grill for 6–8 minutes, or until they are hot and bubbling. Serve warm.

COOK'S TIP

Star anise has a warm, rich flavour – if you can't get it, try ground cloves or ground mixed spice instead.

NUTRITIONAL NOTES

Per portion:

Energy	83Kcals/353kJ
Total fat	2g
Saturated fat	1.3g
Cholesterol	7.17mg
Fibre	1.7g

GRILLED NECTARINES WITH AMARETTO

Amaretto, the sweet almond-flavoured liqueur from Italy, adds a touch of luxury to these delicious low-fat grilled nectarines.

Ingredients

6 ripe nectarines
30ml/2 tbsp clear honey
60ml/4 tbsp Amaretto
half-fat crème fraîche, to serve (optional)

Serves 4

Nutritional Notes

Per portion:

Energy	150Kcals/627kJ
Total fat	0.2g
Saturated fat	0g
Cholesterol	0mg
Fibre	2.7

1 Cut the nectarines in half by running a small sharp knife down the side of each fruit from top to bottom, pushing the knife right through to the stone. Gently ease the nectarine apart and remove and discard the stone. Try not to handle the fruit too firmly as nectarines bruise easily.

2 Place the nectarines cut side up in an ovenproof dish and drizzle 2.5ml/½ tsp honey and 5ml/1 tsp Amaretto over each nectarine half. Preheat the grill until very hot and then grill the fruit until slightly charred. Serve warm with a little half-fat crème fraîche, if you like.

STRAWBERRY CONCHIGLIE SALAD

This is a divinely decadent Italian low-fat dessert, laced with liqueur and luscious raspberry sauce, for all the family to enjoy.

Ingredients

175g/6oz/1½ cups dried conchiglie
a little salt
225g/8oz fresh or frozen raspberries, thawed if frozen
15–30ml/1–2 tbsp caster sugar
lemon juice
450g/1lb small fresh strawberries
15g/½oz flaked almonds
45ml/3 tbsp kirsch

Serves 4

1 Cook the pasta in a large saucepan of boiling lightly salted water, according to the packet instructions, until tender or *al dente*. Drain well and set aside to cool.

2 Purée the raspberries in a blender or food processor and press through a sieve to remove the seeds. Discard the seeds.

3 Add the sugar to the raspberry purée, then place in a saucepan and simmer for 5–6 minutes, stirring occasionally. Add lemon juice to taste. Remove the pan from the heat and set aside to cool.

4 Hull the strawberries and halve if necessary. Toss with the pasta and transfer to a serving bowl.

5 Spread the almonds out on a baking sheet and toast under a hot grill until golden. Set aside to cool.

6 Stir the kirsch into the raspberry sauce and pour over the pasta salad. Scatter the toasted almonds over the top of the salad and serve.

Nutritional Notes

Per portion:

Energy	203Kcals/861kJ
Total fat	1.8g
Saturated fat	0.2g
Cholesterol	0mg
Fibre	3.4g

Cook's Tip

Like all soft fruit, strawberries and raspberries should be used as soon as possible after they are picked. Wash them very gently and use immediately.

Variation

You might like to try making sweet pasta salads with other types of soft fruit such as blackberries and loganberries.

FRESH FIG, APPLE AND DATE DESSERT

Sweet Mediterranean figs and dates combine especially well with crisp dessert apples to create this appetizing low-fat dessert. A hint of almond serves to unite the flavours.

Ingredients

6 large apples
juice of 1/2 lemon
175g/6oz fresh dates
25g/1oz white marzipan
5ml/1 tsp orange flower water
60ml/4 tbsp low-fat natural yogurt
4 ripe green or purple fresh figs
4 whole almonds, toasted

Serves 4

1 Core the apples. Slice them thinly, then cut into thin matchsticks. Put into a bowl, sprinkle with lemon juice to keep them white and set aside.

2 Remove and discard the stones from the dates and cut the flesh into thin strips, then combine with the apple slices. Toss to mix.

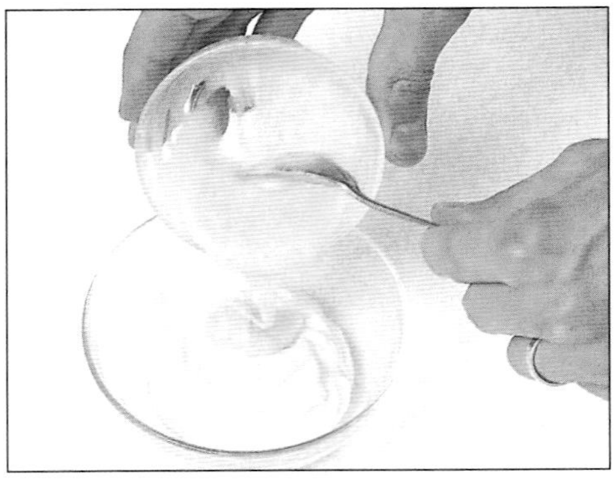

3 In a small bowl, soften the marzipan with the orange flower water and combine this with the yogurt. Mix well.

4 Pile the mixed apples and dates into the centre of four plates. Remove and discard the stem from each of the figs and cut the fruit into quarters without cutting right through the base. Squeeze the base with the thumb and forefinger of each hand to open up the fruit.

5 Place a fig in the centre of each apple and date salad, spoon in some yogurt filling and decorate each portion with a toasted almond. Serve.

Nutritional Notes

Per portion:

Energy	178Kcals/751kJ
Total fat	2.3g
Saturated fat	0.2g
Cholesterol	0.5mg
Fibre	4.4g

Cook's Tips

- Figs are at their best straight off the tree when they are perfectly ripe. Bear in mind that ripe figs are extremely delicate and do not travel well, so take great care not to squash them on the way home. If you buy under-ripe figs, they can be kept at room temperature for a day or two until the skin softens, but they will never develop the fine flavour of tree-ripened figs. Ripe figs should be eaten on the day they are bought.
- When choosing fresh dates, select those that are fat and shiny, with skins that are golden and smooth. You may wish to remove the skin by squeezing the stem end. Most figs, however, have thin skins that are edible.

Variation

For a true Mediterranean touch, use fresh fig or vine leaves, if available, to decorate the serving plates for this dessert.

FIGS WITH RICOTTA CREAM

Fresh, ripe figs are full of natural sweetness and need little adornment. This simple Italian recipe makes the most of their intense flavour and creates a mouthwatering low-fat dessert.

INGREDIENTS

4 ripe, fresh figs
115g/4oz/½ cup ricotta or cottage cheese
45ml/3 tbsp half-fat crème fraîche
15ml/1 tbsp clear honey
2.5ml/½ tsp vanilla essence
freshly grated nutmeg, to decorate

SERVES 4

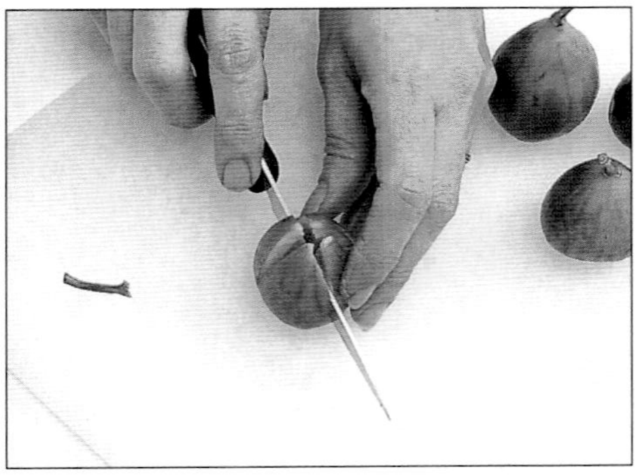

1 Trim the stalks from the figs. Make four cuts through each fig from the stalk end, cutting them almost through but leaving them joined at the base.

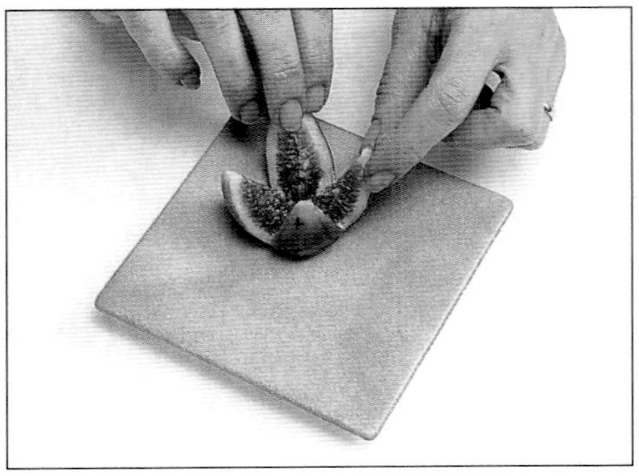

2 Place the figs on serving plates and open them out.

3 In a bowl, mix together the ricotta or cottage cheese, crème fraîche, honey and vanilla essence.

NUTRITIONAL NOTES

Per portion:

Energy	55Kcals/232kJ
Total fat	2g
Saturated fat	1.2g
Cholesterol	6.7mg
Fibre	0g

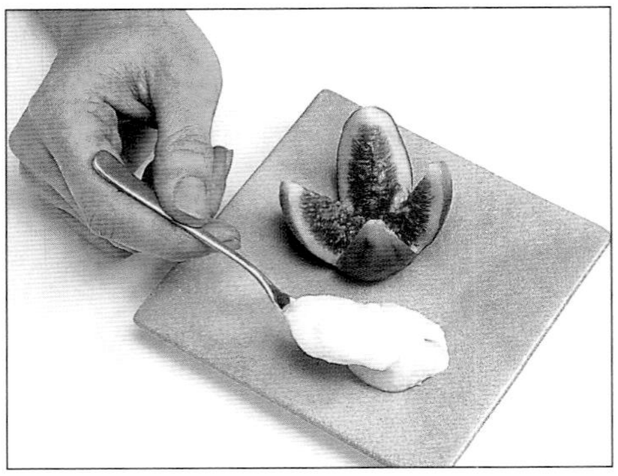

4 Spoon a little ricotta cream on to each plate and sprinkle with grated nutmeg to decorate. Serve.

MANGO AND LIME SORBET IN LIME SHELLS

This richly flavoured virtually fat-free sorbet looks pretty served in the lime shells, but is also good served in scoops for a more traditional presentation.

INGREDIENTS

4 large limes
1 ripe mango
7.5ml/1 1/2 tsp powdered gelatine
2 egg whites
15ml/1 tbsp sugar
pared lime rind strips, to decorate

SERVES 4

NUTRITIONAL NOTES

Per portion:

Energy	50.5Kcals/215kJ
Total fat	0.09g
Saturated fat	0.3g
Cholesterol	0mg
Fibre	1g

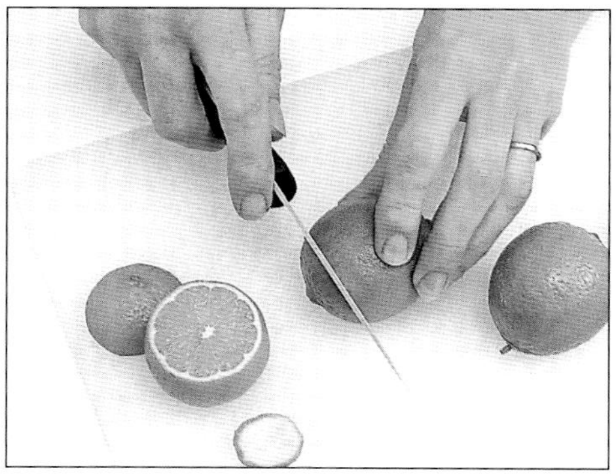

1 Cut a thick slice from the top of each of the limes, and then cut a thin slice from the bottom end so that the limes will stand upright. Squeeze out the juice, then use a small sharp knife to remove all the white membrane from the centres. Discard the membranes. Set the lime shells aside.

2 Peel, halve, stone and chop the mango, then purée the flesh in a blender or food processor with 30ml/2 tbsp of the lime juice. Set aside. Dissolve the gelatine in 45ml/3 tbsp of lime juice in a small bowl placed over a saucepan of simmering water, then stir it into the mango mixture.

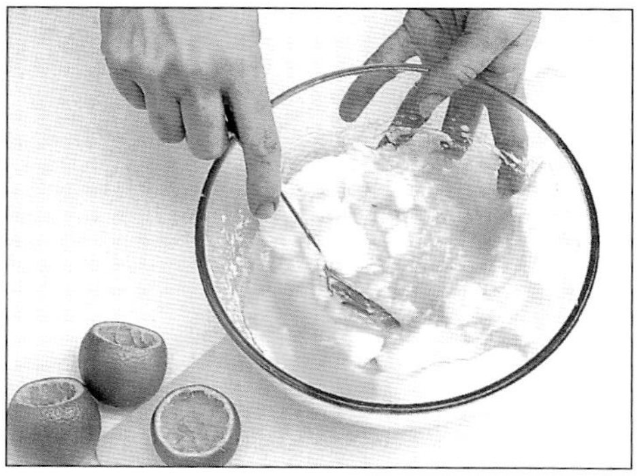

3 Whisk the egg whites in a bowl until they hold soft peaks. Whisk in the sugar, then quickly fold the egg white mixture into the mango mixture. Spoon the mixture into the lime shells. (Any leftover sorbet that will not fit in can be frozen in small ramekins.)

4 Wrap the lime shells in clear film and put in the freezer until the sorbet is firm. Before serving, allow the lime shells to stand at room temperature for about 10 minutes; decorate them with strips of pared lime rind and serve.

BAKED FRUIT COMPOTE

Mixed dried fruits, combined with fruit juice and spices, then oven-baked, make a nutritious and warming Italian-style winter dessert.

INGREDIENTS

115g/4oz/2/3 cup ready-to-eat dried figs
115g/4oz/1/2 cup ready-to-eat dried apricots
50g/2oz/1/2 cup ready-to-eat dried apple rings
50g/2oz/1/4 cup ready-to-eat prunes
50g/2oz/1/2 cup ready-to-eat dried pears
50g/2oz/1/2 cup ready-to-eat dried peaches
300ml/1/2 pint/1 1/4 cups unsweetened apple juice
300ml/1/2 pint/1 1/4 cups unsweetened orange juice
6 cloves
1 cinnamon stick
toasted flaked almonds, to decorate (optional)

SERVES 6

1 Preheat the oven to 180ºC/350ºF/Gas 4. Place the figs, apricots, apple rings, prunes, pears and peaches in a shallow ovenproof dish and stir to mix.

2 Mix together the apple and orange juices and pour over the fruit. Add the cloves and cinnamon stick and stir gently to mix.

3 Bake in the oven for about 30 minutes until the fruit mixture is hot, stirring once or twice during cooking. Remove from the oven, set aside and leave to soak for 20 minutes, then remove and discard the cloves and cinnamon stick.

4 Spoon into serving bowls and serve warm or cold, decorated with toasted flaked almonds, if you like.

NUTRITIONAL NOTES

Per portion:

Energy	174Kcals/744kJ
Total fat	0.8g
Saturated fat	0.05g
Cholesterol	0mg
Fibre	5.16g

MANGO YOGURT ICE

Serve this delicious mango yogurt ice in scoops for a popular and low-fat family dessert.

INGREDIENTS

450g/1lb ripe mango flesh, chopped
300ml/1/2 pint/1 1/4 cups low-fat peach or apricot yogurt
150ml/1/4 pint/2/3 cup Greek yogurt
150ml/1/4 pint/2/3 cup low-fat natural yogurt
25–50g/1–2oz/2–4 tbsp caster sugar
fresh mint sprigs, to decorate

SERVES 6

1 Place the mango flesh in a blender or food processor and blend until smooth. Transfer to a bowl. Add all three yogurts and mix thoroughly.

2 Add enough of the sugar to sweeten to taste and stir to mix. Pour into a shallow, plastic container. Cover and freeze for 1 1/2–2 hours until it is mushy in consistency. Turn the mixture into a chilled bowl and beat until smooth.

3 Return the mixture to the plastic container, cover and freeze until firm. Transfer the ice to the fridge about 30 minutes before serving to allow it to soften a little. Serve in scoops, decorated with fresh mint sprigs.

NUTRITIONAL NOTES

Per portion:

Energy	155Kcals/655kJ
Total fat	2.9g
Saturated fat	1.7g
Cholesterol	6.5mg
Fibre	2.17g

LEMON GRANITA

Nothing is more refreshing on a hot summer's day than an Italian fat-free fresh lemon granita. Try making a lime version as well.

Ingredients

475ml/16fl oz/2 cups water
115g/4oz/1/2 cup sugar
2 large lemons

Serves 4

Nutritional Notes

Per portion:

Energy	114Kcals/488kJ
Total fat	0g
Saturated fat	0g
Cholesterol	0mg
Fibre	0g

1 In a large saucepan, heat the water and the sugar together over a low heat until the sugar dissolves. Bring to the boil, stirring occasionally. Remove the pan from the heat and set aside to cool.

2 Finely grate the rind from 1 lemon, then squeeze the juice from both. Stir the grated lemon rind and juice into the sugar syrup. Pour it into a shallow plastic container or freezer tray, and freeze until it is solid.

3 Plunge the bottom of the frozen container or tray in very hot water for a few seconds. Turn the frozen mixture out into a bowl and chop it into large chunks.

4 Place the mixture in a blender or food processor fitted with metal blades, and process until it forms small crystals. Spoon the granita into serving glasses and serve immediately.

COFFEE GRANITA

Espresso coffee adds a delicious flavour to this appetizing fat-free Italian-style dessert.

Ingredients

475ml/16fl oz/2 cups water
115g/4oz/1/2 cup sugar
250ml/8fl oz/1 cup very strong espresso coffee, cooled

Serves 4

1 Heat the water and sugar together in a saucepan until the sugar dissolves. Bring to the boil, stirring occasionally. Remove the pan from the heat and set aside to cool.

Cook's Tip

If not served immediately, the granita can be frozen again.

2 Stir the cooled coffee and the sugar syrup together. Pour the mixture into a shallow, plastic container and freeze until solid. Plunge the bottom of the frozen container in very hot water for a few seconds. Turn the frozen mixture out into a bowl and chop it into large chunks.

Nutritional Notes

Per portion:

Energy	115Kcals/488kJ
Total fat	0g
Saturated fat	0g
Cholesterol	0mg
Fibre	0g

3 Place the mixture in a blender or food processor fitted with metal blades, and process until it forms small crystals. Spoon the granita into tall serving glasses and serve.

WATERMELON SORBET

A slice of this refreshing Italian fruit sorbet is the perfect way to cool down on a hot sunny day. It also makes an excellent summer starter.

Ingredients

1/2 small watermelon, weighing about 1kg/2 1/4lb
75g/3oz/1/2 cup caster sugar
60ml/4 tbsp cranberry juice or water
30ml/2 tbsp lemon juice
fresh mint sprigs, to decorate

Serves 6

1 Cut the watermelon into six equal-sized wedges. Scoop out the pink flesh from each wedge, discarding the seeds but reserving the shell.

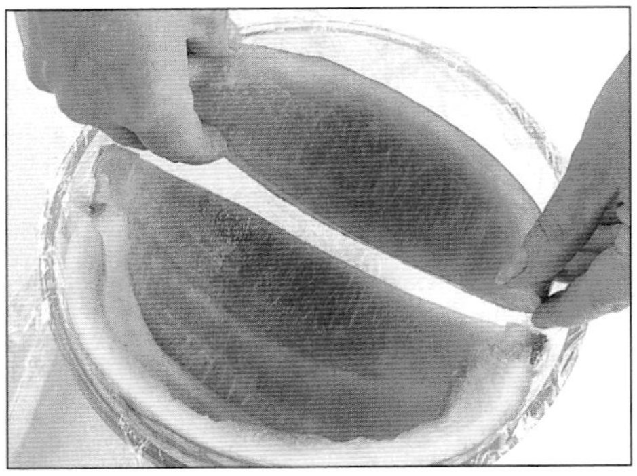

2 Line a freezerproof bowl, about the same size as the melon, with clear film. Arrange the melon skins in the bowl to re-form the shell, fitting them together snugly so that there are no gaps. Put in the freezer.

3 Put the sugar and cranberry juice or water in a saucepan and stir over a low heat until the sugar dissolves. Bring to the boil, then reduce the heat and simmer for 5 minutes. Remove the pan from the heat and set aside to cool.

4 Put the melon flesh and lemon juice in a blender or food processor and blend to a smooth purée. Pour into a bowl, stir in the sugar syrup, then pour into a freezer-proof container. Freeze the mixture for 3–3 1/2 hours, or until slushy.

5 Tip the sorbet into a chilled freezerproof bowl and whisk well to break up the ice crystals. Return to the freezer for a further 30 minutes. Whisk again, then tip into the melon shell and freeze until solid.

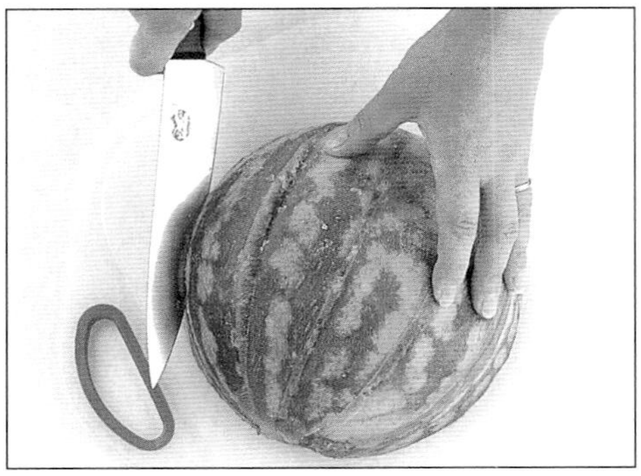

6 Remove the sorbet from the freezer and leave to stand at room temperature for 15 minutes. Take the melon out of the bowl and cut into wedges with a warmed sharp knife. Serve decorated with fresh mint sprigs.

Nutritional Notes

Per portion:

Energy	101Kcals/434kJ
Total fat	0.5g
Saturated fat	0.2g
Cholesterol	0mg
Fibre	0.2g

Cook's Tip

If preferred, this pretty pink sorbet can be served scooped into balls. Do this before the mixture is completely frozen and re-freeze the balls on a baking sheet, ready to serve.

ICED ORANGES

The ultimate virtually fat-free treat – these delectable orange sorbets served in fruit shells create a light and refreshing flavourful dessert.

INGREDIENTS

150g/5oz/⅔ cup sugar
juice of 1 lemon
14 oranges
8 fresh bay leaves, to decorate

SERVES 8

1 Put the sugar in a heavy-based saucepan. Add half the lemon juice, then add 120ml/4fl oz/½ cup water. Cook over a low heat until the sugar has dissolved, stirring. Bring to the boil and boil for 2–3 minutes until the syrup is clear. Remove the pan from the heat and set aside.

2 Slice the tops off eight of the oranges to make "hats". Scoop out the flesh of the oranges and reserve. Freeze the empty orange shells and "hats" until required.

3 Finely grate the rind of the remaining oranges and stir into the syrup. Squeeze the juice from the oranges, and from the reserved flesh. There should be about 750ml/1¼ pints/3 cups of juice. Squeeze another orange or add bought unsweetened orange juice, if necessary, to make up to the correct quantity.

4 Stir the orange juice and remaining lemon juice with 90ml/6 tbsp water into the syrup. Taste, adding more lemon juice or sugar as desired. Pour the mixture into a shallow freezerproof container and freeze for 3 hours.

5 Turn the orange sorbet mixture into a chilled bowl and whisk thoroughly to break up the ice crystals. Return to the container and freeze for a further 4 hours, until firm, but not solid.

6 Pack the frozen mixture into the hollowed-out orange shells, mounding it up, and set the "hats" on top. Freeze the filled sorbet shells until ready to serve. Just before serving, push a skewer into the tops of the "hats" and push in a bay leaf, to decorate.

NUTRITIONAL NOTES

Per portion:

Energy	139Kcals/593kJ
Total fat	0.17g
Saturated fat	0g
Cholesterol	0mg
Fibre	3g

ITALIAN FRUIT SALAD AND ICE CREAM

If you visit Italy in the summer, you will find little pavement fruit shops selling small dishes of macerated soft fruits, which are delectable on their own, but also wonderful with low-fat ice cream.

INGREDIENTS

900g/2lb/8 cups mixed ripe soft fruits, such as strawberries, raspberries, loganberries, redcurrants, blueberries, peaches, apricots, plums and melons
juice of 6–8 oranges
juice of 1 lemon
15ml/1 tbsp liquid pear and apple concentrate
60ml/4 tbsp very low-fat fromage frais
30ml/2 tbsp orange-flavoured liqueur (optional)
fresh mint sprigs, to decorate

SERVES 6

1 Prepare the fruit according to type. Cut it into reasonably small pieces, but not so small that the mixture becomes a mush.

2 Put the fruit in a serving bowl and pour over enough orange juice to cover. Add the lemon juice, stir gently to mix, cover and chill in the fridge for 2 hours.

3 Set half the macerated fruit aside to serve as it is. Purée the remainder in a blender or food processor. Pour the purée into a bowl.

4 Gently warm the pear and apple concentrate in a small saucepan and stir it into the fruit purée. Whip the fromage frais and fold it in to the fruit purée, then add the liqueur, if using.

NUTRITIONAL NOTES

Per portion:

Energy	60Kcals/254kJ
Total fat	0.2g
Saturated fat	0.01g
Cholesterol	0.1mg
Fibre	3.2g

5 Churn the mixture in an ice cream maker. Alternatively, place in a shallow freezerproof container and freeze it until ice crystals form around the edge. Beat the mixture in a chilled bowl until smooth. Repeat the process once or twice, then freeze until firm. Soften slightly in the fridge before serving in scoops. Decorate with mint sprigs and serve with the macerated fruit.

NECTARINE AMARETTO CAKE

Try this delicious Italian-style cake served with a little low-fat fromage frais for dessert, or serve it solo for an afternoon tea treat. The syrup makes it deliciously moist but not soggy.

INGREDIENTS

3 eggs, separated
175g/6oz/generous 3/4 cup caster sugar
finely grated rind and juice of 1 lemon
50g/2oz/1/3 cup semolina
40g/1 1/2 oz/1/3 cup ground almonds
25g/1oz/1/4 cup plain flour
2 nectarines or peaches, halved and stoned
60ml/4 tbsp apricot glaze (see Cook's Tip)

FOR THE SYRUP

75g/3oz/6 tbsp caster sugar
90ml/6 tbsp water
30ml/2 tbsp Amaretto liqueur

SERVES 10

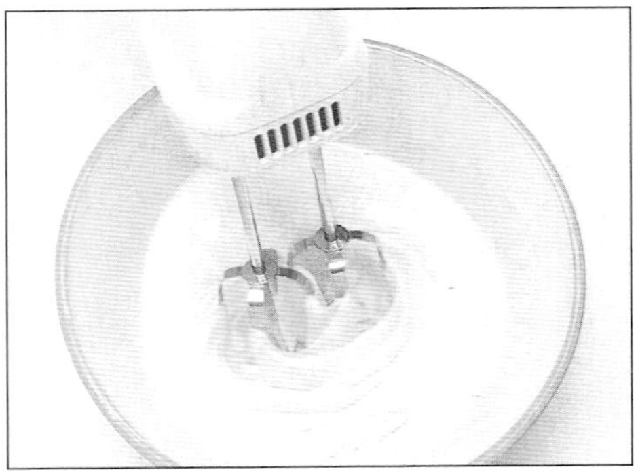

1 Preheat the oven to 180°C/350°F/Gas 4. Lightly grease a 20cm/8in round loose-based cake tin. Whisk the egg yolks, caster sugar, lemon rind and juice in a bowl until thick, pale and creamy.

2 Fold in the semolina, almonds and flour.

3 Whisk the egg whites in a separate bowl until fairly stiff. Using a metal spoon, stir a generous spoonful of the whisked egg whites into the semolina mixture to lighten it, then fold in the remaining egg whites. Spoon the mixture into the prepared cake tin and then level the surface.

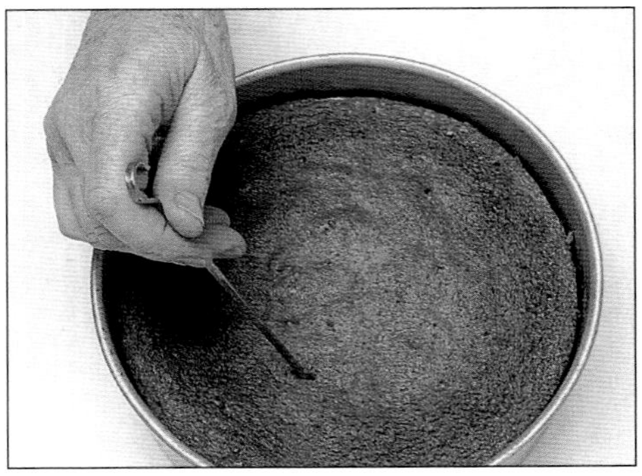

4 Bake in the oven for 30–35 minutes until the centre of the cake springs back when lightly pressed. Remove the cake from the oven and carefully loosen around the edge with a palette knife. Prick the top of the cake all over with a skewer and leave to cool slightly in the tin.

5 Meanwhile, make the syrup. Heat the sugar and water in a small saucepan, stirring until dissolved, then boil without stirring for 2 minutes. Stir in the Amaretto liqueur, then drizzle the syrup slowly over the top of the cake.

6 Remove the cake from the tin and place it on a serving plate. Slice the nectarines or peaches, arrange them over the top of the cake and brush with the warm apricot glaze. Serve warm or cold in slices.

COOK'S TIP

To make apricot glaze, place a few spoonfuls of apricot jam in a small saucepan along with a squeeze of lemon juice. Heat the jam, stirring until it is melted and runny. Pour the melted jam through a wire sieve set over a bowl and stir the jam with a wooden spoon to help it go through. Discard the contents of the sieve. Keep the strained jam/glaze warm and use as required.

NUTRITIONAL NOTES

Per portion:

Energy	165Kcals/701kJ
Total fat	1.8g
Saturated fat	0.5g
Cholesterol	57mg
Fibre	0.4g

CHOCOLATE AMARETTI

These mouthwatering Italian chocolate amaretti are delicious served on their own or with low-fat sorbet, mousse or zabaglione.

INGREDIENTS

150g/5oz/1 cup blanched whole almonds
90g/3½oz/½ cup caster sugar
15ml/1 tbsp unsweetened cocoa powder
30ml/2 tbsp icing sugar
2 egg whites
pinch of cream of tartar
5ml/1 tsp almond essence
15g/½oz flaked almonds, to decorate

MAKES ABOUT 24

1 Preheat oven to 180°C/350°F/Gas 4. Place the whole almonds on a small baking sheet and bake in the oven for 10–12 minutes, stirring occasionally, until the almonds are golden brown. Remove from the oven and set aside to cool to room temperature. Reduce the oven temperature to 160°C/325°F/Gas 3.

2 Line a large baking sheet with non-stick baking parchment or foil and set aside. In a blender or food processor fitted with a metal blade, process the toasted almonds with 45g/1¾oz/¼ cup sugar until the almonds are finely ground but not oily. Transfer to a medium bowl and sift in the cocoa powder and icing sugar; stir to mix. Set aside.

3 In a mixing bowl, beat the egg whites and cream of tartar together, using an electric mixer, until stiff peaks form. Sprinkle in the remaining 45g/1¾oz/¼ cup sugar, a tablespoon at a time, beating well after each addition, and continue beating until the egg whites are glossy and stiff. Beat in the almond essence.

4 Sprinkle the almond-sugar mixture over the whisked egg whites and gently fold them in until just blended. Spoon the mixture into a large piping bag fitted with a plain 1cm/½in nozzle. Pipe the mixture into 4cm/1½in rounds about 2.5cm/1in apart on the prepared baking sheet. Press a flaked almond into the centre of each one.

5 Bake the amaretti in the oven for 12–15 minutes or until they appear crisp. Place the baking sheets on a wire rack and leave to cool for 10 minutes. With a metal palette knife, remove the amaretti and place on a wire rack, then leave to cool completely. When cool, store in an airtight container.

NUTRITIONAL NOTES

Per portion:

Energy	58Kcals/244kJ
Total fat	3.7g
Saturated fat	0.4g
Cholesterol	0mg
Fibre	0.6g

APRICOT AND ALMOND FINGERS

These moist apricot and almond fingers are an irresistible low-fat snack or treat for all to enjoy.

INGREDIENTS

225g/8oz/2 cups self-raising flour
115g/4oz/⅔ cup light muscovado sugar
50g/2oz/⅓ cup semolina
175g/6oz/1 cup ready-to-eat dried apricots, chopped
2 eggs
30ml/2 tbsp malt extract
30ml/2 tbsp clear honey
60ml/4 tbsp skimmed milk
60ml/4 tbsp sunflower oil
few drops of almond essence
30ml/2 tbsp flaked almonds

MAKES 18

1 Preheat the oven to 160°C/325°F/Gas 3. Lightly grease and line a 28 × 18cm/11 × 7in shallow baking tin and set aside. Sift the flour into a bowl and add the sugar, semolina, dried apricots, eggs, malt extract, honey, milk, oil and almond essence. Mix well until smooth.

2 Turn the mixture into the prepared tin, spread to the edges and sprinkle with the flaked almonds.

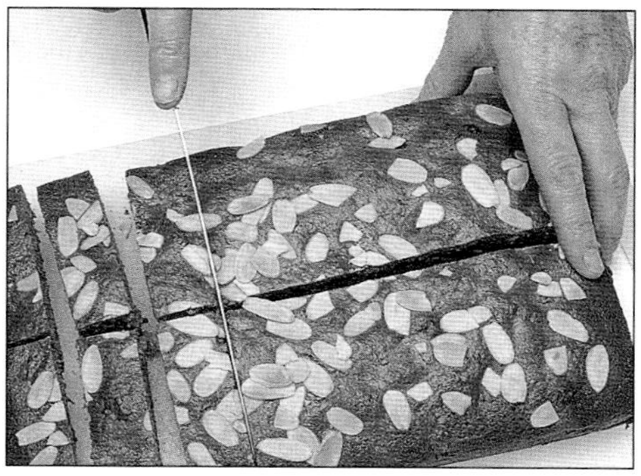

3 Bake in the oven for 30–35 minutes or until the centre of the cake springs back when lightly pressed. Turn out onto a wire rack and allow to cool. Remove and discard the paper, place the cake on a board and cut it into 18 slices with a sharp knife. Store in an airtight container.

NUTRITIONAL NOTES

Per portion:

Energy	153Kcals/641kJ
Total fat	4.56g
Saturated fat	0.61g
Cholesterol	21.5mg
Fibre	1.27g

BISCOTTI

These delicious Italian biscuits are part-baked, sliced to reveal a feast of mixed nuts and then baked again until crisp and golden. They're perfect for rounding off a low-fat Italian meal.

INGREDIENTS

50g/2oz/¼ cup unsalted butter, softened
115g/4oz/½ cup caster sugar
175g/6oz/1½ cups self-raising flour
1.5ml/¼ tsp salt
10ml/2 tsp baking powder
5ml/1 tsp ground coriander
finely grated rind of 1 lemon
50g/2oz/½ cup polenta
1 egg, lightly beaten
10ml/2 tsp brandy or orange-flavour liqueur
50g/2oz/½ cup unblanched almonds
50g/2oz/½ cup pistachio nuts

MAKES 24

1 Preheat the oven to 160°C/325°F/Gas 3. Lightly grease a baking sheet and set aside. Cream together the butter and sugar in a bowl.

2 Sift the flour, salt, baking powder and coriander over the creamed mixture in the bowl. Add the lemon rind, polenta, egg and brandy or liqueur and mix together to make a soft dough.

COOK'S TIP

Use a sharp, serrated knife to slice the cooled biscuits in Step 4, otherwise they will crumble.

3 Add the nuts and mix until evenly combined. Halve the mixture. Shape each half of the dough into a flat sausage about 23cm/9in long and 6cm/2½in wide. Place on the prepared baking sheet. Bake in the oven for about 30 minutes until risen and just firm. Remove from the oven and set aside to cool on a wire rack.

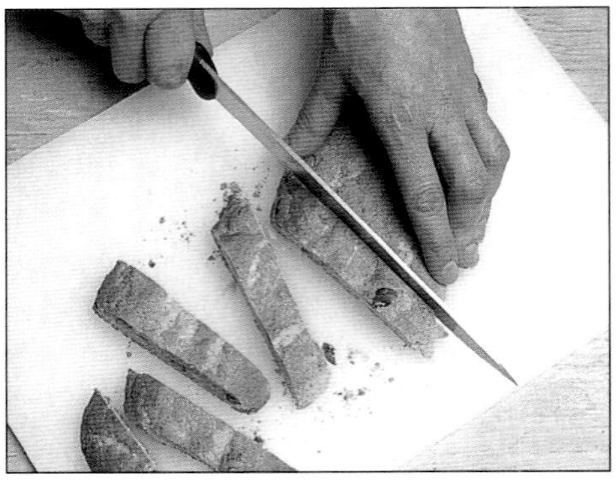

NUTRITIONAL NOTES

Per portion:

Energy	94Kcals/397kJ
Total fat	4.2g
Saturated fat	1.2g
Cholesterol	12.6mg
Fibre	0.2g

4 When cool, cut each sausage diagonally into 12 thin slices. Return to the baking sheet and bake in the oven for a further 10 minutes until crisp.

5 Transfer the biscotti to a wire rack to cool completely. Store in an airtight container for up to one week.

INDEX

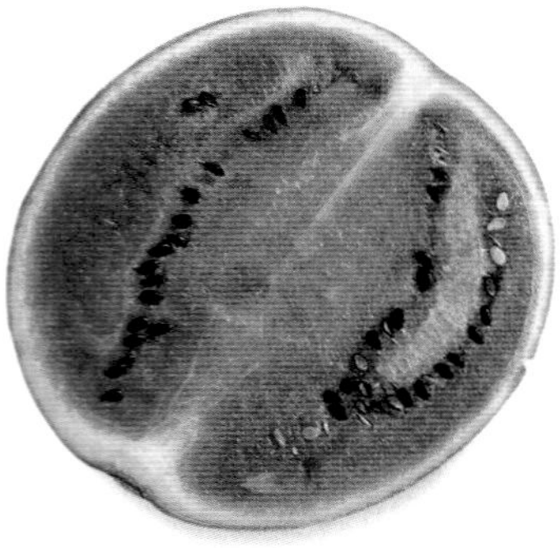

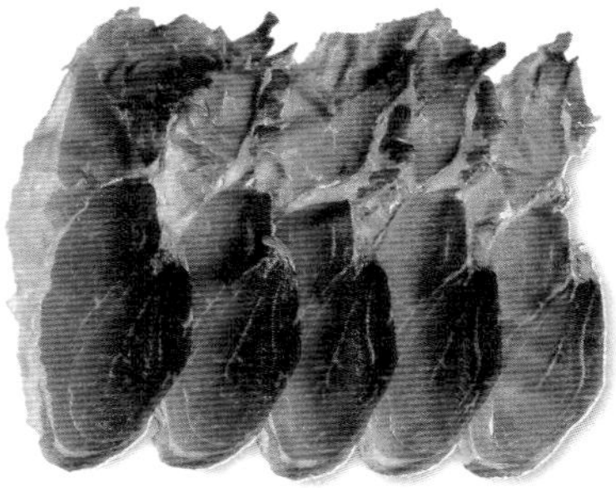

POMODORI all'ISOLANA
Merlini